UNWANTED

WORKERS

UNWANTED

Richard C. Wilcock
and
Walter H. Franke

WORKERS

Permanent Layoffs and Long-Term Unemployment

INSTITUTE OF LABOR AND INDUSTRIAL RELATIONS
UNIVERSITY OF ILLINOIS

OCTAGON BOOKS

A DIVISION OF FARRAR, STRAUS AND GIROUX

New York   1979

To Joe and Pat

OCTAGON BOOKS
A DIVISION OF FARRAR, STRAUS & GIROUX, INC.
19 Union Square West
New York, N.Y. 10003

Library of Congress Cataloging in Publication Data

Wilcock, Richard Carrington.
  Unwanted workers.

  Reprint of the ed. published by Free Press of Glencoe, New York.
  Bibliography: p.
  Includes index.
  1. Unemployed—United States.   I. Franke, Walter Henry, 1928-
joint author.   II. Title.
[HD5724.W443   1979]   331.1′37973   78-23981
ISBN 0-374-98565-0

Manufactured by Braun-Brumfield, Inc.
Ann Arbor, Michigan
Printed in the United States of America

Preface & Acknowledgments

IN THE Great Depression of the 1930's, mass unemployment was a national disaster because of its waste of human resources and vast personal suffering. Now, in the 1960's, unemployment has again become a major national problem, although with changed dimensions. First, unemployment has not been as widespread throughout the population but has hit some groups and some areas much harder than others. Second, there has been a pattern of recession and prosperity, with unemployment rates becoming higher in each successive period of prosperity.

Unemployment has not been returning to "normal" levels after recessions. Following the 1949 recession, unemployment averaged about 3 per cent of the labor force; but after the 1954 recession the average was above 4 per cent, and following the 1958 recession it stabilized above 5 per cent. The prosperity period after the 1960 recession has had an even higher average.

These higher levels of unemployment "in the midst of prosperity" have brought long months of joblessness to hundreds of thousands of experienced workers who are family heads and breadwinners, and they have caused great activity and concern in legislative chambers, union halls, company board rooms, and at the collective bargaining table. Not all who study the problems of unemployment agree on the causes and cures, but there is general agreement that the solution cannot be left entirely to the free play of market forces.

Our concern in this book is primarily with the problems arising when experienced workers are permanently displaced from their jobs and undergo extended periods of joblessness. Such long-term unemployment may be associated either with market changes that take jobs away from an area or with technological changes and automation that eliminate jobs entirely. In either case, many of the displaced workers tend to become "unwanted workers" whose skills and experience are in insufficient demand either locally or nationally.

In Part One we analyze the changing patterns of unemployment and the characteristics of the long-term unemployed in the United States. Our inquiry raises at least two important and related questions, which we analyze in the remainder of the book. To what extent is the long-term unemployment a result of dynamic changes in the structure of industry and of the labor force? To what extent and under what conditions would an acceleration in economic growth solve the problem of long-term unemployment?

In Part Two we present the data from five studies of plant shutdowns in as many communities. We document the economic and social problems of the individuals thrown out of work by permanent layoffs, and we analyze the supply-and-demand factors involved in their difficulties in finding new jobs.

Finally, in Part Three, we examine both existing and proposed measures that are open to government, companies, and unions in attempting to deal with the problem of long-term unemployment. These measures are divided between those intended to reduce the financial burden of unemployment and those directed toward reducing the level and duration of unemployment. We also examine the causes of long-term joblessness in the belief that a correct analysis of these causes is essential to the development of effective public and private policies. Our final conclusion is basically optimistic, because our analysis has convinced us that long-term unemployment *can* be reduced to tolerable levels without endangering the system of free choice that is basic to the American labor market as we know it.

Acknowledgments

Of the many persons who contributed in some way to the completion of this book, we are most in debt to the workers who are its main subject. Although they had nothing directly to gain from doing so, many hundreds of them took the time to fill out questionnaires or answer questions put to them by interviewers. Very rarely were we refused cooperation, even though we imposed on some individuals as many as four different times to ask them scores of questions. We cannot repay them for their cooperation, but we can hope that they and others like them, who find the impersonal labor market a challenge beyond their individual capacities, will derive some benefit from having the story of their difficulties made available for public inspection and consideration.

The studies we are reporting could not have been undertaken without substantial financial assistance. The necessary funds were provided by the Forest Park Foundation of Peoria, Illinois, and the Armour Automation Fund Committee. In addition to agreeing to support the studies at the four closed Armour plants, members of the Armour Committee contributed to the studies by offering comments and suggestions on the questionnaire and interview schedules and on the conduct of other aspects of the research.

At the time of the studies, the Automation Committee was chaired by Clark Kerr, President of the University of California, and the Executive Secretary was Robben W. Fleming, Professor of Law at the University of Illinois. Representatives of Armour and Company on the committee were Harold E. Brooks, Walter E. Clark, Frederick R. Livingston, and William J. Ohl. Representing the United Packinghouse Workers of America, AFL-CIO, were Howard McDermott and Jesse Prosten. The Amalgamated Meat Cutters and Butcher Workmen of North America, AFL-CIO, was represented by Russell E. Dresser and James H. Wishart. Special thanks are due to the members of this committee for their permission to publish the results of the four Armour plant studies, which were done initially for the Committee.

Field work for the four Armour studies was under the supervision of Professors Paul Brinker, University of Oklahoma; Glenn Fisher, North Dakota State College (now at the University of Illinois); Herbert Parnes, Ohio State University; and Irvin Sobel, Washington University. Interviewers under their supervision were: Ernst Stromsdorfer and William Swift (East St. Louis); Bernard Jump, Donald Kress, and Frederick Zeller (Columbus); Lilian Holmsen and Arthur Walters (Fargo); Lewis Abernathy, Walter Smith, and James Weaver (Oklahoma City). The Peoria interviewers were Toby Kahr, Jerry Menzel, and Coenraad Mohr. We commend them all for a good job in a difficult task.

The tedious work of coding the large quantity of data and otherwise assisting in their processing fell upon our graduate students at the Institute of Labor and Industrial Relations. At various times the following students contributed their services to these tasks: Harvey Anderson, Paul Becht, David Booth, Neil Collins, Ed Ghearing, Alan Gibbs, Irwin Ginsburg, John Glass, Philip Graber, Allan Harrison, Edward McCallum, Roy Pawley, Robert Predan, Michael Schwartz, Richard Sears, Hiro Tsuchida, Floyd Whellan, and Douglas Wolfe.

We also benefited greatly from the advice of a number of colleagues. Special thanks are due to Milton Derber (University of Illinois) and Irvin Sobel (Washington University), who read an earlier version of all or most of the manuscript and gave us many helpful criticisms and suggestions. Various chapters are also better than they would otherwise have been because of the comments of W. Ellison Chalmers, Robben W. Fleming, and Adolf Sturmthal (University of Illinois), Sanford Cohen (Butler University), Margaret Gordon (University of California), Jacob Kaufman (Pennsylvania State), John McConnell (Cornell), William Miernyk (Colorado), Arnold Weber (University of Chicago), and Joseph Becker, S.J. (St. Louis University). The services of Robert Ferber (University of Illinois) in helping us to design the interview samples were invaluable. The final product owes a great deal to the very capable editorial hand of Barbara Dennis, the Institute's editor.

For the difficult task of transcribing our handwriting, our thanks go to the typists who completed several versions of the manuscripts: Marian Brinkerhoff, Elaine Collins, Anice Duncan, Darlene Feurer, Sharon Allen, and Gerry Swift. Special thanks also are due Anice Duncan for her work in preparing the illustrations.

Lastly, we wish to express our appreciation for the congenial and stimulating atmosphere of the Institute of Labor and Industrial Relations where we work and for the many ways in which the director, Martin Wagner, was able to facilitate our labors.

In spite of the many helping hands, however, we must accept full responsibility for the final results.

R. C. WILCOCK
W. H. FRANKE

Urbana, Illinois
December, 1962

Contents

PART ONE

◀ INTRODUCTION

1

Changing Patterns
of Unemployment

THE PATTERNS OF UNEMPLOYMENT changed significantly between 1950 and 1962. During those years unemployment rates
crept upward; they were higher in each period of prosperity than
in the previous one. The average unemployed worker in 1962 was
out of a job longer than his counterpart in the early 1950's. Unemployment was particularly heavy among young people just
entering the labor market and among experienced unskilled and
semiskilled manual workers, especially those manual workers who
were older men, Negroes, or poorly educated. In our case studies,
we have found groups of permanently displaced workers with unemployment rates *up to twelve times* the average in their communities. These are the "unwanted workers" of our title.

Economists disagree as to the causes of the higher rates and
longer duration of unemployment. Some hold that there has been
an acceleration of shifts in production and consumption as well
as an acceleration of job-displacing technological change and
automation. These changes in markets and in technology have
created a rising level of "structural" unemployment that cannot
be attributed to the business cycle or a deficiency in demand. A

3

significant reduction of "structural" unemployment would require very extensive programs designed to improve both the job qualifications and the mobility of the jobless.[1]

Others maintain that the primary cause of the upward trend in unemployment has been the failure of the economy to grow at a rate rapid enough to provide jobs under conditions of an expanding labor force and steadily increasing productivity. According to this view, proper monetary and fiscal policies would produce an increase in demand sufficient to reduce unemployment to acceptable levels. The solution to the excessive and extended unemployment characteristic of the postwar prosperity periods, therefore, would be a series of measures that would stimulate economic growth.[2]

In our view, both greater economic growth and a more efficient functioning of the labor market are required to reduce total and long-term unemployment to tolerable levels. Further, we believe that both approaches would be more effective if they were coordinated and if they were based on greater knowledge of the relationship between the characteristics and qualifications of the unemployed and the specific demands for labor.

If the labor market is ignored, measures designed to produce full employment by increasing aggregate demand are likely to be inflationary, as they often have been in the past. On the other hand, measures designed to encourage retraining or relocation and other steps to improve the functioning of the labor market are bound to have disappointing results in reducing unemployment if economic growth is insufficient to create an adequate number of jobs.

Although our analysis has convinced us that attention to both approaches is required to reverse the upward drift of unemployment, this book concentrates on the functioning of the labor market. This is a self-imposed limitation and does not reflect any judgment as to the relative urgency of the two approaches. In our view they are both important.

---

1. For an example of this viewpoint, see Clarence D. Long, "Prosperity Unemployment and Its Relation to Economic Growth and Inflation," *American Economic Review*, Vol. 50, No. 2 (May, 1960), pp. 145–161.

2. For examples of this viewpoint, see Conference on Economic Progress, *Jobs and Growth* (Washington, D.C., May, 1961), 93 pp. and Council of Economic Advisers, *The American Economy in 1961: Problems and Policies*, statement before the Joint Economic Committee, March 6, 1961.

Proposals to stimulate aggregate demand through fiscal and monetary measures usually implicitly assume that the manpower resources required for expansion and economic progress are available or will quickly be developed. Imperfections in the labor market, such as incomplete knowledge of labor requirements and labor supply, obsolete labor skills, and geographic mislocation of workers are either completely ignored or assumed away as minor barriers to growth and full employment.

In our view this is a mistake. The five case studies presented in this book vividly demonstrate a host of barriers to the effective utilization of our manpower resources. Further, the studies illustrate the difficulties encountered by the displaced workers, both in finding jobs and in meeting the financial crisis of unemployment. Too often, concern with the broader aspects of economic development and growth overlook the problem of fitting individuals into our complex and dynamic economic system. In this book, we try to analyze critically the functioning of those parts of the economic system that have to do with the effective utilization of our human resources.

Types of Unemployment and Definitions

Many labels have been used to describe types of unemployment; among the more common are *cyclical, seasonal, frictional, structural, chronic, hard-core, long-term,* and *short-term.* For our purposes, however, we can use two sets of labels. *Cyclical* and *frictional* unemployment are the two basic types in terms of causes of joblessness, although no precise measurements of either are available. *Short-term* and *long-term* indicate duration of joblessness; we find these terms useful both because such data are available and because the division by length of time out of work is meaningful in the development and application of social and economic policies.

CYCLICAL AND FRICTIONAL UNEMPLOYMENT

Cyclical unemployment results from an inadequate level of effective labor demand. Usually considered a product of the recession phase of the business cycle, it may also occur if full employment demand is not achieved during the prosperity phase.

Frictional unemployment, on the other hand, is the product of imperfections in the labor market and cannot be "reduced significantly in the short run by increased aggregate spending."[3] When unemployment has been reduced to the frictional level, increased demand would result in higher wages and prices rather than in higher employment.

Frictional unemployment, therefore, is conceived to be the minimum, noninflationary level that can be achieved in view of the dynamics of the labor market and the characteristics of workers in the market. Seasonal fluctuations in employment, movement of workers into and out of the labor force, and voluntary job mobility are all sources of frictional unemployment. Also contributing to frictional unemployment are (1) involuntary worker displacement from jobs as a result of product shifts, changes in consumer tastes, technological changes, and the like, and (2) the lengthening of unemployment among those workers whose age, race, sex, level of education, physical condition, or obsolescent skills make it difficult for them to find new jobs.

Unemployment resulting from such causes, particularly if it is of long duration, is sometimes called "structural," but it is, in fact, a form of frictional unemployment. In other words, regardless of the specific causes of workers' becoming unemployed—whether discharges, quits, temporary layoffs, or plant shutdowns—the resulting unemployment is frictional if its continuance is not the result of a deficiency in over-all labor demand.

Although the theoretical distinction between cyclical and frictional unemployment is clear, it is difficult to distinguish between the two in actual measurement. The basic difficulty is that, even though we have rather extensive data on the characteristics and numbers of the employed and unemployed, the data on the demand for labor are woefully inadequate. Thus, for any given amount of unemployment, we do not know how much of it is caused by frictions in the labor market that have delayed re-employment and how much by an absolute shortage of job vacancies.

---

3. Joint Economic Committee, *The Extent and Nature of Frictional Unemployment* (Washington, D.C.: The Committee, Eighty-sixth Congress, First Session, Study Paper No. 6, U.S. Government Printing Office, 1959), p. 2.

Some analysts would measure frictional unemployment as the level occurring in a prosperity period that is not markedly inflationary. The assumption is made that the existing level of unemployment in such a period is attributable to the dynamic changes within the economy. This level then becomes the base, with any unemployment over that base being considered cyclical, the result of a deficiency in labor demand.

A major objection to this method of determining frictional unemployment is that it assumes there is an adequate demand for labor at the cyclical peaks in the business cycle. Clearly, this was not true in 1937, when unemployment remained very high, and it was probably not true after the 1954 and 1958 recessions, when unemployment failed to drop to the level of 1951–53.

The difficulty of determining what is cyclical and what is frictional has created a controversy over the acceptable level of unemployment during prosperity, with some saying 4 per cent, others 3 per cent, and others a rate below 3 per cent. Part of the problem is that the available data and tools of economic analysis are not adequate for the purpose of predicting the lowest noninflationary level of unemployment that can be achieved in a free economy. It is our contention, however, that a given level of frictional unemployment is not inevitable and that it can be reduced to some significant degree by public and private measures that will improve the process of matching jobs and workers in the labor market.

SHORT-TERM AND LONG-TERM UNEMPLOYMENT

Since unemployment data do not provide precise measures of cyclical and frictional unemployment, we need to find statistics that will furnish a reasonable substitute. The data that come closest to meeting our needs are those on short-term and long-term unemployment, particularly when analyzed over time. We use the definitions of these terms given by the *Monthly Report on the Labor Force* published by the U.S. Bureau of Labor Statistics. Short-term unemployment is that lasting less than 15 weeks and long-term is that lasting 15 weeks or more. Since there are also data on workers out of work for 27 weeks or more, we shall label these workers as the very long-term unemployed.

These data still leave much to be desired, because they do not distinguish between those whose unemployment is cyclical (resulting from a deficiency in labor demand) and those whose unemployment is frictional (resulting from imperfections in the labor market). Nevertheless, they possess the major virtue of isolating those whose unemployment is of greatest economic and social concern.

We need not be overly concerned about the short-term unemployed. Unemployment insurance, credit, and their own resources make it possible for most of the unemployed to take a few weeks in finding and accepting suitable jobs. The long-term unemployed, on the other hand, who are much more likely to be the victims of permanent layoffs and dislocations in the economy, are the ones who may exhaust their unemployment insurance benefits and face the economic, social, and psychological problems of enforced idleness.

Our particular emphasis in this book is on those experienced workers who are displaced and who become long-term unemployed. Because of their personal characteristics, their geographic location, their lack of education, or their lack of relevant work experience, many of these are "unwanted workers" who need help quite apart from the adequacy of the demand for labor.

Unemployment Trends since World War II

The magnitude of the problem of long-term unemployment is illustrated by an examination of unemployment trends since World War II.

The most notable feature of the over-all unemployment pattern since 1948, as shown in Figure 1, is the steady rise of the unemployment level *in between* the recession periods. From June, 1951, through August, 1953, the average unemployment rate was 3.0 per cent.[4] After the 1954 recession, "prosperity" unemployment

---

4. This period includes the high-level labor demand of the Korean War. Also, in the peacetime half of 1953, it is possible that the Census was underreporting unemployment as a result of a change in the sample. See Clarence D. Long, *The Labor Force under Changing Income and Employment* (Princeton, N.J.: Princeton University Press, 1958), p. 47.

averaged 4.2 per cent between August, 1955, and June, 1957. Then, following the 1958 recession, "prosperity" unemployment was at an average 5.3 per cent level in the 12 months from June 1959, through May, 1960. The 1959–60 prosperity unemployment, therefore, was at a *higher* rate than the recession unemployment of 1949–50 (5.3 compared with 5.2 per cent) and also higher than the 1954 recession rate of 4.9 per cent.

Also noteworthy is the fact that each of the prosperity periods in the 1950's was shorter than the preceding one. The 1951–53 period lasted 27 months; the 1955–57 period lasted 23 months; while in 1959 and 1960 only 12 months elapsed after unemployment stopped falling and the 1960–61 rise in unemployment began. Fortunately, this pattern was broken in the 1961–63 recovery.

The rising trend in unemployment in the periods between recessions has raised the issue of how much of the unemployment is really frictional. An examination of the prosperity periods shown in Figure 1 raises the question of whether the level of frictional unemployment has been rising because of dislocations in the labor market or whether in the 1956, 1959, and early part of the 1961–63 prosperity periods a failure in the rate of economic growth meant an over-all deficiency in labor demand. In our view, it has been a combination of incomplete recovery and structural dislocations in the labor market. In our case studies (Part Two) we investigate the nature of structural barriers to re-employment, and in Chapter 10 we consider the causes of the rising level of unemployment.

THE RISING LEVEL OF LONG-TERM UNEMPLOYMENT

Figure 1 also shows how long-term unemployment rates, along with total unemployment, increased quite dramatically for the "prosperity periods," from less than 0.4 per cent of the civilian labor force in the 1951–53 period to 1.3 per cent of the labor force in the short 1959–60 period. Also, the averages for the 1958 and 1961 recession periods are well above those for the earlier 1949–50 and 1954 recessions. In fact, over the 14-year time span in the chart, long-term unemployment rates increased more rapidly than total unemployment, with the result that long-

Figure 1. UNEMPLOYMENT RATES, BY MONTHS, JANUARY 1949 THROUGH APRIL 1962,
UNITED STATES (SEASONALLY ADJUSTED)

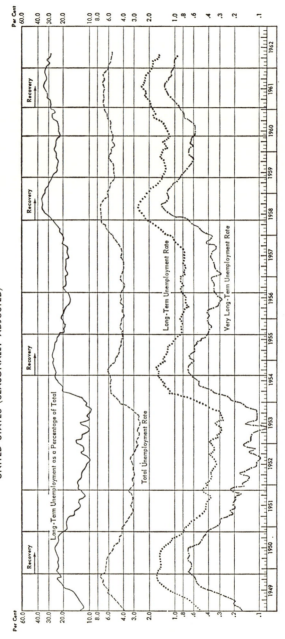

Source: U.S. Bureau of Labor Statistics.

term unemployment gradually made up a significantly larger portion of all unemployment.

This increase in long-term unemployment of 15 weeks or more was matched by an increase in the very long-term unemployment of over six months. Using data for the month of May in four recession years, we find the results in Table 1. In May, 1961, almost

Table 1
Very Long-Term Unemployment During Month of May, Four Recession Years

	Total Unemployment (Millions)	Unemployed 27 Weeks or More (Millions)	Very Long-Term as Proportion of Total (Per Cent)
May, 1949	3.6	0.2	6
May, 1954	3.7	0.4	11
May, 1958	4.9	0.6	12
May, 1961	4.8	0.9	19

one in every five of the unemployed had been out of work for more than six months. In the same month, two of every five had been jobless at least 15 weeks.

Characteristics of the Long-Term Unemployed

The personal and work history characteristics of the long-term unemployed are important in the assessment of the problem of reducing unemployment. Of particular importance are characteristics that hinder employer acceptance.

PERSONAL CHARACTERISTICS

Long-term unemployment falls upon young and old, white and nonwhite, men and women, and workers from all major industrial and occupational groups. Its incidence, however, is much heavier among some groups than others. Older workers, nonwhites, those with low-level skills and education, and workers who were separated from jobs in declining occupations, industries, or areas are particularly hard hit, during both prosperity and recession.[5]

5. Our analysis is based primarily on data presented in Jane L. Meredith, "Long-term Unemployment in the United States," *Monthly Labor Review,* June, 1961, pp. 601–610, and Joint Economic Committee, *op. cit.,* pp. 1–69.

Figure 2 shows the incidence of long-term unemployment among unemployed younger and older men and women in 1957 and 1961. In both years and in each age group, unemployed men were more likely than unemployed women to experience lengthy unemployment. The lower rates for women reflect both the greater tendency of women to leave the labor force when they lose their jobs or after a short period of unemployment and their greater representation in industries and occupations in which long-term unemployment is relatively low. Fewer women, for example, are employed in industries such as manufacturing, construction, and agriculture, which contribute substantially to lengthy unemployment. In contrast, there are higher proportions of women than men in office jobs, in retail stores, in finance, insurance, and real estate establishments and also in service jobs and industries, all of which create unemployment of shorter duration.

Among both men and women, the older workers (those 45 and over) who lose their jobs are unemployed longer than those under age 25. In 1961, for example, 36 per cent of the unemployed men 45 and over had 15 or more weeks of unemployment compared with 28 per cent of those under age 25. The comparable figures for 1957 were 28 per cent and 16 per cent. The differential associated with age is even larger when age groups are compared for those with more than six months of unemployment. In 1957, an average of 14 per cent of the unemployed males aged 45 to 64 but only 5 per cent of the 18-to-24-year-olds experienced a spell of unemployment as long as six months.

While older workers have the highest rates of long-term unemployment, very young workers (those under 25) bear more of the burden of extended joblessness when economic activity declines. Further, considering long-term unemployment as a proportion of the number of persons in various age groups who are in the labor force (rather than as a proportion of those unemployed), extended joblessness is highest for workers under age 25 in both prosperity and recession years. In 1961, for example, 4.4 per cent of the male 18-to-24-year-olds in the labor force were unemployed 15 or more weeks compared with 2.4 per cent of those 45 and over. In 1957 the comparable figures were 1.5 per cent and 1.1 per cent.

Figure 2. PROPORTIONS OF LONG-TERM UNEMPLOYMENT AMONG UNEMPLOYED
PERSONS, BY SEX AND AGE, 1957 AND 1961,[a] UNITED STATES

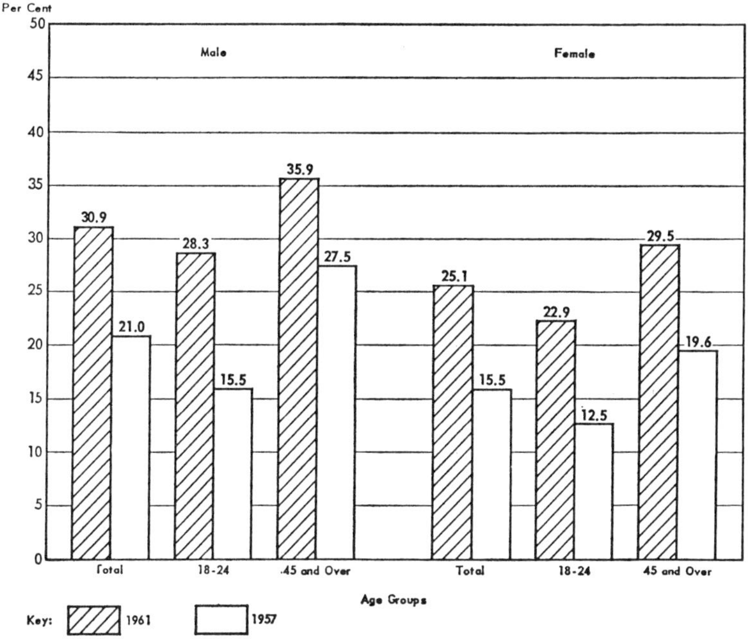

a. First quarter averages.

Source: Jane L. Meredith, "Long-Term Unemployment in the United States," *Monthly Labor Review*, June, 1961, p. 605.

Long-term unemployment is much higher among nonwhites than among whites. In 1961, for example, the long-term unemployment rate for nonwhites in the labor force was 4.5 per cent, while the rate for the white labor force was 2.0 per cent.

Lengthy unemployment is also higher for nonwhites as compared with whites when duration of unemployment is measured on an annual basis rather than for a given spell of unemployment, because nonwhites are more likely to have repeated spells of unemployment during a year. In 1957, for example, 44 per cent of the nonwhites who experienced any unemployment were long-term unemployed (15 or more weeks for the entire year) compared with

33 per cent of the whites. Also, nonwhite workers were a very large proportion of the very long-term unemployed. Although they composed only 11 per cent of the total labor force, nonwhites represented 27 per cent of the workers who had 27 or more weeks of unemployment during the year.

Part of the unemployment of nonwhites is attributable to their higher representation in unskilled and other occupations where the incidence of long-term unemployment is high. Unemployment rates and long-term unemployment, however, are higher for non-whites than whites in all occupations and industries.

Both older workers and nonwhites are more likely than others to be additionally handicapped in job search by low levels of education. Data from special surveys for 1959 show that persons with less than a high school education comprised about three-fourths of those out of work 15 or more weeks, although they made up only one-half of the labor force.[6] In addition to difficulties associated with age and color, therefore, older workers and nonwhites who are out of work are more likely than others to find their unemployment extended by lack of education.

As for marital status, married women have about the same degree of long-term unemployment as other women. Married men, however, have lower unemployment rates and usually less long-term unemployment than other men. In 1960, although married men made up about half of the labor force, they represented only 37 per cent of the long-term unemployed. While the shorter periods of joblessness of married men may have something to do with the greater necessity of their finding new jobs, these shorter periods probably result more from the greater tendency of married men to be employed in more highly skilled occupations and the fact that they have characteristics that make them more employable.

WORK-HISTORY CHARACTERISTICS

Measurement of long-term unemployment by industry has the shortcoming of using for an industry classification the last job at-

6. Arnold Katz, "Educational Attainment of Workers, 1959," *Monthly Labor Review,* February, 1960, pp. 118–119.

tachment of the worker before his current period of unemployment. Thus, an unemployed worker who had spent most of his working life in a coal mine that shut down but who subsequently obtained a temporary job as a night watchman at a chemical plant would be classified in nondurable goods manufacturing rather than coal mining if he were currently unemployed. It could be argued that if his unemployment is lengthy, it might more appropriately be attributed to the coal mining industry than to nondurable goods manufacturing. The data on duration of unemployment by industry, in other words, do not necessarily get to the major industrial cause of long-term unemployment.

Also, which would be preferable, data for single spells of unemployment or data for unemployment over the course of a year? If the first definition is used, long-term unemployment is higher than average in manufacturing—both durable and nondurable— in public administration, among the self-employed, and among unpaid family workers. If, on the other hand, the definition is based on cumulative weeks of unemployment during an entire year, long-term unemployment is above average in agriculture, mining, and construction. The higher rates in these industries during the course of a year reflect the seasonal nature of employment in these industries.

Aside from the long-term unemployment associated with seasonal industries, the major industrial difference is between factory workers and workers in nonmanufacturing industries. The highest proportion of long-term unemployment in 1957 occurred among workers who lost jobs in manufacturing, 23 per cent of whom experienced 15 or more weeks of unemployment. This compares with an average of 19 per cent for all industries combined.

Although published data are not available for duration of unemployment in detailed industry classifications, long-term unemployment in the past few years has apparently been particularly severe in certain durable goods industries—steel, autos, and machinery—and in the textiles sector of nondurable goods manufacturing.

The highest rates of long-term unemployment are associated with industries that have declining employment opportunities as a result of either loss of markets or technological change that displaces workers. When unemployment occurs in these industries, many of the workers are unable to shift easily to jobs in other industries. The problem is often complicated by geographic concentration. Laid-off auto workers, textile workers, or miners are likely to be located in areas dominated by the industries in which they worked and in which employment opportunities are scarce or declining. A combination of both industry and geographic immobility contributes to the lengthy unemployment of many of the jobless.

High unemployment rates and lengthy unemployment are disproportionately high among blue-collar workers—especially when the measure used is total unemployment during the course of a year rather than the length of the current period of unemployment. In 1957, about 37 per cent of the unemployed blue-collar workers (craftsmen, operatives, and nonfarm laborers) had 15 or more weeks of unemployment during the year compared with only 27 per cent of the white-collar workers (professional and managerial, clerical, and sales). The figure was highest for the nonfarm laborers (43 per cent) and smallest for clerical workers (22 per cent). Using the yearly measure, blue-collar and service workers accounted for over three-fourths of the long-term unemployment during the year; white-collar workers accounted for only 15 per cent.

Finally, it should be noted that the probability of re-employment for the jobless is related to how long they have been out of work. Although turnover among the unemployed is quite high each month (an average of 55 per cent in 1957), the longer a person has been out of a job, the less likely he is to be re-employed quickly. In 1957, for example, about 41 per cent of the jobless who in a given month had reported four weeks of unemployment or less had found a job by the time of the next month's survey. In contrast, among those who reported unemployment of 15 weeks or more, only 21 per cent had found a job by the following month.[7] Even in relatively good years, such as 1957, combinations of such factors as low skills and education, middle or advanced

---

7. Joint Economic Committee, *op. cit.,* p. 35.

age, and color of skin reduce the probabilities for re-employment among the long-term unemployed.

A number of the factors that contribute to lengthy joblessness were prevalent in the local labor market situations described in Part Two of this book. A careful examination of the problems of permanently displaced workers in the local community can, we believe, provide considerable insight into both the difficulties and opportunities of special labor market measures designed to reduce both the burden and the incidence of long-term unemployment.

PART TWO

▶ CASE STUDIES

▶ OF

▶ SHUTDOWNS

▶ WITH

▶ PERMANENT

▶ LAYOFFS

2

The Communities,
the Studies,
and the Workers

C HANGES IN MARKETS, in technology, and in the pace of auto-mation have in recent years accelerated the displacement of work-ers from jobs in many industries. The job displacement problem is frequently taken care of through attrition; that is, workers who quit, retire, or die are not replaced and the remaining workers are re-assigned to other jobs as necessary. In such cases, the chief im-pact comes through the failure to hire new employees. Increasingly, however, displacement from jobs has meant permanent layoffs.

The most extreme case of permanent layoff occurs when an en-tire plant closes. Companies decide to close plants for many differ-ent reasons—business failure or decline; dropping a product; re-location to move closer to markets, to obtain lower wages or other costs, or to escape a union contract; and relocation to permit sub-stitution of automated facilities for obsolete equipment.

In this and following chapters we present data on the impact of five plant shutdowns on the workers who were permanently laid off.[1] These data give us an opportunity to analyze the behavior of the American worker and the functioning of the local labor market under stress.

The five communities where the shutdowns occurred vary considerably in population size, industrial composition, and industrial diversity. None was known as a distressed area or an area of chronic unemployment when the shutdowns took place, although two were later designated as labor surplus areas by the U.S. Bureau of Employment Security in the 1960–61 recession. All of the communities had been relatively prosperous and expanding in population. The one qualification to this generalization is that the city of East St. Louis was not sharing in the general prosperity of the Illinois section of the St. Louis standard metropolitan area. East St. Louis was not expanding in population, had been losing some major companies, and was having difficulty attracting new industry. Thus, the immediate labor market area where the Armour plant was located was weak and had relatively high unemployment.

Because of the differences in the five communities and the fact that they were not depressed areas, the studies can be said to provide a variety of evidence for the phenomenon of displacement during "prosperity." The experiences of the displaced workers in these five cities have been repeated in towns and cities throughout the nation, and every indication is that similar situations will continue to develop in other industrialized communities.

The studies serve, therefore, as illustrations of a problem of growing importance—whether the economy can absorb experienced industrial workers whose prior work experiences have lost their meaning because of market and technological changes. The case studies in this part of the book will furnish some of the background for the discussions in Part Three on ways of alleviating the hardships and of reducing the extent of long-term unemployment.

In this chapter, we introduce the case studies by describing briefly the shutdowns, the communities in which they occurred, the research design of the studies, and the characteristics of the displaced workers.

---

1. Armour meatpacking plants in East St. Louis, Ill.: Columbus, Ohio; West Fargo, N.D.; and Oklahoma City, Okla.; and a home laundry equipment plant in East Peoria, Ill.

The Shutdowns

Relatively little advance notice of the shutdowns was given in any of the situations. Each of the four Armour plants began separating workers only one month after the workers, unions, and public were notified that operations would cease. Further, all but a few maintenance workers and those assigned to clean-up crews had been separated from their jobs within a month after the layoffs began. Most of the workers, therefore, had only a month to consider their predicament and make plans for finding new employment. Although notice of the ABC plant shutdown in Peoria was given more than three months before production actually stopped, the Peoria layoffs also took place over a short period of time. About 90 per cent of the production work force was laid off in less than a month.

The brief advance notice and the rapid separation of the workers are probably the most important aspects of the shutdowns because of their direct impact on the displaced workers. The consequences are examined in the subsequent chapters of this part of the book. As background, however, a short account of each shutdown is given here.

THE ABC SHUTDOWN

The ABC Company had been a manufacturer of home laundry equipment in East Peoria, Ill., for more than 50 years. Until 1952 it was owned by a local family; in that year it became a subsidiary of the American Motors Corporation. According to a member of the ABC personnel department, the appliance division of the new parent company had been losing money for a number of years and, with declines in the demand for consumer durable goods, found itself with excess plant capacity. While the ABC plant had been profitable, other plants in the appliance division were being underutilized and had many workers on layoff. After an extensive study, American Motors decided to consolidate operations and move the ABC laundry line to Grand Rapids, Michigan.

When the decision to close the plant was announced early in the fall of 1958, no definite termination date was given. The announcement was not happily received by either the workers or the local management. Local management considered ABC an efficient and profitable plant which deserved a continued life, although they could understand the "business reasons" for the shutdown.

The reaction of the workers was expressed in the form of a strike called by Local 1144 of the United Electrical Workers.[2] The primary issues involved the terms and conditions under which the workers were to be separated from their jobs. An agreement was reached after a few weeks and the workers returned to their jobs. The most important provisions of the agreement were a severance pay arrangement tied in with the pension fund, early retirement for those between 60 and 65 years old, and a preferential hiring clause for any workers interested in employment at the Milwaukee, Kenosha, or Grand Rapids plants of the parent company, when and if openings should occur. Agreement on these items was reached on October 17, 1958, and the company continued to operate until mid-January, 1959. In fact, additional workers were hired to make it possible for the company to fill its remaining orders.

Most of the layoffs began about the middle of January, 1959, and by the end of the month only about 60 of 670 workers were left on the payroll. By February 7, all of the workers other than 20 maintenance and warehouse employees, engaged in the final details of the closing, had been laid off.

THE THREE-CITY SHUTDOWNS

Six Armour meatpacking plants in various parts of the country were closed in July, 1959, and their employees permanently separated from their jobs.[3] Only the East St. Louis, Ill., Columbus, Ohio, and West Fargo, N.D., plants are covered in the studies reported in this volume. Layoffs began early in July, and by the end of the month only 5 or 6 per cent of the production and maintenance workers remained on the payroll. Shortly thereafter they, too, were separated, although a few individuals were transferred to other Armour establishments.

---

2. According to the management, this was an illegal strike in violation of the collective bargaining agreement.
3. Operations at one other plant were partially terminated.

The plants that were closed had not been profitable for some time. They were obsolete and not suited to modern meatpacking technology. Further, the company's analysis of transportation costs for meat, both processed and "on the hoof," population shifts, and livestock distribution indicated a necessity for some geographic redistribution of processing plants.

The closing of the six Armour plants, which terminated the employment of about 5,000 production employees and eliminated more than 20 per cent of the company's total plant capacity, was not unique in the meatpacking industry. Each of the other three members of the industry's so-called "Big Four" has closed down major packinghouses in recent years. As of mid-1961, approximately 30,000 workers had been affected by such closings.[4]

When the decisions to shut down were made, they were carried out quickly. The workers had little time to consider their plans for re-employment or to make adjustments in their family finances to prepare for the impending loss of jobs. In June they had the security of a job they long had held and in which they expected to continue. A month later they were former Armour workers.

THE OKLAHOMA CITY SHUTDOWN

The closing of the Armour plant in Oklahoma City followed the pattern of the three-city shutdowns, but it was even more unexpected. The two major unions that represent most Armour employees, the Amalgamated Meat Cutters and the United Packinghouse Workers, were of the opinion, based on company statements, that after the 1959 shutdowns Armour anticipated no further closings for some time. The unions had so informed their members. Further, the company had given wide publicity to its intention to build a new plant in Oklahoma City. When the announcement was made on June 5, 1960, that the Oklahoma City plant would be permanently closed on July 8, 1960, it came as a shock to workers, union, and community.

The conditions that led to the closing of the Oklahoma City plant illustrate the economic changes that have affected the meat industry

---

4. See Armour Automation Fund Committee, *Progress Report* (Chicago: The Committee, June, 1961), p. 2.

generally.[5] The plant was old and, as a consequence, obsolete and inefficient. It was built in 1910 and sold to Armour in 1923 by another packing firm. For a number of years the plant was successful, but by the mid-1950's it was losing money as a result of the growing obsolescence of its facilities as well as changes in livestock distribution, methods of transportation, and freight rates.

In an attempt to solve the cost problem, the hog kill operation, which had represented about 50 per cent of the plant's production, was dropped in April, 1958. For a number of reasons the cutback did not solve the cost problem. The sheer size of the plant—a million square feet—meant substantial overhead costs even when the plant was operating at full capacity. The central power plant and maintenance and machine shops, for example, were not economical after the hog kill was terminated. A second reason was that most of the cattle processed produced utility type beef, which was not consumed in the area but instead had to be shipped to the east coast. Items produced for the local market, such as sausages and wieners, were only a small proportion of total output. Most of the plant's production, therefore, was subject to the high cost of long-distance shipping. Finally, the presence of Armour plants in Fort Worth and Kansas City limited the local market of the Oklahoma City plant largely to the state of Oklahoma.

Before the termination of the hog kill in the spring of 1958, the plant had about 550 hourly plant employees on its payroll. Although most of them were still carried on the seniority rolls, only about 270 plant maintenance and production workers were still on the active payroll in July, 1960. Both groups, those still working and those on layoff status, were notified in June, 1960, that their jobs would be terminated the following month.

About a month after the plant closed, the Armour Automation Fund Committee initiated a series of steps designed to assist the displaced workers in finding new jobs.[6] The steps included testing

5. The circumstances leading to the shutdown were obtained in an interview with Mr. A. S. Drain, who was General Manager of the Oklahoma City plant.

6. The Armour Automation Fund Committee was organized under a provision of the 1959 collective bargaining contract between Armour and the United Packinghouse Workers and the Amalgamated Meat Cutters Unions. The Automation Committee is tripartite, composed of four representatives

and counseling of the workers, contacts with firms in the community to attempt to find job openings and to acquaint employers with the availability of the former Armour workers, and sponsorship of pilot retraining courses for those who were interested, qualified, and able to benefit. These programs are described and evaluated in the chapters that follow.

The Five Communities

All of the communities where the plant shutdowns took place are standard metropolitan areas, although varying in population from about 100,000 to almost 700,000 (Table 2). Columbus, Ohio (Franklin County), is the largest, having a population of more than two-thirds of a million, and it has also been the fastest-growing, with a population increase of 35.7 per cent between 1950 and 1960. The Oklahoma City standard metropolitan area (Oklahoma, Cleveland, and Canadian counties), with half a million people in 1960, also grew rapidly between 1950 and 1960, expanding by 30.4 per cent. The Illinois section of the St. Louis standard metropolitan area (Madison and St. Clair counties)[7] had just under a half million population in 1960 and expanded by 25.5 per cent between 1950 and 1960. All of these areas during the decade had a growth greater than the 19 per cent average increase for the resident population of the United States as a whole, although the population of the *city* of East St. Louis declined slightly.

The population of the other two areas expanded at somewhat lower rates than the United States average. The Peoria, Ill., area (Peoria and Tazewell counties), with about 290,000 people in 1960, had a population increase of 15.3 per cent over the decade. The Fargo, N.D.–Moorhead, Minn., area achieved the classifica-

---

of the company, two from each of the unions, and an impartial chairman and executive director. The essential clause in the automation agreement was "that the Committee will study the problems of 'automation' . . . and report its findings and recommendations to the company and to the unions for their further consideration in connection with bargaining over a new contract in August of 1961." See Automation Committee, *op. cit.,* p. 1.

7. For simplicity, we subsequently refer to this area as the East St. Louis area.

tion of standard metropolitan area in 1960 by going over 100,000 population. Its population grew by 18.8 per cent between 1950 and 1960.

Table 2
1960 Population—Columbus, Oklahoma City, East St. Louis, Peoria, and Fargo

Standard Metropolitan Statistical Areas	1950 Population	1960 Population	Per Cent Increase	Per Cent Nonwhite, 1960
Columbus, Ohio	503,410	682,962	35.7	11.9
Oklahoma City	392,439	511,833	30.4	9.4
Illinois Section, St. Louis (E. St. Louis)	388,302	487,198	25.5	12.4
Peoria, Ill.	250,512	288,833	15.3	3.6
Fargo, N.D.–Moorhead, Minn.	89,240	106,027	18.8	0.3

Source: U.S. Bureau of the Census, *1960 Census of Population, General Characteristics* (Reports in PC-2 series for individual states).

INDUSTRIAL COMPOSITION

Three of the five cities—Columbus, East St. Louis, and Peoria —have heavy concentrations of employment in manufacturing, particularly in durable goods manufacturing (see Figure 3). The two largest—Columbus and East St. Louis—have a much greater diversity of manufacturing industries than does Peoria. Manufacturing in Peoria is dominated by the nonelectrical machinery industry, which normally employs about 60 per cent of the manufacturing labor force. Other major manufacturing industry groups are food (particularly beverages), primary metals, and fabricated metals.

The East St. Louis area has a great diversity in manufacturing industries. Since much of the manufacturing is durable goods (roughly 60 per cent of manufacturing employment), the area tends to be hit harder than some by employment downturns during recessions. Prominent among the manufacturing industries are petroleum refining, steel and other primary metals, transportation equipment, meatpacking and other food products, and chemicals.

Columbus, Ohio, also has a diversity of manufacturing industries, with considerable emphasis on durable goods manufacturing (about 70 per cent of its manufacturing employment). The major

Figure 3. PERCENTAGE DISTRIBUTION OF NONFARM EMPLOYEES IN MANUFAC-
TURING AND NONMANUFACTURING INDUSTRIES ON DATES OF SHUT-
DOWN, FIVE CITIES

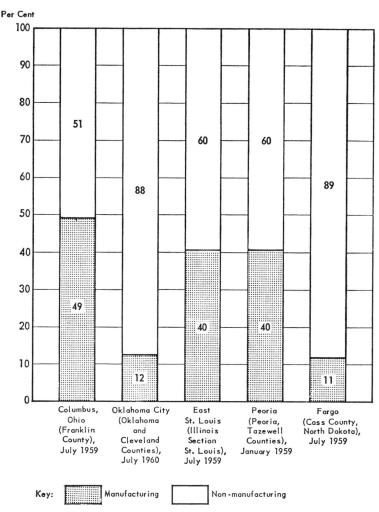

Source: Estimates made by State Employment Service, each state.

manufacturing industry groups are transportation equipment, non-electrical and electrical machinery, fabricated metal products, and food products. Even though it is the state capital, government employment is not a very large proportion of total employment.

Oklahoma City, while falling between Columbus and East St. Louis in population size, is very different in its industrial composition. Manufacturing makes up only about one-eighth of its nonfarm employment. Much more than the other large cities in the studies, Oklahoma City is a government and trading center. In January, 1961, it had 28 per cent of its nonfarm employment in government jobs. Much of this government employment occurs because Oklahoma City is the state capital and also has several major federal installations. Further, as the major city in the state, it has above-average employment in wholesale and retail trade.

Fargo-Moorhead,[8] although only one-fifth the size of Oklahoma City, is somewhat similar in industrial composition, particularly in the small proportion of total employment in manufacturing industries. Fargo is predominantly a trading and commercial center for a geographically large, predominantly rural area of North Dakota and Minnesota. As a result, relatively high proportions of the Fargo jobs are in trade and services.

DISPLACED WORKERS AND THE LOCAL LABOR FORCE

The workers displaced by the ABC and Armour plant shutdowns represent very small proportions of the civilian labor forces in each of the areas. The data in Table 3 show that while the gross figures indicate that a plant shutdown is a minor incident in the economic life of a large community, the impact of the worker displacement on the volume of unemployment can be quite substantial.

The Design of the Studies

In the autumn of 1958, upon learning that the ABC home laundry plant in Peoria was going to be closed permanently, we obtained permission from the company to interview the nonmanagerial

---

8. For simplicity, subsequently referred to as Fargo.

Table 3
Laid-Off Workers Studied as Proportions of Civilian Labor Force and Total Area Unemployment at Time of Shutdowns

Date of Plant Shutdown	Labor Market Area	Estimates of Civilian Labor Force	Estimates of Total Unemployment	WORKERS LAID OFF BY SHUTDOWNS[a]		
				Number	Per Cent of Labor Force	Per Cent of Unemployment
January, 1959	Peoria	116,625	6,300	680[b]	0.6	10.8
July, 1959	Illinois Section, St. Louis (E. St. Louis)	159,525	9,100	1,620	1.0	17.8
July, 1960	Oklahoma City (Oklahoma, Cleveland Counties)	205,000	6,500	270[c]	0.1	4.2
July, 1959	Fargo (Cass County)	27,000[d]	1,200	380	1.4	31.7
July, 1959	Columbus	275,000[d]	8,500[d]	410	0.1	4.8
Totals	Five areas	783,000	31,600	3,360	0.4	10.6

Source: Labor force and unemployment estimates from reports of the public employment service in each area.
[a] Workers included in the five shutdown studies only.
[b] Includes part of the salaried work force.
[c] Those laid off in July, 1960. Some 200 others were laid off over the preceding two years.
[d] Based on authors' rough estimates of labor force participation rates.

work force before the shutdown took place.[9] We had several reasons for interest in such a study. One of us was already engaged in a study of unemployment among older workers in the Peoria labor market area, and the other had recently completed a study for the U.S. Bureau of Labor Statistics on the impact of a major plant shutdown in a depressed area.[10] We saw the possibilities of exploring the impact of a plant shutdown in an area that was not depressed and of obtaining data from the workers on their labor market goals before they were displaced.

To our knowledge, there were no studies of displaced workers in which data had been obtained from the workers after learning of the layoff plans but before the layoff took place. In our view, interviews both before and some time after the plant shutdown would enable us to compare the labor market goals of displaced workers with their success in achieving those goals.

Our objective, therefore, was to obtain reliable data in pre-shutdown interviews and in post-shutdown mail questionnaires and personal interviews that would help us answer the following questions:

1. When workers are displaced, what personal and other factors determine relative success in finding new jobs?

2. When a large group enters the labor market at the same time, how important is the worker's age in finding new employment?

3. Which groups have the highest unemployment? Which are most successful in finding the *type* of work sought? And which are most willing to move to other communities for jobs?

In the spring of 1960, after we had obtained the post-shutdown mail questionnaire data from the ABC workers and were beginning the personal interviews, we were asked by the Armour Automation Fund Committee if we would conduct surveys of the former

---

9. The cost of the study was partially underwritten by the Forest Park Foundation.

10. Walter H. Franke was completing the field work on a study of older workers in the Peoria labor market, a study financed by the Forest Park Foundation of Peoria. The plant shutdown study of Richard C. Wilcock was published as *Impact on Workers and Community of a Plant Shutdown in a Depressed Area* (Washington, D.C.: U.S. Bureau of Labor Statistics, Bulletin No. 1264, June, 1960), 58 pp.

Armour workers in three of the cities where Armour plants had closed in July, 1959. The cities selected for study were East St. Louis, Columbus, and Fargo. Since we had a tested research design available, we were able to launch these studies quickly and thus obtain data as of approximately one year after the shutdowns.

In June, 1960, immediately after Armour and Company's decision to close the Oklahoma City plant, we were requested by the Automation Committee to make a survey in that city. We agreed, and it was decided that we should include an in-plant survey of the workers who were still employed in the Oklahoma City plant. The immediate purpose was to obtain data from the workers that would be useful to the committee and its representatives in formulating plans for job retraining and for helping the workers in their search for jobs. In addition, the in-plant survey would be comparable to the one made in Peoria and would provide us with two sets of before-and-after data.

The general purpose of all the Armour studies was to measure the economic and financial impact of the plant shutdowns on the workers who were displaced from their jobs. Our studies of plant shutdowns were in addition to a number of other studies sponsored by the Armour Automation Committee. All studies were designed to provide the committee with data that would be relevant to discussions between the company and the unions on the economic and employment changes taking place within the meatpacking industry.[11] In authorizing the studies, the committee was fulfilling part of its obligation under the collective bargaining agreement concluded in 1959.[12]

---

11. Other studies included an analysis of interplant transfers in a number of industries (Arnold Weber, Graduate School of Business, University of Chicago); the economics of the meatpacking industry, with particular reference to future employment prospects (Milton Derber, Institute of Labor and Industrial Relations, University of Illinois); an engineering analysis of the skills involved in the maintenance of certain automated equipment (Bernt O. Larson, College of Engineering, University of Illinois); an analysis of the company's severance pay structure in relation to its usefulness to the employees (S. Herbert Unterberger, Philadelphia); and an analysis of advance notice in plant closings (Arnold Weber).

12. Master Agreement between Armour and Company, United Packinghouse Workers of America (AFL-CIO), and Amalgamated Meat Cutters and Butcher Workmen of North America (AFL-CIO), September 1, 1959, to August 31, 1961.

In addition to the general objective, the Armour plant closing studies were designed to answer the following questions:

1. What was the extent of unemployment experienced by the laid-off workers?
2. What classifications of workers experienced the greatest difficulty in finding new jobs?
3. What labor market alternatives were available to the workers at the time the plants closed?
4. What kind of help was furnished to the workers in seeking and finding new employment?
5. How did post-Armour jobs compare with the jobs held at Armour?
6. What impact did the shutdowns have on the economic life of the workers and their families?

THREE-CITY STUDY: EAST ST. LOUIS, COLUMBUS, AND FARGO

The two major sources of data for this study were a mail questionnaire survey of all production and maintenance employees who were in the bargaining units in the three plants at the time of the shutdowns and personal interviews with a sample of the same workers. Most of the mail questionnaires were returned in June, 1960, and most of the personal interviews were conducted in July, 1960.

The mail questionnaire survey was designed to obtain information on the employment and unemployment experience of the workers in the period following their separation from Armour. Initially, questionnaires were sent to all bargaining-unit employees who were eligible for separation pay—a total of 2,411 persons. After two follow-up mailings, 1,837 returns were received. This represents 76 per cent of the total number of workers or 80 per cent of those who received the questionnaires. By obtaining 83 additional questionnaires from nonrespondents selected for personal interviews, we finally had questionnaire data for 1,920 of the workers, or 80 per cent of the total bargaining-unit work forces of the three plants.

Among those who responded to the mail questionnaire, 64 individuals had moved at least 100 miles away from the three local labor market areas. A special questionnaire was sent to these 64 migrants to determine their reasons for moving and their interest in moving back to their former homes. Because of limitations in time, only one mailing was made to the migrants and returns were received from 41 persons, or 64 per cent.

A sample of 243 individuals—99 in East St. Louis, 74 in Columbus, and 70 in Fargo—were selected for personal interviews. The interview survey had two major purposes. One was to gather from a representative group of workers in the three cities more detailed information about their post-shutdown experiences than could be obtained through a mail questionnaire. The other was to check the reliability of the mail questionnaire results.

To meet these objectives the interview sample had to meet two criteria: first, it had to be representative of the total work forces of the three plants; and second, a large enough number of nonrespondents to the mail questionnaire had to be included to test for any difference or bias in the mail questionnaire data due to nonresponse.

The first objective was met by selecting random stratified samples of workers from each city. The East St. Louis sample was stratified by sex, race, and age; the samples for the other two cities by sex and age. To meet the second objective, we decided that half of the interviews in each city should be with respondents and half with nonrespondents.[13]

PEORIA AND OKLAHOMA CITY STUDIES

The designs of the ABC study in Peoria and the Armour study in Oklahoma City are basically the same as the three-city study, but both contain a pre-shutdown survey. The major purpose of the pre-shutdown surveys was to determine, before the layoffs took place, the plans and expectations of the workers for finding new

---

13. One result of these decisions is that the distribution of interview respondents by age, sex, and race differs slightly from the over-all distribution of the work forces. These differences have virtually no effect on the degree to which each subsample represents the population of its group, however. For further discussion, see Appendix A.

jobs, and the extent of the workers' knowledge about labor market conditions and employment opportunities. These data could be compared with post-shutdown survey data. The pre-shutdown questionnaire was completed by 657 of the 670 hourly and salaried workers at ABC and 260 hourly employees at Armour. In both plants, groups of about 15 workers at a time filled out the schedules during working hours and under the supervision of the authors.

In Peoria, the post-shutdown questionnaires were mailed in January, 1960, one year after the shutdown, to the 542 regular production workers at ABC at the time of the shutdown. Excluded from the sample were 79 short-service employees and 36 salaried office workers.[14] After three mailings, the forms were returned by 426 of the 542 production workers. Forty-six of the remaining 116 nonrespondents were later interviewed and completed the mail questionnaire at that time. The ABC questionnaire data, therefore, cover 472 of the 542 persons who qualified for the mail survey sample, or 87 per cent.

In Oklahoma City, the post-shutdown questionnaires were mailed in November, 1960, about four months after the shutdown. As in Peoria, two follow-up forms were sent to nonrespondents. All the returns used were received in November and December, four to five months after the shutdown. Of the 260 persons in the final-layoff group who were included in the in-plant survey, 203 (78 per cent) returned questionnaires by mail. Of the 56 who did not respond, 48 were interviewed in February, 1961, and completed the questionnaires at that time. The remaining nine persons could not be located. Fourteen of the questionnaires were discarded because the individuals were still working for Armour at the time of the questionnaire survey. The mail questionnaire data in this report, therefore, cover 237 out of a possible 246 cases, or 96 per cent of those in the final-layoff group.

The early-layoff group consisted of 200 persons who were still

14. The short-service workers were for the most part persons on temporary layoff from other plants who took the ABC jobs knowing they were only temporary. Since they presumably had regular jobs to go back to, they were eliminated from the sample. The small number of office salaried workers were included in the mail survey but were excluded from the mail questionnaire tabulations to make the Peoria sample comparable with the samples in the other four cities.

in employment status and eligible for separation pay. In this group, 134, or 67 per cent, returned the mail questionnaire.[15]

In Peoria, personal interviews were held with 196 former ABC employees, or about one-third of the laid-off workers. The interviews were held between late May and mid-July of 1960, or about a year and a half after the shutdown. Because they were relatively few and we wished to have them adequately represented, we decided to include in the interview sample all of the salaried employees, all Negroes under 45 years of age, and all of those who had indicated in the pre-shutdown survey that they had jobs lined up.[16] The remaining nonrespondents who were to be interviewed were stratified by age and the remaining respondents were stratified by age and length of unemployment.[17] Each of the stratified groups was sampled randomly. The objectives of the stratification were, first, to insure that groups whose employment experience after the shutdown could be expected to differ were adequately represented in the sample, and second, to obtain interviews with a sufficient number in each of these groups to permit comparisons.

In Oklahoma City, personal interviews were conducted in February, 1961, about seven months after the shutdown, with 111 of the 246 persons in the final-layoff group.[18] The interview sample included all nonrespondents to the mail survey who could be located (48 persons). Respondents were stratified by sex, race, and age and sampled randomly within each stratum. Proportionate numbers were interviewed in the several strata, so that the sex, race,

---

15. The mail questionnaire data obtained from persons in the early-layoff group—those who were already on layoff when the announcement of the closing occurred—were subjected to the same analysis as the data from the final-layoff group. Since there were no substantial differences between the two groups, only the data for the final-layoff group are presented in this book.

16. There were so few Negro employees 45 years old or over we eliminated them from the sample.

17. Length of unemployment was determined from the mail questionnaires. Two strata were sampled—those with less than six months and those with six months or more unemployment in the year following the shutdown.

18. This is about 45 per cent of the final-layoff group. Persons in the early-layoff group were not included in the interview sample.

and age distribution of the interview sample is identical to the distribution of the original work force in these characteristics.

RESURVEY IN 1962

Between January and April, 1962, we conducted a follow-up mail survey of the more than 2,600 respondents in the five cities. With three mailings and checks of nonrespondents by phone and personal visit, we obtained data from over 85 per cent of the original respondents.

In this resurvey, we found out who had left the labor force and why, the extent of unemployment in 1961, the sources of income of those unemployed, and the occupation and industry of those employed. Most importantly, we found out how many had remained "unwanted workers"—three years later in Peoria, two and one-half years later in the three cities, and a year and one-half in Oklahoma City. Some of the data from this resurvey are reported in subsequent chapters.

RELIABILITY OF RESULTS

Although there are some minor differences, the interview data in all of the studies support the results obtained from the mail questionnaires on comparable factual questions. Because the mail questionnaire data were obtained from a much larger proportion of the workers and, for this reason, provide more reliable results when the data are broken down into subgroups, the mail questionnaire data are used in our analysis in those cases where data are available from both sources.

Both the mail questionnaire and personal interview data, however, provide reliable results if the data are treated as close approximations rather than precise numbers. In our interpretation we have tried to limit our major conclusions to differences that are clearly significant. Further, the reliability of the data is attested to by the fact that the sex, race, and age distributions from both interviews and questionnaires are closely similar to company data on the composition of the work forces in the five plants. In each of the studies, therefore, men and women, white and Negro, and younger and older are adequately represented.[19]

Characteristics of the Displaced Workers

Most of the workers included in the studies held semiskilled or unskilled manual jobs at Armour or ABC. A few were in skilled manual occupations or in clerical jobs.[20] The Armour workers were older, on the average, than the ABC workers (see Figure 4) and also had greater length of service with the company. Median length of service for the Armour workers ranged from 10 years at Fargo to 17 years at Oklahoma City (for those in the final-layoff group). Median length of service at ABC was about 7 years.

The typical former Armour worker is a married man with two or three dependents who has had only a grade school education and is over 45 years of age. The chances are better than even that he owns or is paying for a modest home and still has one or two children under 18 dependent upon his support.

The characteristics of the Armour workers vary relatively little among the four cities. The major difference is in the proportion who are Negroes, ranging from 59 per cent in East St. Louis to none in Fargo. In Oklahoma City 36 per cent of the final-layoff group are Negroes, but in Columbus this is the case for only 8 per cent of the displaced workers.[21] Differences in age, proportions married, home ownership, and number of years of school are relatively small from city to city.

Many of the characteristics of the Armour workers made it

19. Some tests of the comparability of the mail questionnaire and personal interview results were made. Results of these tests and additional data on sampling procedures, estimates of sampling error, and procedures both for the field survey work and for coding and processing of data are given in Appendix A. The questions used in the mail questionnaire and personal interview schedules are shown in Appendix B.

20. There were some shop clerical personnel in the bargaining units at Armour and at ABC.

21. In Columbus, Fargo, and East St. Louis, the proportions of Negroes in the work force reflect the proportions in the community at large (in the 1960 Census, the city of East St. Louis had a 44.6 per cent nonwhite population). In Oklahoma City, the proportion of Negroes in the work force was well above the proportion in the community. See Table 2.

Figure 4. PERCENTAGE DISTRIBUTION OF DISPLACED WORKERS, BY SEX, RACE, AGE, AND YEARS OF SCHOOL, FIVE CITIES

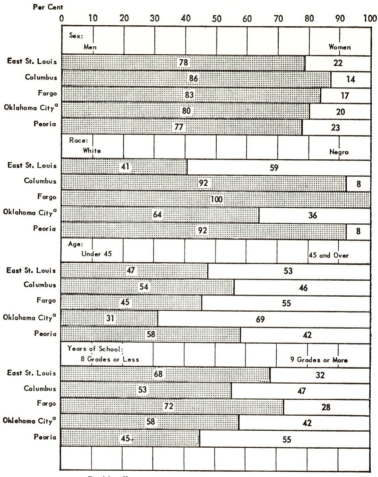

a. Final layoff group.

Source: Mail questionnaire respondents.

fairly predictable that under the best of circumstances they would have difficulty in finding new jobs. Their high average age, their relatively unskilled and nontransferable work experience, and their low level of education are known handicaps in the job market. The Negroes had the additional handicap of race.

The ABC workers, in contrast, were relatively better off. Their average age was not quite 40 at the time of the shutdown, their industrial and occupational experience is more transferable, their average level of education is higher, and only a small proportion are Negroes. Also, as it happened, job opportunities were relatively better in Peoria than in any of the cities where Armour plants closed, with the exception of Columbus.

In spite of the differences between the ABC and Armour workers, we found that workers with similar characteristics had similar labor market experiences and difficulties in each of the cities. Age, sex, race, lack of education, and low skill level were job market handicaps in all five communities. Our findings on this and other aspects of the post-shutdown experiences are presented in the chapters that follow.

3

Unemployment
after the Shutdown

U NDER THE MOST FAVORABLE of circumstances unemployment
of some duration would occur among workers displaced from their
jobs by a plant shutdown. Before accepting new jobs, many workers want time to survey the labor market and locate job openings
that suit their particular skills and interests. In a "perfect" market,
such frictional unemployment would last for only a brief period.
Labor markets are never perfect, however, and even when the
employment level is high some displaced workers may have considerable difficulty finding suitable jobs. When a shutdown occurs
in a period of declining or relatively low economic activity, the
time required to locate new jobs is apt to be greatly lengthened
for many of the workers.

Short-term frictional unemployment is generally recognized as
necessary in a dynamic economy and even desirable because it is
evidence that workers have some freedom of choice in picking new
jobs. Unemployment insurance is almost universally admired as a
device that both encourages labor mobility and provides the unemployed worker with a modest income while he seeks suitable
work. Private contractual arrangements providing severance pay
and supplemental unemployment benefits are designed to add to

the minimum level of support for a limited period of time for eligible workers. Neither public nor private programs, however, are expected to extend beyond periods generally associated with frictional and short-run cyclical unemployment. No programs are designed to support an unemployed worker indefinitely.

Almost all of the production and maintenance workers in the five plants included in this study received severance pay and, if unemployed after their separation, unemployment compensation. Many of them, however, experienced unemployment far more extensive than the short-term frictional variety that the existing private and public programs are designed to combat.

Extent of Long-Term Unemployment

In order to evaluate the unemployment experience of the displaced workers in the five cities, we shall discuss (1) the initial period of unemployment before they found their first jobs, (2) the total amount of their unemployment during the first year, and (3) the extent of unemployment at various times from a half year to three years after the shutdowns.

THE INITIAL PERIOD OF UNEMPLOYMENT

Workers facing an imminent separation from their jobs are themselves aware that they may not find a new job immediately. Prior to the shutdowns in Peoria and Oklahoma City, the workers were asked to estimate how long they would be unemployed before they found a new job. In both cities about half thought they would have a new job in less than three months; the other half thought it would take longer, with 13 per cent in Peoria and 27 per cent in Oklahoma City guessing it would take more than six months. Since the survey in Peoria was done toward the end of the 1957–58 recession and the one in Oklahoma City during the 1960 recession, the half who were anticipating a relatively lengthy job search were undoubtedly influenced by what they perceived to be unfavorable job prospects at the time.

How long it actually took the displaced workers to find their first jobs after the shutdowns is summarized in Figure 5. The

workers in the five cities obviously had greatly different employment experiences. While only 17 per cent of the East St. Louis
workers found jobs in less than three months, over half of the
Peoria workers (55 per cent) did so—about as they had predicted
in the pre-shutdown survey. Conversely, almost half of the workers in East St. Louis (49 per cent) but only 11 per cent of those in
Peoria had no regular job in the entire year following the shutdown; that is, they had no job that lasted as long as a month.

Figure 5. NUMBER OF MONTHS TO FIRST JOB AFTER PLANT SHUTDOWNS, DIS-
PLACED WORKERS, FIVE CITIES (IN PER CENTS)

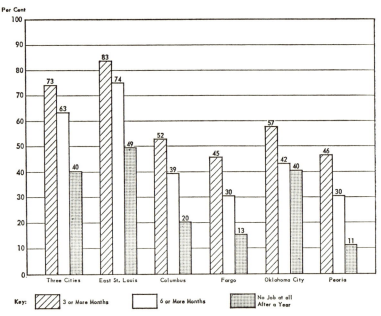

Source: Mail questionnaire data, except Oklahoma City. Source for Oklahoma City was
personal interview data obtained about seven months after the shutdown. For the
other cities, the data were obtained about one year after the shutdown.

The workers who required three months or more to find a job
are those who approximate the 15-week definition of the long-
term unemployed used by the U.S. Labor Department. At least
40 per cent of the workers in each city, and in East St. Louis over

80 per cent, required three months or more to find work after separation from their jobs.

In addition to showing a great deal of long-term unemployment among the displaced workers, the data indicate that those who failed to find jobs quickly found it increasingly difficult to leave the ranks of the unemployed. To be sure, more and more workers found jobs as time passed. But, with the exception of East St. Louis, more workers in each city found jobs in the first two months after their layoff than in all of the following months. As Table 4 shows, between 42 and 55 per cent of the workers in each city, again excluding East St. Louis, found a job within two months. In the succeeding ten or more months only about an additional one-third of the workers were able to obtain employment.[1]

Table 4
Time Required to Find First Post-Shutdown Job, Five Cities

	East St. Louis	Columbus	Fargo	Okla. City	Peoria
Per cent who found jobs in first two months	17	47	55	42	55
Per cent who found jobs in remainder of year	34	33	32	18	34
Per cent who found job during year—total	51	80	87	60	89

The major explanation for this phenomenon would appear to be that those workers with skills, experience, or other characteristics most in demand are quickly hired while those who remain unemployed either have fewer skills to offer or have characteristics that place them at a disadvantage in the labor market. The long-term unemployed include, in other words, a large proportion of "unwanted workers."

Although we have no specific evidence on the point, it may be that the employment possibilities of the long-term unemployed are reduced merely by virtue of their being without a job for a long time. Employers might conclude, for example, that there must be

1. The proportion who had found a job after two months in Oklahoma City was only 18 per cent. Only seven months had passed after the shutdown when the workers were interviewed, however, compared with twelve months in the other cities.

something wrong with such a worker and hesitate to employ him. Or the worker himself might conclude either the same thing or that no suitable jobs are available. As a result he might become discouraged in his job search and thus prolong his unemployment. The post-shutdown pattern of job search, discussed in Chapter 5, shows that this did occur for some of the displaced workers.

For substantial proportions of workers in all five cities, therefore, finding a new job was difficult and required a long time. At least 30 per cent of the displaced workers in each of the cities required at least six months to find their first jobs. Some of them will probably never work again. Preliminary tabulations of data from our 1962 resurvey show that two and one-half to three years after the shutdowns, the proportions of workers still in the labor force who had not worked at all since the shutdowns ranged from 3 per cent in Peoria to about 30 per cent in East St. Louis.[2] In addition, quite large numbers in East St. Louis and Fargo had left the labor force without ever finding a job. For most of those in these groups the prospects for regular employment in the future are poor.

DURATION OF UNEMPLOYMENT

Information on the initial period of unemployment does not tell the complete story of the extent of unemployment following the shutdowns. Some workers accepted only temporary jobs and were soon out of work again. Others were involved in layoffs from their first jobs and experienced another period of unemployment. In the three cities, for example, one out of every three of the former Armour workers who found a job was not working on the same job a year after the shutdown. In Peoria, a majority of the workers found jobs in less than two months, but a year after the shut-

2. The proportions for Fargo and Columbus are 6 per cent and 11 per cent, respectively. In Oklahoma City, about 22 per cent had not worked at all at the resurvey time a year and a half after the shutdown. These proportions may be compared with the 9 per cent of car shop workers who were unable to find any employment during the two years following the plant shutdown in Mt. Vernon, Ill., which was a depressed area. See Richard C. Wilcock, *Impact on Workers and Community of a Plant Shutdown in a Depressed Area* (Washington, D.C.: U.S. Bureau of Labor Statistics, Bulletin No. 1264, June, 1960), p. 28.

down almost 40 per cent of those who had worked at all were no longer employed on their first post-shutdown job.

A minority of the displaced workers, varying from less than one out of ten in East St. Louis to a little over one in four in Peoria, had no unemployment at all during the year following the shutdowns.[3] The median length of unemployment varied from 11 to 12 months in East St. Louis to two months in Peoria, reflecting again the great differences among the cities. In Columbus and Fargo the median time out of work was five to six months.

Although job prospects were far brighter for the ABC workers in Peoria than for the meatpacking workers in the other cities, a substantial proportion of them also had extended unemployment. About one in four were out of work more than six months (see Figure 6). Among the former Armour employees in the three cities, however, almost two out of three workers had over six months of unemployment. Again, it is clear from Figure 6 that those who had more than a few months without work were also likely to have very protracted unemployment.

LABOR FORCE STATUS

The labor force status of any group of workers at a particular point in time will depend to a considerable extent on the existing demand for labor. If the studies in the five cities had been done at time periods other than the ones used, quite different results might have been obtained. Nevertheless, a year is a long time, and the labor force status attained by the workers a year after the plants were closed suggests the general labor market adjustment the workers were able to make.

The percentage of workers with jobs a year after the shutdowns varies from 33 per cent in East St. Louis to 76 per cent in Peoria. Most of the others were unemployed. Only small minorities in each community left the labor force. They comprised about equal proportions of women doing housework in their own homes, persons unable to work because of health or other personal reasons, and persons who retired because of age (see Table 5).

3. These include a few who were out of the labor force for the entire period following the shutdowns.

Figure 6. PROPORTIONS OF DISPLACED WORKERS WITH OVER TWO MONTHS OF
UNEMPLOYMENT DURING THE YEAR AFTER THE SHUTDOWNS, FOUR CITIES

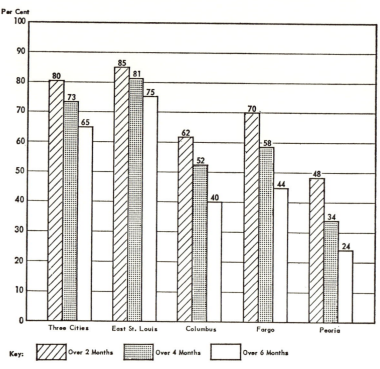

Source: Mail questionnaire data.

The variation among the cities in the proportions who had left
the labor market suggests that the general state of the economy is a
factor in the decision not to look for work. In Peoria, where job
prospects were most favorable, only 2 per cent had left the labor
force, while for East St. Louis, where community unemployment
was heaviest, the figure is 7 per cent. The personal characteristics
of the workers are also important. The relatively high proportion
(10 per cent) of the Oklahoma City workers out of the labor force
is largely the result of the high percentage of women, 27 per cent,
who were not looking for work, although the 1962 resurvey shows
that a number of these later re-entered the labor force. Also, the

Table 5
Labor Force Status at Time of Mail Questionnaire, Workers
Displaced by Plant Shutdowns, by City
(in Per Cent)

Labor Force Status	Total	THREE CITIES[a]			Okla. City[b]	Peoria ABC[a]
		East St. Louis	Columbus	Fargo		
	(N = 1,920)	(N = 1,331)	(N = 290)	(N = 299)	(N = 237)	(N = 472)
Employed	42	33	63	65	42	76
Unemployed	51	60	32	29	48	22
Out of labor force	7	7	5	6	10	2

Source: Mail questionnaire data.
[a] Approximately one year after shutdowns.
[b] Approximately five months after the shutdown.

higher proportion of older workers in the East St. Louis plant, many of whom left the labor force, was a factor in the higher rate of labor force withdrawal in that city.

Of greater significance than the numbers of workers who, voluntarily or involuntarily, left the labor force is the exceedingly high incidence of unemployment among the displaced workers a year after the shutdowns. In East St. Louis, the unemployment rate among the displaced meatpacking workers was 12 times as high as the unemployment rate in the East St. Louis labor market generally. In Columbus, it was 8 times the community rate; in Fargo, 9 times; in Oklahoma City, 13; and in Peoria, 6.

That these high unemployment rates are not a temporary phenomenon or due to unique circumstances present during the survey period is revealed by the fact that the high rates of unemployment persisted to the time of our 1962 resurvey. The picture improved relatively little during the year and a half between surveys. Figure 7 compares unemployment rates among the displaced workers for the original surveys and the 1962 resurvey. Early in 1962, the unemployment rate among the East St. Louis workers was still over 50 per cent. The rates in Fargo and Peoria had fallen hardly at all. In Columbus and Oklahoma City, the rates had fallen somewhat more but were still very high.

Not only did unemployment remain high, but in East St. Louis, Fargo, and Peoria there was a further exodus from the labor force after the original surveys. The proportions who were out of the

Figure 7. UNEMPLOYMENT RATES, YEAR AFTER SHUTDOWN,[a] AND SPRING, 1962, FIVE CITIES

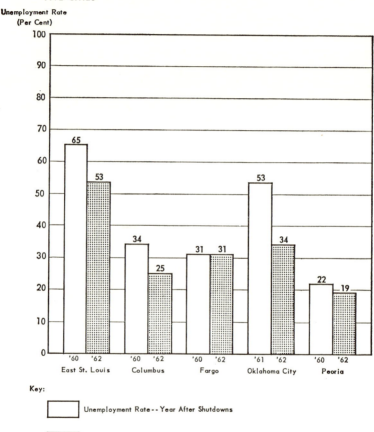

Key:

◻ Unemployment Rate -- Year After Shutdowns

▦ Unemployment Rate -- Spring, 1962, Survey

a. Seven months after shutdown in Oklahoma City.

Source: Mail questionnaire and resurvey data.

labor force in the spring of 1962 were about 13 per cent in East St. Louis and Fargo and 8 per cent in Peoria.

The abnormally high unemployment rates reflect the severe consequences of the permanent loss of job rights caused by plant shutdowns. Although many experienced workers who become unemployed retain their job rights and the hope of returning to their employers, those who are permanently displaced, like new entrants into the labor force, have no job security. Further, many have the disadvantage of advanced age, low levels of education, obsolete skills, and lack of experience in job hunting. The resurvey shows that the passage of time did not significantly lessen the impact of these disadvantages.

The Incidence of Long-Term Unemployment— Who Are the Long-Term Unemployed?

Long-term unemployment was not confined to one or even a few groups of workers. Regardless of the classifications of workers used, there were "unwanted workers" in every group. Prolonged unemployment was more heavily concentrated, however, in some groups than in others (see Table 6).

SEX

Well over half of the displaced women workers in each city reported unemployment of more than six months. In Peoria, the proportion of women among the very long-term unemployed was more than three times that of men; in Fargo and Columbus it was almost two times the proportion of men. The high rates appear in part to be due to factors peculiar to these cities limiting the employment prospects for women, particularly at pay rates they were accustomed to. The heavy machinery industry, which employs relatively few women, dominates the employment market in Peoria. Therefore, few factory jobs for women were available. In Fargo, many of the men were able to find jobs in agriculture and construction, an opportunity not available to women. But the high unemployment rates for women in all of the cities indicate that there are also more general causes.

The male-female differential in duration of unemployment is in large part the result of the inability of many women to find any job at all during the year after the shutdowns. The proportion of women unemployed for the entire period was three times that of men in Fargo (33 per cent compared with 11 per cent), about

Table 6
Number of Months of Unemployment during Year after
Shutdowns by Sex, Race, Age, and City[a]
(in Per Cent)

Months of Unemployment	SEX		RACE		AGE	
	Male	Female	White	Negro	Under 45	45 and Over
Less than 3 months						
East St. Louis	15	11	22	8	15	13
Columbus	41	20	39	25	44	31
Fargo	34	10	—	—	38	24
Peoria	58	30	53	38	57	44
3–6 months						
East St. Louis	11	7	16	7	11	10
Columbus	23	15	22	17	22	20
Fargo	27	23	—	—	28	25
Peoria	27	15	24	30	23	26
More than 6 months						
East St. Louis	74	82	62	85	74	77
Columbus	36	65	39	58	33	49
Fargo	39	67	—	—	34	51
Peoria	15	55	23	32	20	30
Number of cases						
East St. Louis	1,031	282	536	776	606	695
Columbus	249	40	265	24	153	131
Fargo	244	51	—	—	130	164
Peoria	359	107	429	37	272	194

Source: Mail questionnaire data.
[a] Oklahoma City is not included because of noncomparability of time periods.

twice that of men in Columbus (40 per cent compared with 19) and Oklahoma City (77 per cent compared with 41), and six times that of men in Peoria (30 per cent compared with 5). For those women who did find jobs, their period of unemployment, in general, was not much different than that of the men.

The data on wages received by women (see Chapter 6) suggest the possibility that those who found jobs did so because they were willing to work for very low pay. It may be that the large proportions of women who found no work reflect unwillingness and less necessity among this group to accept low-paying jobs of the types available to them in their communities. The choice of working or not working, particularly for married women, is undoubtedly strongly influenced by the "net gain" that results from employment.

The costs of being employed, such as babysitting, transportation, and additional clothing, make employment unattractive if the pay is low. At the factory wages they were getting on their old jobs, employment was well worth the cost and effort. At the lower rates for jobs open to them outside of factory work, working was perhaps not so attractive.

Analysis of unemployment among women is always complicated by the difficulty of determining whether a particular individual is in or out of the labor force at any given time. Women, much more frequently than men, are part of the "secondary" labor force; that is, many are in the labor force only under the "right" conditions.[4] Nevertheless, all of the women included in these studies had been steadily employed for some time before the plants closed down. It is reasonable, therefore, to believe that almost all who said they sought new jobs actually did so and thus to accept the data on their protracted unemployment as accurate.

RACE

Negroes made up a large proportion of the work force only in the Armour plants at East St. Louis (58 per cent) and Oklahoma City (37 per cent). Only 9 per cent of the workers in the Armour plant in Columbus and 8 per cent in the ABC plant in Peoria were Negroes. Most of the Negroes were men—all in Oklahoma City and Peoria, 86 per cent in East St. Louis, and 83 per cent in Columbus.

The race differential in unemployment shown in Table 6 tends to understate the actual differences in the experiences of whites and Negroes. The reason is that the data for whites more than for Negroes reflect the unfavorable labor market experience of women. Nevertheless, the data show that long-term unemployment was much more extensive among Negroes than among whites. In East St. Louis, where Negroes were a majority of the employees, 85 per cent of the Negroes had more than six months of unemployment, as compared with 61 per cent of the whites. Among male

4. See Richard C. Wilcock, "The Secondary Labor Force and the Measurement of Unemployment," in *The Measurement and Behavior of Unemployment*, National Bureau of Economic Research (Princeton, N.J.: Princeton University Press, 1957), pp. 167–210.

interviewees only in Oklahoma City, 59 per cent of the Negroes compared with 46 per cent of the whites were unemployed seven months after the shutdown. In Peoria, 32 per cent of the Negro men compared with only 15 per cent of all men experienced more than six months unemployment. The pattern is similar for Columbus. And in the two cities of East St. Louis and Columbus combined, twice as many Negroes as whites (60 per cent compared with 30 per cent) were unemployed for the entire period after leaving Armour.

Unemployment among Negroes, then, was particularly severe, even though on the average they were younger and about as well educated as the whites.[5] The percentage of Negroes and whites under age 45 and the percentage with more than an eighth-grade education were as shown in Table 7.

Table 7
Age and Education Differences, by Race, Displaced Workers,
Four Cities

CITY	PER CENT UNDER AGE 45		PER CENT WITH MORE THAN EIGHTH-GRADE EDUCATION	
	Negroes	Whites	Negroes	Whites
Peoria	91	56	52	57
Oklahoma City	38	27	44	43
East St. Louis	51	42	33	29
Columbus	61	53	58	45

In each city the Negroes were considerably younger than the whites and, except in Peoria, they had more years of schooling. Since youth and education are ordinarily advantages in the job market, it appears that the greater difficulty experienced by Negroes in finding jobs may be attributed primarily to discrimination. Limitation of job opportunities for Negroes through exclusion from many types of jobs, plus the reluctance or refusal of some

---

5. Judgment of relative level of education of whites and Negroes depends somewhat upon the selection of a dividing line. In East St. Louis, for example, while more Negroes than whites had nine or more years of schooling, the reverse is true if the measure is eight or more years of school. The median years of school completed was about the same for each group. We have no way of judging the quality of education received by the two groups.

employers to hire them for any type of work, made the re-employment problems of the Negroes formidable indeed.

AGE

The results of these studies confirm what every other labor market study has found—namely, that once an older worker loses his job he has a difficult time finding a new one. In all five cities, long-term unemployment was more prevalent among workers aged 45 and over than among those younger (see Table 6). In Columbus, Fargo, and Peoria, unemployment of more than six months duration among older workers was 50 per cent higher than for workers under age 45. The difference between the two groups in East St. Louis was small, mainly because nearly everyone did so poorly and because of the dominance of the race differential. The proportion of older workers unemployed seven months after the shutdown in Oklahoma City was substantially higher (56 per cent) than the percentage of younger workers (41 per cent).

In Peoria, there was a substantial increase in long-term unemployment at about age 35, after which the relationships between age and unemployment change very little. In East St. Louis, where more than 70 per cent of all the workers were unemployed for over six months, the age factor made a difference only after age 55. In Columbus, age became a factor at age 45, beyond which there was little change, and in Fargo long-term unemployment increased at age 35 and again at age 55.

In spite of the variation in pattern among the cities, the relationship between age and unemployment is clear. In each city, approximately twice the proportion of workers aged 55 and over were unemployed for the entire year following the shutdowns as were workers under age 35. In Peoria, the ratio was five to one. As examples, the ABC workers with no jobs increased from 5 per cent of those under age 35 to 27 per cent of those aged 55 and over, and in East St. Louis the percentage with no jobs jumped from 30 per cent in the under-age-35 group to 59 per cent of those 55 and over.

These results, as well as those of other studies, leave no doubt that many of the older workers are at a disadvantage when seeking work. The reasons are complex. While employers generally praise the stability, reliability, productivity, and quality of workmanship of their older workers, at the same time they are reluctant to hire older applicants when openings are available. Increased insurance and pension costs, promotion-from-within policies, declining physical and mental abilities, slow recovery from illness or injury, and a multitude of other factors are cited as reasons for their reluctance. Whatever the merits of these arguments, and many students of the problem are inclined to minimize them, they do not justify blanket exclusion of the older worker from access to jobs. Yet considerable evidence exists that many firms set arbitrary maximum hiring ages beyond which they seldom, if ever, employ.

Part of the problem of older workers, on the other hand, is related to personal and work history characteristics. Such factors as poor health, physical disabilities, lack of education, narrow experience (experience limited to meatpacking, for example), and skill that is obsolete or little in demand are prevalent to a greater degree among older workers.

AGE AND EDUCATION

The older workers involved in the five plant closings, for example, had, on the average, considerably less education than their younger fellow workers. In each of the meatpacking plants about four out of five workers aged 55 and over did not go beyond grade school in their formal education. This was also true of over half of the older ABC workers. In the five cities, between 60 and 80 per cent of those aged 45 to 54 had no more than an eighth-grade education. Among workers under age 35, on the other hand, only about 40 per cent failed to go beyond the eighth grade. In each city, the level of education was less in successively higher age groups.

Aside from any questions of employer discrimination against them, it is clear that some older workers are not qualified educationally for a great many jobs. Except for those with skills or trades highly in demand, most are probably restricted to unskilled and semiskilled manual jobs and service occupations. Since employment in jobs of these types is not expanding as rapidly as in other occupations or in the labor force generally, the older worker, unless he is capable of and receives training in skills more in demand, will continue to face great barriers to employment once out of a job.

While education is an important factor in the re-employment experience of workers in all age groups, it seems to be more of a differentiating factor for younger workers. The data for Oklahoma City and Peoria, which we analyzed by age and education combined, show that either advanced age or lack of education often results in lengthy unemployment, but that for older workers long-term unemployment was as common for those with more years of school as for those with fewer. In contrast, among the younger workers, those with at least a ninth-grade education had much less long-term unemployment than those with less schooling. For example, among workers under age 45 in Peoria, 11 per cent of those with a grade school education or less had no work in the year following the shutdown, compared with only 4 per cent of those with more schooling. Among older workers, however, the comparable figures for the two education groups are nearly identical: 14 per cent and 17 per cent. The pattern was about the same in Oklahoma City. The data suggest that the degree of education bears little relation to the employment prospects of the older manual worker.[6]

SKILL AND TRAINING

The workers' skill level at Armour and at ABC is not as consistently related to unemployment as one might expect, although in general the skilled workers had less unemployment than the unskilled, semiskilled, and service workers. Since relatively few of the packinghouse workers were able to obtain work in meat-

---

6. Some authors have argued that there is no discrimination against the older worker and that whatever employment difficulties he may have are primarily his own fault for not being prepared for the changes taking place in industry. See, for example, Joseph A. Metzger, "The Older Worker's Contribution to His Own Unemployment," *Personnel Journal,* Vol. 40, No. 1 (May 1, 1961), pp. 19–21 ff. Our evidence does not support the Metzger position.

packing, the skills they had were often of little advantage in the job market.[7] Similarly, some of the former ABC workers may have found that skills useful in making washing machines were not useful to other industries in the area. The proportions of skilled, semiskilled, and unskilled workers who had no work at all after the shutdowns were as follows:

	East St. Louis	Columbus	Fargo	Oklahoma City	Peoria
Skilled	21	10	18	20	12
Semiskilled	44	18	15	38	11
Unskilled and service workers	52	25	11	56	8

Workers who had served an apprenticeship or had taken other kinds of formal vocational or trade-related training did somewhat better in finding new jobs than those who had only their job experience as an occupational background. About 44 per cent of the 94 former ABC workers who had such training obtained a new job in less than two weeks compared with only half that proportion, 22 per cent, who had no specialized training. And 61 per cent with training, compared with 53 per cent of those without it, found a job in less than three months. The experience of the former packinghouse workers was similar. Of the 40 former Armour workers in Oklahoma City who prior to the shutdown had obtained training in some trade, 30 per cent found new employment in less than two weeks. The comparable figure for those without training was 17 per cent. Similarly, 58 per cent with training compared with 35 per cent without it found a new job in less than three months.

Although the specialized trade and occupational training obtained by these workers served to their advantage when they were displaced from their jobs, few had such training. The data suggest, however, that efforts to upgrade the labor force through occupational training are well worth investigation and experimentation.

---

7. Skill classifications were based on occupational classifications in: U.S. Bureau of the Census, 1950 Census of Population, *Index of Occupations and Industries* (Washington, D.C.: U.S. Government Printing Office, 1950), except in Oklahoma City. In Oklahoma City the classifications were based primarily on the wage rate they were receiving at Armour.

THE OKLAHOMA CITY RETRAINING PROGRAM

A modest experiment in retraining was conducted by the Armour Automation Committee following the plant shutdown in Oklahoma City. The Committee partially underwrote courses offered in local trade and vocational schools for workers who requested retraining and who showed promise of benefiting from the courses. The courses made available were limited to those related to skills that were in demand in the area. Further, there was a maximum contribution for tuition and costs of $150 per person. About 60 persons were given training of some kind under the program.

Forty-six of the trainees were in the final-layoff group, and we received completed questionnaires from 41 of them in our 1962 resurvey. Nineteen (46 per cent) of them were under age 45 and 22 (54 per cent) were aged 45 and over. Data on their post-shutdown experience provide a partial basis for assessing the results of the retraining experiment.

In the spring of 1962, unemployment among the trainees was higher than for the Oklahoma City displaced workers generally. Forty-six per cent were unemployed at that time, compared with 34 per cent of the entire group of displaced workers. The unemployment rate was 37 per cent for those under age 45 and 54 per cent for those aged 45 and over.

Among the 22 individuals with retraining who were working in the spring of 1962, only 4 of the 12 younger workers and 2 of the 10 older workers had jobs that appeared to be related to their special training.

Although this is an unimpressive record, a number of factors need to be considered in assessing the poor results of the retraining program. First, the displaced meatpacking workers, as a group, were below average in education and industrial qualifications. Second, the trainees were a particularly hard-to-place group. Of the 46 trainees in the final-layoff group, 20 were women and 13 were Negro men. As our analysis of unemployment in Oklahoma City has shown, the women and Negroes found it particularly difficult to find employment after the shutdown. Finally, the training provided was, in most instances, quite limited. Because the Automation Committee limited its subsidy to a maximum of $150 per person, most of the courses were of relatively short duration.

In view of these factors, the Oklahoma City experiment cannot be considered an adequate test of retraining possibilities. We cannot tell from this experiment whether longer periods of retraining and related education would have been any more successful. Nor can we tell what the effect of better local market conditions might have been.[8] The Automation Committee, itself, in its progress report, noted that retraining on a "crash" basis is not likely to be very successful, and that a continuing education program designed to develop ability and skills over a period of time is required.

LOCATION

Nearly all of the long-term unemployed were still living in their home communities a year after the shutdowns. Few migrated to new locations in search of jobs. In the three cities, for example, fewer than 4 per cent of all of the displaced workers had moved to locations more than 100 miles from the three-city areas. Migration was also slight in Oklahoma City and Peoria. Our resurvey in 1962, however, shows a substantial increase in migration after the first year.

A comparison of the unemployment experience of the three-city migrants with the three-city workers in general indicates that those who did relocate had far less unemployment. Nearly twice as many migrants (78 per cent) were working a year after the shutdowns as three-city workers generally (42 per cent). Further, only 17 per cent had been unemployed for the entire year following the shutdowns, compared with 40 per cent of the entire group of three-city respondents. The migrants also obtained their first jobs in a much shorter time. Over half found their first jobs in less than three months, while only 28 per cent of the mail respondents could obtain a job in this length of time. Thus, because they found it either possible or desirable to move, the migrants were, to a large extent, able to avoid lengthy unemployment.

---

8. See Chapter 9 for a further discussion of the retraining experiment with former Armour workers in Oklahoma City.

THE UNWANTED WORKERS

"Unwanted workers" were found in every grouping of personal and occupational characteristics. Workers in some groups, however, found the job market particularly difficult. If unwanted workers are defined as those who could find no jobs at all during the year after their employers closed shop, the data in Table 8 summarize the groups in which they were concentrated. The pattern is much the same when other measures of long-term unemployment are used.

Table 8
Personal Characteristics of Those Who Found No Jobs and of Total Mail Questionnaire Respondents, by City
(in Per Cent)

Personal Characteristics	THREE CITIES No Job	THREE CITIES Mail Respondents	OKLAHOMA CITY No Job	OKLAHOMA CITY Mail Respondents	PEORIA No Job	PEORIA Mail Respondents
Male	75	80	73	80	36	77
Female	25	20	27	20	64	23
White	36	58	66	64	94	92
Negro	64	42	34	36	6	8
Under 45	40	48	23	31	32	58
45 and over	60	52	77	69	68	42
Unskilled	58	49	43	33	20	29
Semiskilled	38	43	54	61	60	57
Skilled	3	5	3	6	10	8
Other	2	3	—	—	10	5
Eighth grade or less	73	65	65	58	60	42[a]
Ninth grade or more	27	35	35	42	40	58[a]
Married	76	82	80	85	68	77[a]
Other	24	18	20	15	32	23[a]

Source: Mail questionnaire data and company records.
[a] Based on in-plant survey sample.

In each of the cities, but particularly in Peoria, women to a greater degree than men were unable to find new employment. While only 23 per cent of the displaced ABC workers were women, 64 per cent of those without jobs were women.

The Negroes were unemployed for much longer periods than whites. In East St. Louis and Columbus, for example, twice as many Negroes as whites were unemployed for the entire period after leaving Armour. While only 4 out of 10 workers in the three cities were Negroes, Negroes made up more than 6 out of 10 of those who found no work in the year following the shutdown.

In each city, more workers over the age of 45 than younger went without jobs; also, the older ones who found jobs took longer to do so. In Peoria, for example, although only 42 per cent of the workers were 45 or older, 68 per cent of those who found no job were over this age.

The workers' employment experience is also related to their skill level. Except in Peoria and Fargo, the unskilled were more likely than the semiskilled or skilled to have difficulty finding new work.

In general, workers with the least education had the most unemployment. The effect of education on unemployment is most striking in Peoria. Forty-two per cent of the ABC workers had eight years of schooling or less, but 60 per cent of those without jobs came from this group. Although the differences are not large, in each city more of the unmarried workers were jobless than those who were married.

In many cases, workers possessed combinations of characteristics, all of which operated to their disadvantage. Older workers, for example, not only faced an age barrier to employment but also were more likely to be less educated than younger workers. Many of the Armour workers were not only beyond their "prime" years and lacking in education but had skills that were useful primarily in an industry of declining job opportunities in their communities. Thus, for many, their years of experience in an occupation were of little use as an aid in finding new jobs or starting new careers.

Causes of the Intercity Differences

We have already given a number of examples of intercity differences in unemployment experience, but we have not yet attempted a full explanation for the variations that occurred.

THE LEVEL OF ECONOMIC ACTIVITY

Of major importance is the difference among the cities in the general level of labor demand. In this respect, the ABC workers benefited from the most favorable conditions. A general pick-up of economic activity in Peoria occurred at about the time of the shutdown. Unemployment in November, 1958, had been 6.6 per cent of the labor force. In January, 1959, the month of the shutdown, the rate dropped to 5.4 per cent and fell to a postwar low of 1.6 per cent by September, 1959. Unemployment increased later, but in January, 1960, one year after the shutdown, only 3.8 per cent of the labor force was unemployed.

Thus, during most of the first year following their separation from ABC, the Peoria workers were seeking work under very favorable labor market conditions. In East St. Louis, on the other hand, the unemployment rate was 4.6 per cent in July, 1959, the month the plant closed there, and again in September. After that it was not below 5 per cent during the post-shutdown year, rising to a high of 6.8 per cent in March, 1960. Unemployment rates in the other three cities were, for the most part, between the extremes of Peoria and East St. Louis.

The experience of the ABC workers was favorably affected by the high demand for labor in their community. And clearly the packinghouse workers in Columbus, Fargo, and Oklahoma City did better than those in East St. Louis because of more favorable economic conditions. But it is also clear that the differences in business activity do not account entirely for the differences in unemployment. The jobless rate for the displaced workers in East St. Louis as compared with the rates in Columbus and Fargo was higher than one would expect from a comparison of the three community rates. At the other extreme, the fact that 22 per cent of the ABC workers were unemployed a year after the plant shutdown indicates that even a "full employment" economy is not sufficient to clear the market of "unwanted workers."

NATURE OF THE WORK FORCE

The personal characteristics of displaced workers can have a decided effect on their labor market experiences. In most repects, the Peoria workers had more advantages than workers in the other cities.

They were, on the average, considerably younger and better

educated than the former Armour workers. The median age of the ABC workers was a little under 40; in the three cities the average worker was over 45 and in Oklahoma City the average age was 50. Almost two-thirds of the workers in the three cities had only a grade school education compared with only 42 per cent in Peoria.

The Peoria workers also had somewhat greater occupational skills than did the former Armour workers. A much smaller proportion were unskilled laborers, and the proportion classified as skilled workers was about six times as great. In addition, the skills and experience gained in the electrical machinery industry were more easily transferable to other industries than were the meat-packing skills. Further, the ABC workers tended to have a more varied work background. While average tenure at Armour was about 12 years in the three cities and 17 years in Oklahoma City, it was only about six and one-half years at ABC. Many of the Armour workers had spent their entire working lives at Armour. All of these factors help explain the more favorable post-shutdown experience of the ABC workers.

The major characteristic that differentiated the East St. Louis workers from the other Armour workers, as well as those at ABC, was the high proportion of Negroes. No group of workers underwent more prolonged unemployment than did the Negroes in East St. Louis. Although the white workers in East St. Louis also had more long-term unemployment than those in Columbus and Fargo, the experience of the Negroes contributed substantially to the overall unfavorable experience of the displaced workers there, relative to the other two cities.

In almost all respects, the East St. Louis workers started their search for work more handicapped than the Peoria workers or, for that matter, the Armour workers in the other closed plants. They were, on the average, older, less educated, and less skilled, and more of them had the handicap of color.

THE NATURE OF THE DEMAND FOR LABOR

The distribution of employment in the communities seems to have had less effect on the amount of unemployment following the shutdowns than the general level of economic activity and the characteristics of the workers. East St. Louis, Columbus, Oklahoma City, and Peoria are all metropolitan areas, and with the exception of Oklahoma City, all have heavy concentrations of employment in manufacturing, a factor which should have been helpful to the displaced workers in finding new jobs. Manufacturing in East St. Louis and Columbus is quite diversified, but in Peoria manufacturing employment is dominated by the nonelectrical machinery industry. Oklahoma City and Fargo, on the other hand, provide relatively little employment in manufacturing, although they have above-average employment in government establishments and in distributive industries. These differences in industrial distribution, and thus in the demand for labor, appear to have had relatively little relationship to the extent of unemployment among the displaced workers. Industrial composition, however, affected the kinds of jobs found, as we shall show in Chapter 6.

The particular characteristics of the demand for labor did have some effect. The workers in Fargo seem to have benefited from the relative prevalence of jobs in agriculture and construction in that area. In these industries, the job opportunities were largely at the unskilled level and did not require skills or experience beyond that possessed by the former Armour workers. The benefits from the existence of these jobs may not have been permanent, because of their seasonal character, but in the short run they reduced unemployment for the Fargo workers.

In Columbus, the existence of packinghouse jobs increased somewhat the employment opportunities of the displaced workers. And the existence of job opportunities in durable goods industries in Peoria was advantageous to the ABC workers with their experience in the electrical machinery industry.

The three factors discussed seem to have been the most important determinants of the extent of unemployment, but not the only ones. For example, differences in employer hiring policies and the types and quality of job-finding aid available to the workers had some influence on the relative success of the displaced workers in the labor market (see Chapter 5).

Long-Term Unemployment—A Summary

Three facts stand out concerning the post-shutdown unemployment experiences of the displaced workers. One is the great extent of long-term unemployment subsequent to the layoffs. Another is the differential impact of the shutdowns on unemployment among various groups of workers. The third is that although a high level of labor demand is a prerequisite to minimizing the extent of long-term unemployment, it is not a sufficient solution by itself.

Very substantial proportions of the workers, varying from 24 per cent in Peoria to 73 per cent in East St. Louis, had more than six months of unemployment in the year following the shutdowns. Many worked on no regular job at all. The number was small in Peoria, 11 per cent; but in East St. Louis one-half were unable to find a job that lasted a month or more. That the problem of unemployment after a permanent displacement of workers is a persistent one is reflected in the high rates of unemployment among the workers a year after the shutdowns—65 per cent in East St. Louis, 34 per cent in Columbus, 31 per cent in Fargo, 53 per cent in Oklahoma City (seven months after the shutdown), and 22 per cent in Peoria. The unemployment rates were not much lower two and one-half to three years after the shutdowns (a year and one-half for Oklahoma City). Some of the reduction in unemployment that did occur over the longer time span was the result of withdrawals from the labor force.

Protracted unemployment, however, was not spread evenly among the workers. In each of the five cities, long-term unemployment rates were higher for women, older workers, Negroes, the less educated, and the less skilled. Which of these personal characteristics was of the most critical importance in its effect on unemployment is not clear. Workers often possessed a number of characteristics in combination, all of which were handicaps in locating a job. Combinations of advanced age, low level of education, and lack of skill were common. Any one of these characteristics reduced greatly the chances of finding new work; in combination they produced bleak job prospects and in many cases an "unwanted worker."

Finally, although the favorable economic conditions in Peoria appear to have been crucial in keeping long-term unemployment at a level far below that in the other cities, substantial numbers of the ABC workers experienced lengthy joblessness. One in four was unemployed for more than six months during the year following the shutdown. And three years after the shutdown, the unemployment rate among former ABC workers was still nearly 20 per cent. These results suggest that although high labor demand is very important, experienced workers displaced from their jobs need special attention if extensive long-term unemployment is to be avoided or even reduced to tolerable levels.

How typical were the labor market experiences of the displaced workers in the five cities? Other studies of workers permanently displaced by plant shutdowns suggest that the long-term unemployment is not exceptional.[9] Miernyk, in his study of displaced workers in six textile mill shutdowns in New England, for example, found over 40 per cent of the workers unemployed a year or more after the shutdowns.[10] Two years after the closing of the International Harvester plants in Auburn, New York, on the other hand, only 8 per cent were unemployed, and the average duration of unemployment had been about 20 weeks.[11] The layoffs in this case extended, however, over a considerable period of time. Moreover, in Auburn a committee was formed and acted to bring in new industry to the area.

Nine months after the closing of an automotive instruments and gauges manufacturing plant in La Crosse, Wisconsin, 40 per cent of the workers were reported as unemployed.[12] Automobile workers separated over a period of time from a permanently closed Packard plant in Detroit had similar difficulty finding work during the year or two following their separation. About 22 per cent had not worked at all after leaving Packard.[13]

---

9. Comparison with other studies is difficult because the time periods involved usually differ and because in a number of studies workers were separated from their jobs over relatively long periods. In such cases, there is no fixed period over which to measure unemployment. In addition, some studies do not specify the time periods involved.

10. William H. Miernyk, *Inter-Industry Labor Mobility* (Boston: Bureau of Business and Economic Research, Northeastern University, 1955), p. 17.

11. Leonard P. Adams and Robert L. Aronson, *Workers and Industrial Change* (Ithaca, N.Y.: Cornell University, 1957), pp. 39–41.

12. Wisconsin State Employment Service, *La Crosse Reemployment Study,* September, 1960, p. 3 (mimeo).

13. H. L. Sheppard, L. A. Ferman, and S. Faber, *Too Old to Work—Too Young to Retire* (Washington, D.C.: Special Committee on Unemployment Problems, Committee Print, December, 1959), p. 15.

The study of displaced car shop workers in Mt. Vernon, Illinois, an area of surplus labor, found that more than two years after the closing of the shops, 54 per cent of the workers had experienced six months or more of unemployment and 31 per cent a year or more. At the time of the survey 12 per cent were still unemployed and 12 per cent underemployed.[14] Other shutdowns studies have also found extensive unemployment but covered periods too short to be comparable with those reported here.[15]

Thus, studies of permanent displacement of workers in meatpacking, electrical machinery, textiles, automobile manufacturing, farm equipment manufacturing, and railroad car manufacturing have almost invariably reported extensive unemployment following plant shutdowns. Those which have analyzed the incidence of long-term unemployment among various groups report findings similar to ours. Although the impact of a shutdown on the displaced workers will vary with economic conditions, the characteristics of the workers, and the types of employment opportunities in the community, long-term unemployment can be expected to accompany plant shutdowns in almost every circumstance.

The high rates of unemployment among the displaced workers in the five cities were far above those in the communities generally and well beyond what would be considered tolerable if they existed on a wider scale. Unemployment of this magnitude emphasizes the need for special attention to the "unwanted workers" who are swept aside by economic change. In recent years, there has been increasing recognition of the need for special efforts to solve or at least mitigate the impact of chronic unemployment in depressed areas. Similar recognition of the extensiveness and severity of unemployment that can occur among specific groups in almost any labor market area and involve substantial numbers of workers would appear to be equally important.

---

14. Richard C. Wilcock, *op. cit.* (1960), p. 47.
15. See, for example, Charles A. Myers and George P. Schultz, *The Dynamics of a Labor Market* (Englewood Cliffs, N.J.: Prentice-Hall, Inc., 1951), and testimony of the Textile Workers Union of America, AFL-CIO, by Wesley W. Cook, contained in *Unemployment Compensation,* Hearings before the Committee on Ways and Means, House of Representatives, Eighty-sixth Congress, First Session, April, 1959, pp. 579–680.

4

The Personal Impact
of Unemployment

MOST OF THE DISPLACED WORKERS underwent severe economic strain, if not hardship, as a result of the permanent layoffs. They had protracted periods of unemployment, their incomes were low while they were out of work, and many of those who found new jobs went to work at lower wages. More importantly, perhaps, these same factors had significant effects not only on the workers' social status and family life, but also on their attitudes toward their former company and union and toward society. Those who had the experience of interviewing the displaced workers were indelibly impressed by the deleterious effects of long-term unemployment on individual well-being and morale.

The high proportion of breadwinners among the laid-off workers is one measure of the economic impact of long-term unemployment. Almost all of the men in the five cities (ranging from 93 to 97 per cent) were heads of households and primarily responsible for the financial support of their families. Further, about one-half of the displaced women in each of the cities were either breadwinners or at least major sources of family income and support.

Both the long-term and short-term unemployed typically had heavy family responsibilities. The families of the breadwinners averaged between three and four members. For the five cities combined, about 90 per cent of the workers reported they had at least one person dependent upon them for support and about 60 per cent had at least two dependents. Among the ABC workers, who had less total unemployment than the Armour workers, 59 per cent of those out of work less than three months had two or more dependents and 41 per cent of the very long-term unemployed (more than six months) had that many dependents. In East St. Louis, where unemployment was highest, 47 per cent of the very long-term unemployed had two or more dependents. Since the very long-term unemployed were older, on the average, than their fellow workers, they were somewhat more likely to have no dependents (e.g., widowers) or only one.

Sources of Income While Unemployed

UNEMPLOYMENT INSURANCE

During the year following the shutdowns the displaced unemployed had two major sources of income—unemployment insurance and severance pay. A large majority applied for and received unemployment compensation: in East St. Louis and Peoria, four out of five drew benefits; in Columbus and Fargo the proportion was three out of four.

Only in Oklahoma City were there any restrictions on eligibility. Under an Oklahoma unemployment insurance ruling, severance pay was considered wages and even when it was taken in a lump sum, the worker was not permitted to draw compensation for the number of weeks for which his severance pay was calculated. A worker in the final-layoff group with average length of service was disqualified for 18 weeks; anyone with the company for 30 years was disqualified for nine months. Because of this ruling, only 43 per cent of the final-layoff group had received any unemployment insurance at the time of the interview survey (seven to eight months after the shutdown) and only 7 per cent had collected for more than ten weeks. Although benefits were delayed, the proportions who eventually drew them were comparable to the other cities.

In contrast to the unusual situation in Oklahoma, large numbers in the other cities received benefits for an extended period during the first year after layoff. In the three other Armour cities more than three out of four (78 per cent), and in Peoria almost half (46 per cent), had more than 15 weeks of compensation. Negroes and older workers drew benefits for particularly long periods of time. In the three cities, for example, about two-thirds of both older workers and Negroes were on unemployment insurance for 26 weeks or more compared with half of the younger workers and two-fifths of the whites. Some workers reported more than 26 weeks of compensation, in most cases as the result of extended benefits under the Temporary Unemployment Compensation Act of 1958.

Exhaustion of unemployment insurance benefits was much higher in East St. Louis than in any of the other cities. In East St. Louis, Columbus, and Fargo combined, over half (57 per cent) exhausted their benefits during the year after the shutdown, but the rate of exhaustion was twice as high in East St. Louis as in the other two cities. In Peoria, most of the workers had jobs within six months and as a result only 8 per cent exhausted their unemployment insurance. In Oklahoma City, because of the delay in paying unemployment insurance, exhaustions were infrequent during the first year.

In all five cities the median weekly amount of unemployment benefits was between $32 and $33, with three out of four beneficiaries collecting between $30 and $40. For the time it was received, therefore, unemployment insurance replaced only a little more than a third of the wages at either Armour or ABC. Both the amount of benefits and the extent of wage loss were comparable to the average experience of insured unemployed in the nation for 1960.[1]

SEVERANCE PAY

Severance or separation pay has as its major purpose an easing of the burden of permanent layoff, since it is generally expected

1. U.S. Bureau of Employment Security, *Unemployment Insurance: State Laws and Experience,* (Washington, D.C.: U.S. Government Printing Office, April, 1961), table 9.

that a laid-off worker will not find a new job immediately and may very well have to accept new employment at lower earnings. The severance pay can also be viewed as a source of income for financing job search and, possibly, geographic relocation. Finally, the separation pay may also be thought of as compensation for permanently losing a job to which the worker has devoted his time and effort, and it is not surprising that almost all severance pay plans provide that the amounts increase with tenure in the company. It differs from unemployment compensation in at least three important respects: it is paid directly by the company to the workers, it has no relation to length of unemployment, and it bears a closer relationship to prior earnings.

The 1959–61 severance pay plan at Armour, as negotiated with the United Packinghouse Workers and the Amalgamated Meat Cutters, was above the all-industry average in amount of payment and provided a major source of income for the displaced Armour workers. All employees with a year or more of continuous service who were separated from the company because of a permanent reduction in force were eligible for the allowance. Payments were computed on the basis of 40 hours per week at the employee's regular rate according to a graduated scale which provided, for example, one week's pay for one year of service, 3½ weeks' pay for six years, 7½ weeks' pay for ten years, and another 1½ weeks' pay for each year of continuous service above ten years.

This scale meant that an East St. Louis worker with a median length of service of 15 years and with median pay received over $1,300; the comparable worker in Columbus or in Fargo, where average tenure was lower, received about $925 and $660, respectively. In Oklahoma City a worker in the final-layoff group who had average tenure (17 years) received severance pay of approximately $1,675. The typical worker in the early-layoff group received about $925.

At ABC there was no separation allowance plan in the company's agreement with the United Electrical, Radio, and Machine Workers. As part of the settlement after a strike called to protest the arrangements for the shutdown, however, the pension plan was modified to provide a sliding scale of lump-sum payments to those not eligible for pensions. The scale ranged from $20 for each year of credited service for those with less than four years' tenure to $40 for each year of credited service for those with ten or more years of service. The median payment under this agreement was $210, which is the sum for seven years of credited service. The comparable Armour payment for seven years of service would have been approximately $400 at the median wage.

These payments at ABC were in lieu of pension rights, and the recipients thereby lost all credited service toward the pension. In ᵗʰis respect, the plan was the same as at Armour because payment of the separation allowance at Armour meant the employee was permanently separated from the company and lost his credited service.

Both Armour and ABC made provisions for early retirement. At ABC, it was a full pension at age 60 for those with at least 15 years of credited service. At Armour, it was a reduced pension at age 60 (and 55 for women) for workers with ten years of credited service. In addition, provisions were made in the Armour shutdown situations for retirement of men aged 58 to 60.

Separation pay and unemployment insurance combined provided the average Armour worker in East St. Louis and Oklahoma City with approximately half his usual Armour wages for a year. The total was less than half a year's wages in Columbus and Fargo, where average tenure with the company was less. Since separation pay was relatively minor for the ABC workers, the remainder of the discussion is confined to the Armour workers.

Actually, few of the long-term unemployed were able to spread the income from unemployment compensation and severance pay over a full year, because for many the separation allowance was fairly quickly used up in paying debts and everyday living expenses, and unemployment insurance soon became the sole source of income. As a result, many of the long-term jobless had little or no income after their unemployment benefits were exhausted. For those able to conserve a substantial part of their severance pay, however, income was enough to prevent severe economic hardship, at least for a year. Continued unemployment after a year resulted in a more desperate financial situation.

USE OF SEVERANCE PAY

The relatively rapid evaporation of severance pay for the Armour workers is indicated by Figure 8. A good deal of it went to pay debts, which for the most part were incurred prior to the notification of the plant closings. A major complaint of the Armour workers from all four of the plants studied was that company credit union loans were called in immediately after the shutdowns and a significant amount of their severance pay had to be used to repay these loans. The credit unions, on their part, maintained that the collection was necessary to protect the savings of other workers. Other creditors also tended to demand payment when the layoffs were announced because of the prospective financial insecurity of the displaced workers.

Major use of severance pay for debts was almost twice as heavy for those who became unemployed for long periods as compared with those with less unemployment, which meant that the average long-term unemployed worker had no major source of income after exhausting unemployment insurance. In East St. Louis, for example, more than half of the long-term unemployed had used all or most of their severance pay on back debts.

Other than payment of existing debts, the workers used the severance pay primarily for everyday living costs. A minority, however, were able to make some large expenditures they otherwise could not have attempted—heavier payments on home mortgages and on major household repairs, for example. In the three cities, 15 per cent reported such uses, as did 20 per cent in Oklahoma City. Further, one out of every eight (12 per cent) of the former Armour workers was able to put money in the bank for future needs.

As shown in Figure 8, the pattern of severance pay usage was quite similar in each city. The major differences were by race and age. Negroes in East St. Louis and in Oklahoma City were more than twice as likely as white workers to use their severance pay for debt payments. Older workers were less likely than younger workers to need the severance pay for debts, and consequently more of them could put money in the bank or make payments on their mortgages.

Figure 8. PERCENTAGE DISTRIBUTION OF DISPLACED ARMOUR WORKERS, BY USE
OF SEVERANCE PAY, FOUR CITIES

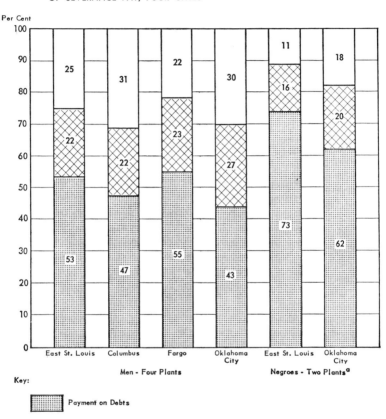

Key:

Payment on Debts

Household Expenses

Other: Mortgage Payments, Savings, and Other

a. In Oklahoma City, all men; in East St. Louis, mostly men.

Source: Personal interview data.

Since the severance pay was used primarily for debts and every-day living expenses, relatively little was left over for other pur-poses. In the three cities, for example, only 2½ per cent said they spent any of it on job training courses, and in Oklahoma City, where the activities of the Armour Automation Committee stimu-lated an interest in retraining, only 3 per cent used any of their separation pay for this purpose. The proportions who spent any of the severance pay on household appliances, automobiles, and vaca-tions were also very small in all four cities, although many used it for debts previously incurred on consumer durables. A sub-stantially higher proportion, however, applied some of the money to mortgage payments (18 per cent).[2]

OTHER SOURCES OF INCOME

In all of the studies, only small proportions of workers had non-wage sources of income. Further, those who were primary bread-winners were less likely to have nonwage income than those partly dependent on the income of others.

For the minority who did have other income, the most usual sources were rental income, income from farms or other businesses, and, for a few, social security or other pension payments. In gen-eral, the high proportion of breadwinners, the number of de-pendents, and the paucity of nonwage income show that almost all of the workers required regular wage employment to maintain an adequate standard of living.

EMPLOYMENT OF WIFE

Another source of family income for some of the male dis-placed workers was the wage or salary earnings of the wife or, more rarely, another member of the family. In some cases, the wife went to work as a result of the prolonged unemployment of the husband.[3] In the three cities, among the husbands who were

---

2. For a discussion of the influence of severance pay and unemployment insurance on job search, see Chapter 5.
3. This phenomenon was observed during the depression of the 1930's and can occur in localized as well as in general depressions. See W. S. Woytinsky, *Additional Workers and the Volume of Unemployment in the*

married and living with their wives, 26 per cent had wives who were working prior to the Armour layoff, while 46 per cent had wives who had worked after the shutdowns. Thus, 20 per cent of all the wives began to work after the layoff and, of these, three out of four, according to the interviews, had gone to work to help out with the family budget. Since another 8 per cent of the three-city wives had unsuccessfully sought work after the shutdown, a total of 28 per cent came into the labor force after the shutdown— most of them because of the long-term unemployment of the family breadwinner.

In Oklahoma City and Peoria, higher proportions of the wives of the displaced workers already had jobs prior to the plant shutdowns, which probably explains the smaller proportions of wives who went to work to help out after the shutdowns. Compared with the 15 per cent of wives in the three cities who went to work to help out, it was 6 per cent in Oklahoma City and 8 per cent in Peoria. In all three studies, however, a large proportion of those who started work did so because of lower family income. For Peoria, a comparison was made of long- and short-term unemployed men as to whether their wives were working, but the difference was nominal. The long-term unemployed among the women, on the other hand, were much more likely than the short-term unemployed to have working husbands.

A large proportion of the women who worked at Armour and ABC were married and living with their husbands. In the three cities, for example, 74 per cent were married and living with their husbands. The unemployment rate for these husbands was almost 10 per cent. A third of the three-city women who had worked at Armour had either no husbands or husbands who were unemployed. About half of the women in these categories said they were solely dependent on their own income for a living.

Depression (New York: Social Science Research Council, 1940). Woytinsky argued that labor force and unemployment are both increased by the job seeking of secondary earners when the breadwinner is unemployed. Long, on the other hand, has contended that as many or more leave the labor force because of the scarcity of jobs as enter because of family financial difficulties. See Clarence D. Long, *The Labor Force under Changing Income and Employment* (Princeton, N.J.: Princeton University Press, 1958), p. 181.

INCOME SOURCES OF UNEMPLOYED—1962 RESURVEY

The 1962 mail resurvey in the five cities shows that approximately two-thirds of the unemployed (excluding those on temporary layoff) had some income from unemployment insurance, wages of others in the family, relief payments, or some combination of these. Fewer had income from unemployment insurance than from the other sources. If Oklahoma City is excluded, five out of six were *not* drawing any benefits. The major reason is that most of these unemployed had not earned enough in post-shutdown covered employment to be eligible for benefits. In Oklahoma City, four out of five of the jobless *were* drawing benefits; this shows the effect of their delayed eligibility resulting from the ruling that the Armour severance pay was wages income. For the five cities combined, about four of every ten who were receiving unemployment benefits had no other source of income.

A minority of the unemployed (about 30 per cent) had some family income from the wages of others in the family group. In about half of these cases, the wages of other family members (usually husband or wife) were the only income source. Intercity differences were slight.

In Columbus and East St. Louis, a third or more of the unemployed reported income from various types of relief. In Fargo, Peoria, and Oklahoma City, only one in ten reported income from relief. The intercity differences probably reflect the fact that relief payments to families with unemployed members depend a great deal upon administrative rulings and practices in the particular states and local communities.

The Family Financial Situation

Our discussion of sources of income after the plant shutdowns would suggest that the families of displaced workers, particularly those whose breadwinners were out of work for a long time, would have some difficulty in making ends meet. In each of the studies, the interview respondents were asked:

As far as family finances are concerned, which of the following would you say best describes your situation since you left Armour (ABC)?

Would you say that: You have had a great deal of difficulty, . . . some difficulty, . . . little or no difficulty?

The responses (Figure 9) correlate very closely with the extent of unemployment. In each city, the long-term unemployed experienced more financial problems than those who found jobs more quickly. Workers in East St. Louis had the highest degree of financial hardship, as one would expect since East St. Louis had the most long-term unemployed.

In Oklahoma City, in spite of the fact that the interview study was held seven to eight months after the shutdown rather than a year later as in the other cities, the level of family financial difficulty was high for both whites and Negroes and was relatively low only for those who found jobs in a matter of weeks. The primary explanation for this is the unemployment insurance ruling making the workers ineligible for benefits for the number of weeks covered by their severance pay.

Although older workers had longer unemployment than younger, the older workers—particularly those 55 and over—were less likely to indicate family financial difficulties. Two reasons are suggested: (1) the older workers generally had much higher separation pay and (2) they were likely to have fewer dependents. A large majority of the 55-and-older group had grown children with only the wife or husband at home. A number were widowers or widows. Finally, the older workers were more likely to have some savings and to have their homes paid for. Negroes, as a group, however, had a great deal of family financial difficulty.

ADJUSTMENTS TO LOWER INCOME

We also inquired into the kind of financial adjustments the families made after the shutdowns. Our finding is that spending had to be reduced not only on luxuries but also on what were considered "necessities." Further, among those who had savings to use, a large majority found it necessary either to dip into them or use them up. Two out of three of the ABC workers and four out of five of the Armour workers either used their savings or had none to use. That the ABC workers were somewhat less likely to use their savings reflects their lower rate of unemployment.

Figure 9. SELF-EVALUATION OF FAMILY FINANCIAL SITUATION BY DISPLACED
WORKERS ONE YEAR AFTER THE SHUTDOWN,[a] BY RACE AND LENGTH
OF UNEMPLOYMENT, EAST ST. LOUIS, OKLAHOMA CITY, AND PEORIA
(IN PER CENTS)

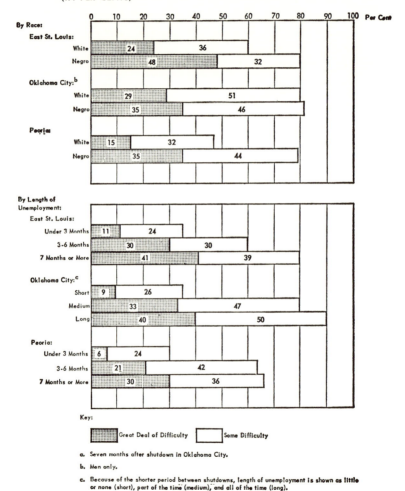

a. Seven months after shutdown in Oklahoma City.

b. Men only.

c. Because of the shorter period between shutdowns, length of unemployment is shown as little or none (short), part of the time (medium), and all of the time (long).

Source: Personal interview data.

A less frequent form of financial adjustment was the canceling, cashing in, or borrowing on insurance policies (12 per cent in Peoria, 20 per cent in Columbus and Fargo, 28 per cent in Oklahoma City, and 31 per cent in East St. Louis). The necessity of doing this was greatest for the long-term unemployed. In East St. Louis, almost all who cashed in or borrowed on insurance had at least three months unemployment and most were out of work seven months or more.

The necessity of selling personal property to meet family expenses (automobile, refrigerator, TV, or other large durable goods) varied even more markedly with the extent of unemployment, ranging from a high of 26 per cent in East St. Louis to 4 per cent in Peoria. Also, very few found it necessary to move to less expensive living quarters: 10 per cent in East St. Louis, 7 per cent in Columbus and Oklahoma City, 6 per cent in Fargo, and 4 per cent in Peoria.

The more drastic types of financial adjustment, therefore, were not too common, at least during the first year after the shutdown. Most of the workers were able to retain insurance, homes, and major items of personal property. Many, however, did have to reduce their everyday spending quite sharply. The number of former Armour workers who had to cut down on spending was close to 80 per cent in East St. Louis and Oklahoma City, and between 50 and 60 per cent in Columbus and Fargo.

In the three-city study, 46 per cent said the major reduction was in the purchase of necessities (food, clothing, medical care, and the like); 30 per cent reported an across-the-board reduction in spending; and the remaining 24 per cent referred to less-essential items such as social life, recreation, and personal items, or to the deferral of major expenditures, including home repairs and the purchase of appliances. The proportion of long-term unemployed (three months or more) who had to reduce spending was almost double that of those with less unemployment. The ways in which spending was reduced were quite similar in Oklahoma City.

Another type of adjustment to reduced family income seemed to occur among Negroes, but our data on this are impressionistic. The East St. Louis interviewers commented that the Negro community operated to some extent as an extended family system by seeing to it that less fortunate members received the minimum of food, clothing, and shelter. Sterner has reported that the practice of providing some support to relatives and friends is higher among Negroes than whites at any given income level.[4]

The interviewers also had the impression that there was some income in the Negro community that the respondents did not wish to report. We did not attempt to probe into the question of income from "shady occupations" but we believe that such income was minor and involved only a few individuals.[5]

CHANGE IN VACATION PATTERNS

Vacation trips have become a major custom for American manual workers, particularly since the widespread growth of paid vacations. As shown in Figure 10, large majorities of the Armour and ABC workers normally went on vacation trips. The impact of the shutdowns on these vacations provides a dramatic index of the extent to which many of the families had to adjust their habits to their reduced standard of living.

In the three cities, 35 per cent took vacation trips during the summer of 1959 when the plants closed and when many had severance pay to use, but in 1960 the proportion dropped off markedly. Only 13 per cent of those interviewed were planning trips in 1960 and only 4 per cent were planning to go as far as 500 miles from home. In Peoria, where higher proportions found jobs, more had vacation plans for the second summer after the shutdown. While 26 per cent of the former ABC workers took trips during the summer of 1959, a half-year after the shutdown, 37 per cent were planning trips for the summer of 1960, a year and a half after the layoff.

Effects on Social Status and Morale

In addition to the problem of adjusting to lower family incomes, the layoffs created two other types of problems for the displaced workers. One was that of finding suitable work or, in many cases,

4. Richard Sterner, *The Negro's Share* (New York: Harper & Brothers, 1943), pp. 163, 165.

5. See Arnold Rose, *The Negro in America* (Boston: The Beacon Press, 1956), p. 113, for a discussion of "shady occupations" among Negroes in big cities.

Figure 10. PERCENTAGE OF DISPLACED WORKERS WHO USUALLY TOOK VACATION
TRIPS AND WHO TOOK VACATION TRIP DURING YEAR AFTER SHUT-
DOWN, FIVE CITIES

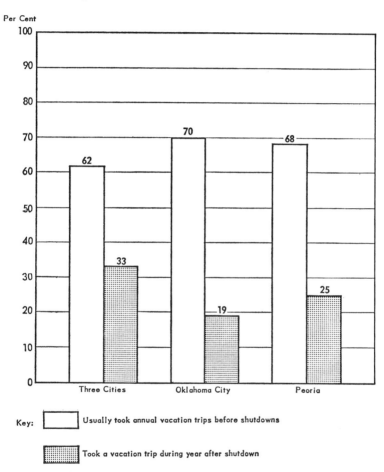

Source: Personal interview data.

any type of work. This we shall discuss in the following chapter.
The other was the problem of social and psychological adjustment
to being separated from long-time jobs, entering the labor market
unprepared, and undergoing the frustrations and humiliation of
unsuccessful job search.

PERSONAL REACTION TO NEWS OF THE SHUTDOWN

At the time they were first notified, about half of the workers in each of the four Armour studies had difficulty in believing that the plants would really close permanently. Also, in the Peoria study, about half expressed either surprise or regret.[6] A substantial minority in all of the studies, however, said they had expected the shutdown. Apparently they were better prepared than the others for the shock. Those with less unemployment were more inclined than the long-term unemployed to be casual about the shutdown and to say they had been able to take it as a matter of course.

In the four Armour plants, where only one month's notification of the shutdown was given, the combination of shock and suddenness meant that approximately half of the workers did not know what to do or at least found themselves unable to take any immediate action in searching for a new job. Since most had done no job hunting for years, the prospect was a difficult one to face, particularly since they were generally aware of the relative scarcity of jobs. As a result of inaction, confusion, bewilderment, and the scarcity of jobs, initial job hunting was ineffective; only a little over 6 per cent of the former Armour workers were able to get a line on specific jobs prior to the final layoff.

THE PSYCHOLOGICAL IMPACT ON THE WORKER

AND HIS FAMILY

Those who found work quickly had the problem of adjusting to their new jobs, new fellow workers, and, in many cases, to lower wages. Their adjustment problems were relatively minor, however, compared to the difficulties of those who went month after month without turning up a job. The unemployed man or woman who is

---

6. A high degree of surprise, disbelief, and regret seems to be quite common in plant shutdown situations. See also Richard C. Wilcock, *Impact on Workers and Community of a Plant Shutdown in a Depressed Area* (Washington, D.C.: U.S. Bureau of Labor Statistics, Bulletin No. 1264, June, 1960), p. 3, and H. L. Sheppard, L. A. Ferman, and S. Faber, *Too Old to Work—Too Young to Retire* (Washington, D.C.: Special Committee on Unemployment Problems, Committee Print, December, 1959), p. 8.

the head of a family and a breadwinner faces not only the financial hardships we have discussed but also serious social and psychological problems.

The unemployed man or woman who is responsible for his own livelihood and that of others can come to feel that there is no place in industry for him. He can lose confidence in himself. In his search for a scapegoat he may take his frustration out on his family. As the wife of a former Armour worker put it:

My husband never used to get upset at anything, but since the shutdown he's been hell on me and on the kids.

Even more likely is a feeling of bitterness toward the system that permits a man to work in a plant for many years only to be displaced from his job and to find that his age and industrial experience count against him in the job market. Quite a few expressed themselves as strongly as the man who said:

It's little better than shooting me to throw me out of a job at 55. Who's going to hire me when there are any number of younger men looking for work?

For the older worker, particularly, lengthy unemployment is apt to be a traumatic shock. His age, as a result of long company service and the seniority system, had given him an advantage in moving to higher-paying jobs. When permanently laid off, however, age suddenly becomes an economic disadvantage.

Other factors contribute to bitterness, lack of confidence, and sagging morale. The unemployed worker loses his daily association with fellow workers. This loss means not only the disappearance of human relationships built up over a period of years but also the end of a meaningful institutional relationship. While he had his job, he may not have regarded it as much more than a source of livelihood. When he is severed from the job, however, he discovers that he has lost, in addition to the income and the activity, his institutional base in the economic and social system. Like Queequeg, he is adrift, "hopelessly holding up hope in the midst of despair."

Further, lengthy unemployment tends to have a stigma attached to it, and the unemployed breadwinner can easily exaggerate this stigma. As one of the interviewers for the Armour studies put it:

You're not able to keep up your end of social obligations. Friends are reluctant to include you in plans for parties, trips, and other things that involve spending money. You become aware of the fact that some friends are avoiding you because they feel sorry for you. Others avoid you because they don't want to hear your sad story or because they're afraid you might want to borrow money. As one fellow remarked, "It's hard to keep wearing the pants in the family when you're not making no money." This is an experience many of them have had whose wives and children still have jobs. They have seen their authority as head of the family slip away when they no longer provide support.[7]

The long-term unemployed worker may become isolated from community organizations. Lack of income, as well as embarrassment, may cause him to withdraw from lodges, recreational groups, political organizations, and even his church. Union membership is also apt to cease. The dangers of this kind of withdrawal and isolation existed during the mass unemployment of the 1930's and have returned for those groups hardest hit by unemployment in recent years. A statement written 25 years ago describes the problem:

Withdrawn from the group contacts which have given them a sense of social status and integrity, unemployed workers and their families finally come to be completely separated from society both in physical reality and in spiritual attitude. If this condition persists over an extended period they are likely to become active enemies of a social order which has deprived them not only of an income but, consequently, of all the other relationships which have made their lives valuable.[8]

---

7. James H. Weaver, one of the interviewers in Oklahoma City.

8. "Social Wastage Due to Unemployment," economic brief in support of the New York State unemployment insurance law before the U.S. Supreme Court, October, 1936, reprinted in *Readings in Unemployment* (Washington, D.C.: Special Committee on Unemployment Problems, U.S. Senate, U.S. Government Printing Office, 1960), p. 187. See also, in the same book, pp. 180–302, and Harold L. Sheppard and others, *op. cit.,* Chap. 7, pp. 49–53.

Much could be said about the psychological impact of long-term unemployment on the individual worker and his family, but our studies did not attempt to measure this factor directly. Nevertheless, it is worth noting that, even though the questions were largely limited to labor market behavior and the economic impact of the shutdowns, the noneconomic, personal effects of displacement and joblessness constantly appeared in the interview responses, in comments written at the end of the mail questionnaire, and in the reports of the interviewers. It is difficult to read statements such as the following, written by the respondents, without visualizing both the immediate and potential harm to the worker and his family if the employment situation does not improve.

I am 45 years old and businesses are reluctant to hire me—and I have five children in school.

Since jobs are so few there is a lot of discrimination. Whenever you find a place where they are hiring, they always hire the white man first.

I have a hard time trying to feed my children.

My son was in college and he had to come home. I was unable to pay his tuition.

A son graduated from high school in 1959. He got one year of college. Another son graduated in 1960. Neither is getting to go to college this year.

We tried for a loan and was turned down. The loan was for unpaid bills.

It has forced my wife to work when she wasn't able. I haven't been able to help her any with the bills or any other expenses.

My wife had to leave the children and go to work.

I am trusting the Lord will give me strength and courage to carry me through this crisis.

I wish in some way you could help me get a job.[9]

_____

9. A number of those who returned mail questionnaires asked for help in finding jobs, even though it was specifically stated that the survey had no connection with the location of jobs.

Attitudes toward Company, Union, and Government

In all five of the cities, a large majority of the displaced workers had not only liked the wages at Armour or ABC but also the type of work and the work environment. Because of this, the shutdowns produced mixed feelings about the companies and the unions involved. In discussions with the interviewers, many workers would make harsh statements about the company and/or the union but at the same time indicate their eagerness to return if that were possible.

Because of all the losses involved, it is to be expected that many of the workers would want to assign blame for the closings, although in each of the cities there was a minority who felt the shutdowns were an unavoidable consequence of industrial life. The Armour workers, however, had developed a strong feeling of job ownership and economic security. The general expectation had been that they had jobs that would last until retirement age. The ABC workers, on the other hand, were more likely to accept economic insecurity as a way of life. They had substantially less seniority, on the average, than the Armour workers and had experienced more job mobility in their working careers.

CRITICISM OF SHUTDOWN PROCEDURES

Little of value can be obtained from a discussion of the workers' assessment of responsibility for the shutdowns, but some lessons can be learned from their evaluation of some of the mistakes made by company and union in the process of closing the plants. The major complaint of the Armour workers was that the company provided only one month's notice of the closings. Many felt they should have had at least a year's notice so that they could have prepared themselves for unemployment by reducing their debts and avoiding major new obligations and so that they could also have begun earlier to look or prepare for other employment.

Another frequent criticism, as previously mentioned, was that the plant credit union called in outstanding loans and closed very quickly. In several of the plants, the credit unions demanded payment as soon as the severance pay checks were distributed. Many of the workers didn't see why the credit unions could not have been continued, enabling them to pay off loans over a longer time.

The unions also came in for criticism. Many of the workers complained that the local's treasury went to the International rather than being kept for their own collective or individual use, where it might have done them some good. In one of the cities, some of the workers charged that a building fund for the local was taken by the International.

VIEWS ON POST-SHUTDOWN RESPONSIBILITIES

In the Peoria study, we obtained the views of the workers on who, if anyone, was responsible for helping workers who are displaced by a plant shutdown. The first of a series of questions was:

Who do you think should try to do something to help in this kind of problem [i.e., a plant shutdown]?

The responses to this open-end question show, first, a fairly high degree of acceptance of a plant shutdown as part of the scheme of things and, second, considerable uncertainty about where responsibility lies for doing something about plant shutdowns and their aftermath. Forty-three per cent didn't know who should do something, although only 10 per cent said nothing should be done. Among those who did have an opinion, about a fourth thought "government" (i.e., federal or state) should do something, another fourth thought local business groups or the "community" should take action, and a third thought it was up to the company. The remainder mentioned the union and the state employment service.[10]

_____

10. These results differ considerably from those in the Packard study (Harold L. Sheppard and others, *op. cit.*, p. 41). In that study, in response to a similar question, nine out of ten named some group, and "government" was mentioned twice as often as unions and four times more frequently than management. Two factors may account for the difference: (1) The Packard workers had had more experience with government contracts and many thought that the government could give contracts to Packard to keep it going, and (2) the Peoria workers may be more "provincial" and "conservative" in spite of belonging to a left-wing union.

Whatever their answer to the open-end question, the respondents were asked what government should do to help. The results are compared in Table 9 with those obtained in the study of laid-off Packard workers in Detroit. The more "conservative" character of the ABC workers is indicated by the higher proportion who thought government should do nothing and the higher proportion who didn't know what government should do. A sizable minority, however, felt that government should help workers find jobs or else save jobs by preventing companies from relocating plants.

Table 9
**Workers' Recommendations for Governmental Action on
Plant Shutdowns
(in Per Cent)**

Action Recommended	ABC Workers (N = 193)	Packard Workers (N = 321)
Do nothing	21	6
Don't know	30	6
Find or make jobs	20	15
Stop company from moving	14	5
Lower taxes	5	12
More defense contracts	3	21
Other	7	35

Source: ABC: personal interview data; Packard: Harold L. Sheppard and others, *Too Old to Work—Too Young to Retire* (Washington, D.C.: U.S. Government Printing Office, 1960), p. 41.

The differences between the Packard and ABC workers probably reflect in part the substantial differences in age and unemployment experience of the two groups. The Packard workers were actually more similar to the Armour workers than to the ABC workers in age, length of service with the company, and length of unemployment after the shutdown. Although we do not have precise data for the Armour workers on what government should do about plant shutdowns, the comments of some of them suggest that they would also be more comparable to the Packard workers in believing the government should assume responsibility for helping displaced workers.

The ABC workers were also asked whether the company and union did all they could to help the workers after the shutdown.

First, it should be noted that the workers were of the opinion that there was more opportunity for the company to help than the union. With this qualification, the results are that 71 per cent thought the union did all it could (16 per cent said it did not and 13 per cent didn't know—some of the latter were not union members). In contrast, only 35 per cent thought the company did all it could and 49 per cent that it did not (another 7 per cent said the local management did all it could but not the parent company, and 9 per cent failed to express an opinion).

When asked what else the company might have done, 36 per cent had specific suggestions: help in locating jobs, particularly for older workers (49 per cent); keeping the plant operating (22 per cent); more transfers to Grand Rapids (16 per cent); financial help (9 per cent); and earlier notice of the plant closing (4 per cent).

The higher proportion who thought the union did all it could reflects, in part, a low level of expectation. Many of the workers, however, were satisfied with the fact that the union had conducted the pre-shutdown strike that resulted in the severance pay arrangement. Of those who gave a reason for saying the union did all it could, about half mentioned the severance pay or the strike. The other half mentioned such actions as efforts to keep the plant from moving or to persuade another firm to move in, help in locating jobs, and advice to workers on the pension plan. The smaller group who felt the union didn't do much gave such diverse reasons as that the union was too weak, didn't help locate jobs, or "sold out" to the company.

Summary

The extensive unemployment described in the previous chapter had far-reaching economic, social, and psychological effects on the displaced workers and their families. Since most of the workers were breadwinners with primary responsibility for families of three to four persons, on the average, the loss of income during lengthy unemployment meant a serious curtailment of living standards. For the continuously unemployed the combination of unemployment insurance and severance pay meant that, for the first year after the shutdown, income was one-half or less of what it had been at Armour or ABC. A second year of unemployment, as our follow-up survey indicates, meant drastically reduced economic circumstances.

Severance pay was only of short-term benefit for many of the workers because they were forced to use it quickly to pay accumulated debts and to meet everyday living expenses. Longer notification of the shutdowns might have enabled more of the workers to reduce their debts while they were still employed, thus prolonging the time for which severance pay would have helped.

Few had any other nonwage sources of income, and most such income was minor. A substantial proportion of the men, however, had wives or other family members who were working, and in each of the cities there were some wives who went to work after the shutdowns in order to contribute to the family income.

A large majority reported some difficulty in family finances in the year after the shutdown; the degree of difficulty was considerably greater for the long-term unemployed. Measures of family financial problems include the need for utilizing savings, reduction in the level of spending on both necessities and luxuries, and, in far fewer cases, cashing in insurance, selling personal property, and changing dwelling places. Finally, as another indicator of reduced circumstances and forced change in habits, there was a drastic decline in vacation trips as a result of the permanent layoffs and subsequent unemployment.

The economic and financial hardships were accompanied by the social and psychological problems associated with prolonged unemployment. Permanent layoffs after years of company tenure meant a traumatic shock, particularly for the long-tenure Armour workers. Facing a labor market in which jobs were scarce was a difficult experience for many, particularly for those who suddenly discovered they had become "old" in the eyes of potential employers.

No attempt was made to measure precisely the psychological effects of prolonged joblessness but the seriousness of these effects was evident in the written-in comments on the mail questionnaires, in the personal interviews, and in the observations of the interviewers. Anger, resentment, bitterness, frustration, and bewilderment are a few of the words used by the interviewers to describe the emotions of many of the unemployed. One interviewer described some of the respondents as "blighted men." The long-term unemployed had been uprooted from a productive institutional tie and a seemingly secure place in society and, as a result, had become isolated from the work environment and a large part of their usual human associations.

In view of all this, there was surprisingly little radicalism or rejection of the social and economic system. Many accepted economic insecurity as part of the American way of life, and few had very specific ideas about what could be done to help them in the labor market. At least at the time of the interviews, which were generally a year or less after the shutdowns, many of the long-term unemployed had not yet given up hope. Nevertheless, a significant number of those who believed their age was against them—and a few of these were not yet 40—were greatly concerned about whether they would ever find decent jobs again.

5

The Search
for Work

THE DISPLACED WORKERS were, for the most part, not very successful in their job search. We have already described some of their personal handicaps in the labor market. In addition, they faced competition with each other for scarce manual and service jobs, since in each city they all entered the labor market at about the same time. To make matters worse, most of them were inexperienced in job hunting, not having faced the problem for many years. They lacked knowledge of job opportunities and there seemed to be no agencies, whether public or private, that were able to furnish much help.

In this chapter, we shall explore the process of job search, including an analysis of job information available to displaced workers, the reasons why some workers became long-term unemployed and others did not, the ways in which they hunted for jobs, the scope and geographic extent of their job inquiries, and the amount and type of job-seeking assistance they received and believed they could have used. The effect of severance pay and unemployment insurance on job search will also be briefly explored.

Of greatest interest, perhaps, from the standpoint of realistic help for the long-term unemployed is the question of willingness to migrate to other communities for employment. This question is investigated primarily in terms of worker interest and willingness to move, and of the conditions for moving, to company plants in other areas.

The Workers' Perception of the Job Market

The five cities differed significantly not only in population and degree of industrial diversification but also in the relative availability of job openings during the year after the plant closings. The displaced workers, although they did not have detailed knowledge of the local job markets, were generally aware of whether jobs for which they might qualify were scarce or plentiful. Their perception of the job market, however vague or distorted, influenced the ways in which they looked for work, where they looked, and also the extent of their interest in possible transfer to other plants of the same company.

PERCEPTIONS OF JOB OPPORTUNITIES

Although no attempt was made to catalog completely the job market knowledge of the laid-off workers, the Armour workers were asked in the post-shutdown interviews:

> When your job at Armour was terminated and you had to find another job, what possibilities were open to you?

The purpose of the question was to obtain a measure of the employment situation as seen by the workers at the time they were thrust into the job market after years of continuous service with one company and with only one month's notification. Although the question required that they reconstruct at the time of the interview what they had seen as possibilities almost a year earlier, the evidence is that their memories of actions and reactions at the time of the shutdowns were quite vivid. The answers provide a general assessment of what these workers thought was "possible" just after the shutdowns.

A majority of the workers were either quite vague about the types of work available or thought job opportunities were poor or even nonexistent. There were substantial differences among the four cities, however, in the perception of job possibilities. These differences seem to be related to three major factors—the general level of job opportunities in the local labor market area, the area's population, and the degree of industrial complexity. At the time of the shutdowns, job opportunities were poorest in East St. Louis and Fargo, and this is reflected by the 40 per cent in these cities who saw job possibilities as poor, nonexistent, or unknown. The proportions in Columbus and in Oklahoma City who saw job opportunities as poor were much smaller, but in those cities the job picture was considerably brighter at the time of the shutdowns, although in Oklahoma City it later worsened. In none of the cities, however, were there many who were able to line up new jobs by the time the plants closed. The highest proportion (13 per cent of the men) was in Fargo.

Oklahoma City differs from the other cities in that a far higher proportion said they saw job possibilities in meatpacking or meatcutting. In the interview sample, 51 per cent (55 per cent of the men and 36 per cent of the women; 49 per cent of the whites and 56 per cent of the Negroes) mentioned either meatpacking or meatcutting in wholesale and retail trade. The comparable figure for the other three cities is only 9 per cent. The difference may be accounted for in that (1) the meat industry forms a larger portion of total employment in Oklahoma City than in the other cities, and (2) some of the Oklahoma City workers seemed to be anticipating help from the company and from the Armour Automation Fund Committee. In fact, the Oklahoma City workers, in contrast to the three-city workers, appeared to be more optimistic about job prospects than the facts warranted; it seems quite probable that the existence of the committee and the fund, along with the related publicity, did much to raise their hopes.

After responding to the question on the job possibilities open to them at the time of the shutdowns, those being interviewed were asked why they gave the answers they did. Among those who said they had anticipated difficulties in finding jobs, two major types of explanations were offered—scarcity of jobs and personal limitations. In East St. Louis and Fargo, job scarcity was mentioned more often than personal limitations (age, health, lack of experience or training). In Columbus and Oklahoma City, on the other hand, where job prospects appeared better, personal limitations were mentioned more frequently than scarcity of jobs. Age was mentioned far more often than any other personal handicap, but mostly by workers over 45 years of age. Only a few Negroes mentioned race as a problem. Those Negroes who had anticipated difficulty in the labor market generally attributed it to age, scarcity of jobs, or lack of skill or education.

WHY THE LONG-TERM UNEMPLOYED FELT THEY COULD NOT FIND JOBS

In each of the five cities, the long-term unemployed who were interviewed were asked why they thought they were unable to find jobs more quickly.[1] Figure 11 shows that two reasons dominate the workers' own evaluations—the scarcity of jobs and age as a barrier to employment.

The data show that in the cities where the employment situation was less favorable, East St. Louis and Fargo, male workers were most likely to mention the general scarcity of jobs as a reason for lengthy joblessness. Columbus and Peoria had the most favorable employment situation, and in those cities the long-term unemployed among the men mentioned job scarcity less often than personal limitations, such as age or lack of education. None of this seems to reflect any significant differences among the cities with respect to employer hiring practices. What it does seem to mean is that where unemployment is high workers will blame the lack of jobs for their unemployment but where jobs are more plentiful the unemployed are more likely to attribute their joblessness to personal characteristics.

In Oklahoma City, the average age of the workers in the final-layoff group was substantially higher than in the other cities, which is probably the major explanation for the frequent mention of age by the male long-term unemployed in that city. In Fargo, how-

---

1. In the ABC study, the question applied to those who had not found a job in three months; in the Armour study, the question was asked of those with at least two months of unemployment. Since most of the respondents to this question had at least 15 weeks of joblessness, we have labeled them the long-term unemployed.

Figure 11. PERCENTAGE DISTRIBUTION OF LONG-TERM UNEMPLOYED MEN, BY
MAJOR EXPLANATIONS FOR INABILITY TO FIND WORK, FIVE CITIES

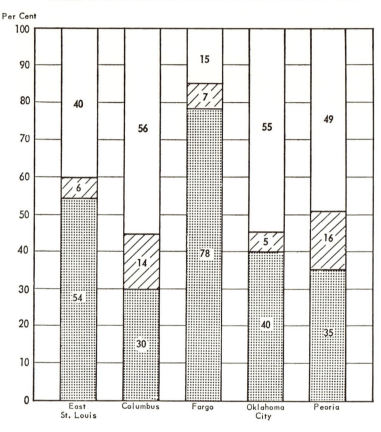

Key:

Age as a barrier to employment

Other personal limitations (sex, race, health, lack of education, skill or experience)

Jobs not available

Source: Personal interview data.

ever, where the average age was also fairly high, age was mentioned in only 15 per cent of the cases. Apparently, most of the men with substantial unemployment in Fargo believed that jobs were scarce for workers of any age and that age itself was not a major factor. Fargo is a much smaller community than the others, and a higher proportion of the workers have rural backgrounds. Traditionally, in such communities, age is not a serious barrier to employment in farming and other nonindustrial jobs. The evidence of the study, however, is that the older men in Fargo were no more successful in finding jobs relative to younger men than were the older workers in the other cities.

The mention of age as a barrier increased rapidly with the age of the unemployed worker. In the three cities, for example, 17 per cent of the long-term unemployed under 45 mentioned age as a barrier, contrasted with 51 per cent of those 45 through 54 years of age and 71 per cent of those 55 or over. The consciousness of age as a problem and, indeed, the traumatic experience of quite suddenly coming to realize that one was "old," at least insofar as finding a job is concerned, are revealed in the following quotations.

I worked at Armour 23 years. Now I am too old to get a new job and not old enough for retirement.

Since I am 40 years of age, I've found it difficult to find work. So many places do not want a man over 35 years of age.

I am in my 40's and they just don't want anyone that is 40 years old. I'm just as able to work as anyone that is in the 20's.

The dominance of the concern with age is reflected in the small proportions who mentioned any other personal factor as a handicap in finding work. In East St. Louis, Oklahoma City, and Peoria, only 5 per cent of the Negro long-term unemployed mentioned race as the major factor that explained their unemployment. Among women, none of the former Armour workers mentioned their sex as the major reason for lengthy unemployment, and only 9 per cent of the former ABC women workers did so. In the five cities combined, only 2½ per cent gave their state of health as the major reason, and only 6 per cent mentioned lack of education, experience, or skills. Intercity variations were slight on these factors. In none of the studies was there any mention of obsolescence of skills, as such, although some referred to the scarcity of jobs in their "line of work."[2]

The fact that only a few attributed their unemployment to their race, their sex, or their lack of education or relevant work experience does not mean that these workers considered these factors as of no importance. What it does mean is that most of the workers were realistic in their job search. The displaced workers for the most part looked for jobs for which they were qualified and at companies where they had some reasonable expectation of being hired. Negroes tended to look for types of work held by Negroes and women looked for jobs held by women. Whether they liked it or not, they sensed that this is how the labor market functions and they had no choice but to conform. Unwillingness to mention race or sex as a cause of unemployment may, however, have been a factor in the responses.

In contrast, age was mentioned frequently, by white and Negro, and by men and women. In the view of the older workers themselves, their job-hunting difficulties were due more to age than to any other factors. A number of them became completely discouraged in their job search.

Those who found jobs quickly did not often attribute their success to their particular qualifications or characteristics. Among the short-term unemployed in Peoria, for example, almost half said they were just lucky or had the right connections (referral by friends, relatives, or their employer). Only 20 per cent attributed their success to having the right qualifications (jobs available in their line of work or in places they had previously worked), and only 16 per cent gave as the major reason the fact that they had looked hard for jobs.

Interest in Transfer to Other Plants

Since Armour has a number of meatpacking plants and ABC was owned by a large corporation that also manufactures appliances

---

2. In Figure 11, these answers are coded as "jobs not available." This particular response was important only in Columbus and Fargo (10 and 8 per cent, respectively).

in Grand Rapids, Michigan, there was in each of the five cities at least some possibility of transfer to other plants in the same company. The degree of interest of the displaced workers in such transfer may be thought of as another measure of their perception of the opportunities in the local job market.

If a typical manual worker were given a choice between doing a familiar type of work in another area and a different type of work at decent wages within reasonable commuting distance of his home, he would choose the latter.[3] In other words, interest in remaining in the same town with one's family, friends, and familiar associations normally far outweighs, for production workers, interest in retaining the particular job or working for the same company. The presumption, therefore, is that willingness to move must be, to a large degree, an index of dissatisfaction with present employment (primarily wages) or the lack of employment. At the same time, the possibility of transfer within the company is a good test of willingness to relocate in another labor market area.

Because the circumstances with respect to the possibilities of transfer differed in each of the three studies, the data on interest in transfer are presented separately.

THE THREE CITIES

In East St. Louis, Columbus, and Fargo little hope of transfer was held out to any of the bargaining-unit workers and, consequently, the following question in the interviews was quite hypothetical:

If you had been offered a job at another Armour meatpacking plant in another city, would you have taken it if:
  (a) Armour had offered you a job at about the same rate of pay as you were making here?
  (b) The above *and* you could have kept your seniority rights?

3. See Richard C. Wilcock, *Impact on Workers and Community of a Plant Shutdown in a Depressed Area* (Washington, D.C.: U.S. Bureau of Labor Statistics, Bulletin No. 1264, 1960), Chap. 3, pp. 20–25. A majority of out-of-town workers (those with jobs in other areas who kept their families in the local area) and of migrants (those who had moved away) preferred jobs in the "home town" even when the work and pay were less satisfactory.

(c) Both of the above *and* the Company had paid part of your
moving costs to a new location?[4]

Part (b) of the question was asked only if the answer to (a) was
"no," and part (c) was asked only if the answer to (b) was "no."
The respondents were also asked the reason for saying "no" to any
part of the question.

The interest in transfer shown by the responses may be exag-
gerated because it is much easier to *say* that one would transfer
to another city than it would to be *make* the move.[5] Expressed
willingness to move, however, was found to be greater among men
than women, nonmarried than married, Negro than white, and
long-term unemployed than short-term unemployed. The major
causal factors would appear to be unemployment or the inability
to obtain satisfactory employment, both of which varied with personal characteristics.

The most significant aspect of the data in Table 10 is that a
rather substantial majority of all the laid-off workers indicated
they would have moved to another Armour plant in another city.
This demonstrates, on the one hand, satisfaction with the Armour
jobs and pay and, on the other, the extent to which the workers,
during the year after they were laid off, either were unable to find
jobs or could only find jobs at much lower pay.

A fairly high degree of willingness to move is shown by the fact
that a majority said they would move at the same pay without
reference to seniority or moving costs. Mention of seniority rights
added 13 per cent to the total (somewhat more men than women),
but mention of moving costs did not budge those who were not

---

4. They were also asked whether they had any chance to stay with
Armour by transfer to another plant. Only seven men (3.6 per cent) and
no women reported having such a chance.

5. See Margaret Gordon and Ann H. McCorry, "Plant Relocation and
Job Security—A Case Study," *Industrial and Labor Relations Review,* Vol.
11, No. 1 (October, 1957), pp. 13–36. Of those who announced an intention
to transfer from San Francisco to Los Angeles, only two-thirds actually did.
Proportions were highest among those, such as Negroes and older men, who
expected greatest difficulty in the local labor market. Also of interest is the
fact that only one-third of the employees originally indicated they would
transfer, presumably because the local employment situation was far better
than it was in the three cities.

Table 10
Willingness to Accept an Armour Job in Another City at Time of Layoff, by Sex, Race, Age, Years of School, Marital Status, Number of Dependents, and Whether Employed when Interviewed (in Per Cent)

	Sex							Race	
	THREE CITIES			EAST ST. LOUIS		COLUM-BUS	FAR-GO	EAST ST. LOUIS	
	Total	Men	Women	Men	Women	Men	Men	White	Negro
	(N = 243)	(N = 192)	(N = 51)	(N = 68)	(N = 31)	(N = 64)	(N = 60)	(N = 54)	(N = 45)
1. Not willing to move	31	28	41	19	45	30	37	46	4
2. Would move at same pay	56	58	49	68	45	50	55	43	82
3. Would move at same pay *plus* retention of seniority	13	14	10	13	10	20	8	11	14
4. Total of 2 and 3	69	72	59	81	55	70	63	54	96

	Age							
	THREE CITIES		EAST ST. LOUIS		COLUMBUS		FARGO	
	Under 45	45 & Over	Under 45	45 & Over	Under 45	45 & Over	Under 45	45 & Over
	(N = 119)	(N = 123)	(N = 47)	(N = 51)	(N = 37)	(N = 37)	(N = 35)	(N = 35)
1. Not willing to move	33	28	34	20	24	32	40	37
2. Would move at same pay	50	62	53	69	49	57	49	57
3. Would move at same pay *plus* retention of seniority	17	10	13	11	27	11	11	6
4. Total of 2 and 3	67	72	66	80	76	68	60	63

	Years of School			Marital Status		Whether Now Employed	
	THREE CITIES			THREE CITIES		THREE CITIES	
	7 or Less	8-11	12 or More	Married	Other	Employed	Unemployed
	(N = 54)	(N = 147)	(N = 31)	(N = 198)	(N = 45)	(N = 143)	(N = 90)
1. Not willing to move	15	33	48	33	20	39	14
2. Would move at same pay	70	56	39	54	67	46	62
3. Would move at same pay *plus* retention of seniority	15	11	13	13	13	15	24
4. Total of 2 and 3	85	67	52	67	80	61	86

Source: Personal interview data.

interested in moving at the same pay or at the same pay with retention of seniority. It is possible that probing by the interviewers would have added a few for whom moving costs would have made the difference, but it is significant that none of those interviewed voluntarily changed their minds when the added incentive of moving costs was mentioned.

The results suggest that the major inducement to transfer would have been a familiar job without loss of pay. If faced with the actual decision it is probable, however, that smaller numbers would have accepted transfer and that retention of seniority would have loomed larger in the workers' minds. The effect of lower-paying jobs and of unemployment is nonetheless quite evident. Interest in transfer was highest among those who had the most unemployment and those who were currently unemployed.

Women were an exception. Even though they had higher unemployment than men, many had husbands working in the local area or they were dependent on the husband's decision. East St. Louis Negro men were more willing to transfer than Columbus or Fargo men because of their higher level of unemployment. Differences among white men in the three cities were small. Similarly, older workers more frequently expressed willingness to move than younger because of their greater difficulty in finding employment. The less-educated were also more willing to move.

Altogether, only one-third said they would not move to another job. Their reasons for *not* wanting to move were, in order, family and friends in the area, no guarantee of steady work or seniority if moved, home ownership, preferring to live in the local area, and husband working locally. Minor reasons were age, health, and not wanting to work for Armour any more. Many of these reasons would undoubtedly also apply to those who said they would transfer. The difference is that the latter saw more pressing reasons for accepting a transfer, if offered.

OKLAHOMA CITY

The plant shutdown in this city took place a year after the three-city shutdowns and also after the Armour Automation Fund Committee had been in operation for a year. The local officers of the

Packinghouse Workers Union and undoubtedly a large percentage of the bargaining-unit employees were aware of the existence of the committee, and some expectations had been built up with respect to the help that might be forthcoming in finding jobs, in retraining, and in transfer. However, only 18 per cent of the workers interviewed before the shutdown said they had applied or planned to apply for transfer to another Armour plant. Almost all of them were men, with roughly equal proportions of whites and Negroes. Not quite half thought the transfer was possible, with whites almost three times more likely than Negroes to see it as a realistic possibility.

In the weeks before the shutdown, therefore, only a small minority were interested in transfer to another plant. The low level of interest was undoubtedly due in part to the belief that few transfers would be offered to hourly-rated workers. In addition, however, the workers at that time thought that job possibilities in the local market were reasonably good; therefore, the relative lack of interest also illustrates the strong desire for local-area jobs.

Because of the conflicting motivations that determined the interest in transfers, the relative attachment to community and to company (including industry and occupation) was also measured in other ways in the in-plant survey. One was a hypothetical choice between a meatpacking job in another city 200 miles or more away at the Armour pay scale and a local meatpacking job at 40 cents an hour less. Given this choice, 73 per cent said they would take the local job and 26 per cent the distant job at higher pay. Given the same differential in pay, but for a nonmeatpacking job, 76 per cent chose the local job at lower pay and 22 per cent the distant job at higher pay. Whether the distant job was in meatpacking or something else made very little difference; local jobs were strongly preferred, even at lower pay and in nonmeatpacking occupations.

Because reluctance to move could be partly the result of the costs of moving, the workers were also asked whether they would take a job in another city (200 or more miles away) if their moving costs were paid and if they received their Armour pay scale. In addition, they were asked if they would go *without* moving costs but at pay 40 cents an hour *more* than at Armour. The results are as follows:

Job in Distant City	*Would Move*	*Would Not*
Moving cost paid; Armour pay level	49%	51%
Moving costs not paid; wage rate 40¢ higher	46%	54%

Economic incentives, therefore, in the form either of moving costs or higher pay, significantly increased the proportions willing to move. Those who were in higher pay brackets at Armour were more responsive to either incentive, but differences related to age, race, and education were slight.

The above questions were asked before the plant had closed. At the time of the post-layoff interviews, the possibility had been raised that some of the workers would have the chance of accepting Armour jobs in Kansas City under a January, 1961, agreement between the company and the unions that was proposed by the Automation Fund Committee. As jobs opened up in the Kansas City plant, Oklahoma City workers would be given preference in hiring. Those who accepted would have their moving costs paid, but for layoff and severance-pay purposes they would have the status of new employees.

INTEREST IN KANSAS CITY JOB

In view of the difficult employment situation in Oklahoma City, one would expect the eligible workers to be torn between the desire to remain in the home community (since most were long-time residents) and the economic pull of an Armour meatpacking job in Kansas City. Further, doubts about the permanence of the Kansas City job could also be expected.

These expectations are confirmed by the interview data, which show that 54 per cent believed they would accept an offer,[6] and Table 11 shows that most of the reasons given are economic— needing the income or a steady job and needing or wanting the pay and benefits. For those who said they would turn down an

---

6. The interview results (February, 1961) are very similar to and tend to confirm the replies to the Committee (January, 1961), as follows:

	Total	MEN All	MEN White	Negro	Women
Indicated interest in K.C. job in reply to Committee (N = 304)	50%	53%	—	—	36%
Said would take a job, personal interviews (N = 111)	54%	57%	54%	61%	36%

offer, however, personal reasons were almost as important as economic reasons. These personal reasons for staying in Oklahoma City (family, friends, home, age, and so forth) were undoubtedly important to most of the workers—those who said they wouldn't move as well as those who said they would. Acceptance of job offers in Kansas City, therefore, would mean that economic necessity outweighed personal considerations.

Table 11
Tabulation of Reasons Given for Wanting to Take or Not to Take a Job in Kansas City
(in Per Cent)

Reason Would Take (N = 64)		Reason Would Not Take (N = 44)	
Needs the income or no work locally	30	Because of family, friends, and	
For the pay	17	"home"	18
Likes the work, familiar work	20	Concern about steadiness of K.C. job	23
Needs "steady" work	14	Home ownership and/or spouse	
Because of the benefits including		working locally	16
pension rights	10	Doesn't want to leave present job	11
Family-connected reasons[a]	3	Financial reasons[b]	9
Other	6	Personal reasons[c]	11
		Other	11

Source: Personal interview data.
[a] Two women: one will go if husband does, the other because she has no family locally.
[b] Concern about returning severance pay; concern about cost of moving.
[c] Doesn't wish to move because of age or health.

As of May, 1962, sufficient job openings had not occurred in Kansas City to test the relationship between stated willingness and actual decisions to move. At the time the possibility was first raised, however, substantial numbers were at least predisposed to accept Armour jobs in Kansas City if offers were made.

COMPARISON WITH IN-PLANT SURVEY

We have seen that in February, 1961, 54 per cent said they would take a Kansas City Armour job. In June, 1960, before the plant closed, 49 per cent had said they would take a job in a distant city at their Armour pay scale if their moving costs were paid. Because these proportions are so close, we decided to match the individuals to see if the same ones were involved at both times. We found that the make-up of the groups had shifted. Among those saying they would accept a Kansas City job offer, only one in three had indicated earlier, in the pre-shutdown survey, he would take an out-of-area job with pay similar to that at Armour and with moving costs. Again, only one in three of those ready to go to Kansas City had in a forced-choice question in the pre-shutdown survey chosen an out-of-town meatpacking job at the Armour pay scale in preference to a job in Oklahoma City at 40 cents an hour below his Armour pay.

Thus, two out of three of those interested in the Kansas City jobs had, because of unemployment and/or dissatisfaction with their post-Armour employment, changed their minds about leaving the community. Some of their reasons for a change in view are indicated by their answers to the question on why they would accept a job offer in Kansas City—Armour pay is better, like the company or opportunities in the company, need the work, and believe the job would be steady (see Table 11).

Although some had been predisposed to consider a transfer to another Armour plant, the major reasons for serious consideration eight months after the shutdown were either unemployment or else dissatisfaction with the pay or other conditions of current employment. Of those who had either no regular work or substantial unemployment, about three out of five said they would accept a transfer; the major reasons given were "need the work," it would be a steady job, the pay or fringe benefits would be good, and the opportunities with Armour would be better than in their current employment.

Other factors were of lesser importance. Fewer women than men, of course, were interested in transfer. For men, the question of whether their wives had jobs appears to have had little influence. In fact, a somewhat higher proportion of those whose wives had jobs (67 per cent) were interested in transfer than of those whose wives were not working (55 per cent). An explanation for this would require a detailed evaluation of the employment and unemployment experience of each man. The probability, however, is that those with working wives had had a more difficult experience in the labor market and consequently were more interested in transfer. Also, the incentive for transfer might be high where the wife is employed and the husband is either unemployed or in a low-paying job.

Differences with respect to race and age are slight. Home ownership, however, is related to interest in jobs at the Kansas City plant. Of those interviewed, less than half of the home owners said they would accept a job, while three out of four of those who rented expressed interest in going to Kansas City. The greater interest of renters in Kansas City jobs may have been for other reasons, such as higher unemployment, but home ownership was given as one of the reasons for staying in Oklahoma City by those who thought they would not accept a Kansas City job.

PEORIA

The Peoria workers also thought that few transfers would be offered to another company plant and preferred local area jobs, if they could be found, to jobs that required moving to another community. Unlike the Armour workers, however, they tended to identify the company as consisting entirely of the local plant (which had previously been true) and seemed to view the Grand Rapids plant as belonging to an entirely different company. Nevertheless, the uncertainties of finding a new job locally led 14 per cent of the workers to apply for work in Grand Rapids, even though two-thirds of these didn't think they had much chance of a job offer. Most of the applicants were white men. Also, the applicants tended to be unskilled, under 45, and with only grade school education.

In the interviews that were held more than a year after the shutdown, the workers were asked whether they had given any thought to trying to get a job in Grand Rapids. The reasons given by the four out of five who said they had not seriously considered it suggest that desire to stay in the local community was the dominant reason (60 per cent) but that other reasons were also important. A number believed that no job offers would be made (26 per cent said "they weren't hiring" or "they only wanted high-rated personnel"). And 13 per cent said they didn't consider it because they would not regain their seniority. For a worker without strong attachment to company or occupation, a local job with beginning seniority would be preferable to an out-of-area job with his old company and in his old type of work that required starting from the bottom of the seniority ladder.

When the respondents were asked about the Grand Rapids plant, with the hypothetical premise that jobs were available for the taking, the degree of interest in going increased substantially, however. The question was essentially the same as one asked in the three-city study. Only 42 per cent said they would definitely not go under any of the hypothetical conditions specified, and 49 per cent said they would—30 per cent for the same type of work they had at ABC; another 17 per cent if full seniority rights were offered; and an additional 2 per cent if moving costs were added to seniority. The remaining 9 per cent thought they might go but were not sure.

Two major factors are associated with the answers to the hypothetical question on a transfer to Grand Rapids—post-shutdown labor market experience and ties to home and family. The latter was, on the whole, more important. Women and older workers had more unemployment than men and younger workers but indicated greater reluctance to consider transfer because of family ties and home ownership. Among the workers who were 25 years old and over, 70 per cent owned or were buying their homes—61 per cent of those in the 25–44 age group and 81 per cent of those 45 and over. Older workers might be more reluctant to move in any event, but home ownership helped "tie them down."

Confirmation for this conclusion is found when home ownership, age, and interest in a Grand Rapids job are cross-classified. In every age group, a higher proportion of those renting homes were ready to transfer than of those who were home owners. Further, among home owners, interest in transfer was as high for those over 45 as it was for the younger workers, while among those who rented, interest in transfer was actually *higher* among older workers.

Except for the women and for the older workers who owned their homes, the groups with the highest unemployment rates were most interested in transfer—Negroes, those with only grade school education, and those who were in the unskilled and semi-skilled labor grades at ABC. The offsetting influences of home and family ties versus unemployment experience, however, created the odd result that those who had short-term unemployment were as interested in transfer as those who had long-term unemployment.

COMPARISONS OF THE THREE STUDIES

For Armour workers laid off in the summer of 1959 (that is, those in East St. Louis, Columbus, and Fargo) and for the ABC workers laid off in January, 1959, the possibility of transfer to jobs in other plants of their companies seemed rather remote. Nevertheless, when they were asked whether they would take such jobs, fairly high proportions in each of the cities indicated they would accept, with a majority of those interested in transfer being willing to move without seniority protection or moving allowances.

The probability is that not all who indicated interest in transfer would actually move if an offer were made. Nonetheless, the proportions are impressive and provide an index of the unfortunate post-shutdown employment experiences in the local labor markets for large numbers of the displaced workers. The impact of these experiences is shown most clearly in the data for Peoria and Oklahoma City, where pre-shutdown surveys were made. As shown in Figure 12, interest in transfer was far higher at the time of the post-shutdown interviews than it had been in the month prior to layoff when hopes were high for local-area employment.

The Oklahoma City experience is particularly valuable because shortly before the post-shutdown interviews the displaced workers had received letters outlining the possibility of Armour plant jobs in Kansas City—transfers that would include moving costs but with new-employee status with respect to layoffs. With this prospect in mind, 57 per cent of the men indicated they would accept an offer. Had we asked the hypothetical question used in the other four cities, it seems probable that an even higher proportion would have shown willingness to transfer. That question included the retention of seniority rights. Since the Kansas City possibility included no seniority protection, 57 per cent is a high response.

Several other generalizations appear to be warranted by the data. Interest in transfer is related to the state of the local labor market. Thus, in East St. Louis, Fargo, and Oklahoma City, the propor-

Figure 12. PROPORTIONS OF MALE WORKERS INTERESTED IN TRANSFER TO A
DISTANT PLANT OF THE SAME COMPANY—BEFORE THE SHUTDOWN
AND SOME TIME AFTER THE SHUTDOWN, FIVE CITIES

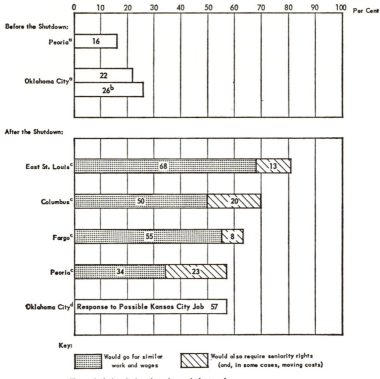

Key:

▓ Would go for similar work and wages   ▨ Would also require seniority rights (and, in some cases, moving costs)

a. Those who had applied or planned to apply for transfer.

b. Those who chose the first alternative in the following forced-choice question: "If you had this choice, which would you do: move to another city (200 or more miles away) for a meatpacking job at the same pay you now get, or take a meatpacking job in Oklahoma City at 40 cents an hour less than you now get."

c. This was the question as to whether the respondents "would have taken" an Armour job in another city, if offered, and if (1) it paid the same rate, (2) paid the same rate and the worker kept his seniority, and (3) both of the above and part of moving costs to the new location were paid.

d. This is the response to the question of whether would take a job in the Kansas City Armour plant, if offered, for those who had a letter explaining the possibility.

Source: In-plant survey and personal interview data.

tions indicating willingness to transfer without seniority protection were higher than they were in Columbus and Peoria where the employment opportunities were better. In Columbus and Peoria, higher proportions specified seniority protection as a condition.

In all of the cities men were more willing than women to transfer, because in most cases they were the breadwinners and their jobs determined family location. Finally, home ownership was a major deterrent to transfer. In Columbus, Oklahoma City, and Peoria, a smaller proportion of workers 45 and over than of younger workers said they would transfer, and this seemed to be partly the result of a higher rate of home ownership. In East St. Louis and Fargo, however, higher proportions of older workers said they would transfer, presumably because the high rates of unemployment overcame the influence of home ownership and the reluctance of older workers to break their local ties.

Methods and Extent of Job Search

In contrast to the situation in many plant shutdowns where the workers are notified of the closing date many months in advance, neither the Armour nor the ABC workers had much warning. This, combined with a labor surplus in manual and service jobs in the areas, meant that there were few quits prior to the shutdowns and also that few workers were able to line up new jobs before being laid off.[7] In the three cities, 6 per cent had found jobs before the shutdown and in Oklahoma City the figure was 8 per cent. In Peoria, a number of short-service workers (less than half a year) were able to return to their previous employers, but if these are excluded only 6 per cent lined up jobs before the plant closed.

Almost all of the displaced Armour workers remained on the

---

7. Practically no Armour workers quit because they feared loss of severance pay and pension rights. Some very short-service ABC workers quit to return to previous employers. In a study of a textile mill closing in 1948, about 10 per cent quit within five weeks of the announcement of the pending layoff. See Charles A. Myers and George P. Shultz, *The Dynamics of a Labor Market* (Englewood Cliffs, N.J.: Prentice-Hall, Inc., 1951), p. 21. In a gradual closing of an International Harvester plant in Auburn, New York, in 1949–50, 16 per cent quit their jobs. See Leonard P. Adams and Robert L. Aronson, *Workers and Industrial Change* (Ithaca, N.Y.: Cornell University Press, 1957), p. 27.

job until final layoff, and approximately half took no action on job search until after the shutdowns took place. The others, however, did start to do something in the month between the announcement and the shutdown. In Oklahoma City, in addition to those who lined up jobs, 45 per cent had started looking or obtaining advice from the company, the union, or friends. In the three cities, 34 per cent had started to look or obtain advice before the shutdown.

In all of the cities, there was fear, reluctance, and a lack of know-how concerning the problem of finding a new job. This was more true of the Armour workers than of those at ABC because at Armour length of service was greater and the workers undoubtedly had had a greater feeling of security in their jobs.

HOW THEY LOOKED FOR WORK

Most of the workers found it necessary to seek jobs on their own and used the time-honored methods of "plant-gate" application, consulting with friends and relatives, and, if possible, obtaining an informal recommendation from a relative, friend, or neighbor. Almost all were looking for full-time work, but many indicated a willingness to accept part-time work if that was all they could find.

In the two studies that included pre-shutdown surveys, the workers were asked how they would look for work after the shutdown. The results (Table 12) show that in both Oklahoma City and Peoria the workers expected to make extensive use of direct applications to companies, want ads, and the public employment service. Differences between men and women, white and Negro, were slight.

Table 12
How Expected to Look for Work—In-plant Surveys, Oklahoma City and Peoria
(in Per Cent)

	Oklahoma City	Peoria
Use the state employment service	76	59
Apply directly to companies	77	85
Read want ads	66	53

Among the five cities, the number of direct applications that were made with employers varied considerably, with the highest numbers in Columbus and East St. Louis and much lower numbers in Fargo, Oklahoma City, and Peoria. The variation appears to be related more to differences in industrial diversification and employer size than to differences in area unemployment. Job opportunities were considerably better in Columbus than in East St. Louis, but in both areas there are a large number of major employers who would attract applications. On the other hand, Oklahoma City and Peoria, although they are standard metropolitan areas, have less industrial diversity and fewer large employers, which would seem to be the main reason why their workers applied at fewer places. Fargo is a much smaller area than the others, and one would expect a smaller number of job applications. The long-term unemployed, in general, applied for work at more places than the short-term unemployed but not at as many more as one would expect, given the length of time out of work.

In all of the cities, however, informal methods of job search were dominant. Further, for those who became long-term unemployed, there was a tendency to stop making the rounds after a while and to rely on the hope that something would turn up from companies where applications had been filed or to wait for the "grapevine" to supply information that a certain company was hiring. As one of the East St. Louis interviewers described it: "When the first frantic period of job seeking was over, people tended to settle down at home, reluctant to pound the pavement or waste precious dollars driving around fruitlessly—hence, the heavy reliance on the grapevine and upon friends and relatives."

When jobs did turn up, they generally were accepted. In the three-city study only 12 per cent of those interviewed reported having turned down any jobs during the year after the shutdown, and in Oklahoma City only 14 per cent had rejected any job offers. When jobs were turned down, in most instances it was because wage rates were "too low"; that is, either below minimum expectations or, more rarely, below what the job was "worth." Less frequent reasons were physical inability to do the work, poor working conditions, and in very few cases the necessity of leaving the local area.

The great majority of all the displaced workers (90 per cent or more in each city) preferred employment in the local area within commuting distance of their homes, and in each city from 80 to 90 per cent of the job hunters confined their search to the local labor market area. Those who looked or applied for jobs in other areas varied from approximately 10 per cent in East St. Louis and Oklahoma City to about 15 per cent in Columbus and Peoria and around 20 per cent in Fargo. Most of these workers also looked for work in the local area.

In the two pre-shutdown surveys, the proportions of those who thought they would look for work outside the area (as well as in the area) are higher than the proportions of those interviewed who did, in fact, look for out-of-area jobs. In Oklahoma City, 25 per cent in the in-plant survey anticipated some out-of-area search but only 9 per cent of those interviewed said later that they had done so. In Peoria, the comparable percentages are 29 and 15 per cent. This is further evidence of the reluctance to migrate and of a fairly common notion that the job market for one's particular skills is not likely to be better anywhere else. Three out of four of the Peoria workers, for example, thought their chances of finding a job quickly were better in Peoria than elsewhere.

JOB-SEEKING ASSISTANCE

In our discussion of methods of job seeking, little has been said about use of the public employment service, the company, or the union because none of them furnished more than minor assistance in job search. As shown by the pre-shutdown survey in Oklahoma City, however, expectations of assistance before layoff were far higher than subsequently realized. While 76 per cent had expected help from the employment service (pre-shutdown survey), only 9 per cent later said they received any help. A majority had expected help from either company or union; only 1 per cent later reported any.

The workers were also asked in the pre-shutdown survey which organization or group they expected to be of greatest help. Their replies were: state employment service, 27 per cent; the union, 23 per cent; the company, 20 per cent; friends or relatives, 20 per cent; other, 10 per cent. They were apparently not very much aware of the Automation Committee at that time, but in the post-shutdown interviews 20 per cent said the committee had helped them.

In the pre-shutdown survey in Peoria, expectations were not as high. Of those planning to look for a new job, 57 per cent thought they would use the Illinois State Employment Service, 33 per cent expected help from the company, 19 per cent from the union, and 32 per cent from friends or relatives. These proportions are significantly lower than those in Oklahoma City and probably reflect the fact that more of the ABC workers had experienced recent layoffs and were able to make a more realistic appraisal of the kind of help they could expect. On the other hand, the expectations of the Armour workers may have been raised by discussions and rumors about the automation agreement between the company and union.

In all of the cities the evidence is that the workers were largely on their own in the job market. In spite of the fact that significant numbers had indicated expectations of help that were not realized, it is our view that it would be more accurate to say that the workers were *hopeful* that the company, union, and public employment service would be able to help them find jobs. They did not seem to think that there was any strict obligation on the part of company, union, or employment service to find work for them. Thus, we interpret the data on expectations to mean that many of the workers would have liked and welcomed more and better job information as well as recommendations and referrals to jobs, but that they were not greatly surprised when they found themselves largely on their own. Some felt, however, that the company was at least obligated to make prompt replies to letters of inquiry from prospective employers.

A majority of the Armour respondents reported that they received *no* help from any source—company, union, employment service, or other agencies. In fact, only 6 per cent reported specific help from their union, 9 per cent from the company, and 13 per cent from the state employment service. Equally small proportions said the union and company tried to help in a general way or that the company or union helped others, even if not the respondent. We have shown data, for men, on help they received and "needed" in Figure 13.

Because the Armour Automation Fund Committee was not a factor in East St. Louis, Columbus, and Fargo, a detailed analysis of help received has to separate the three cities from Oklahoma City.

Three Cities. In the three cities, the responses on help received are for the most part quite similar for the various subgroups. For example, on help provided by the union, there are only minor differences between men and women, white and Negro, younger and older (under and over 45 years of age), and married and unmarried.

On assistance provided by the company, the differences are somewhat greater. Smaller percentages of women than men said the company helped them in any specific way. Negroes in East St. Louis reported less help from the company than did white workers and were also less likely to think that the company had helped others. Semiskilled operatives were less likely than skilled workers to say that they were helped. More married persons than unmarried said the company helped them; one explanation may be the higher proportion of Negroes in the unmarried group (single, widowed, divorced, and separated). Only 63 per cent of the Negroes were married, with spouse present, compared with 86 per cent of the whites.

Most reports of specific assistance by the company came from the men in Columbus, where one out of four said they had some help in finding jobs. These men were helped by the individual efforts of staff members in the personnel department who recommended many employees to other employers.

Workers over 45 were more likely than younger workers to report that the company tried to help or had helped others, but the older workers reported less help from the state employment service in both Columbus and Fargo. State employment services are faced with employer preferences in hiring; therefore it is not surprising that East St. Louis Negroes reported the least help from the employment service (only one case) and that those who were skilled workers at Armour reported more help than those who had lesser skills. Fargo men apparently had more help from the public em-

Figure 13. PROPORTIONS OF MALE ARMOUR WORKERS WHO RECEIVED VARIOUS
TYPES OF JOB-SEEKING HELP AND PROPORTIONS WHO "NEEDED"
ADDITIONAL HELP, FOUR CITIES

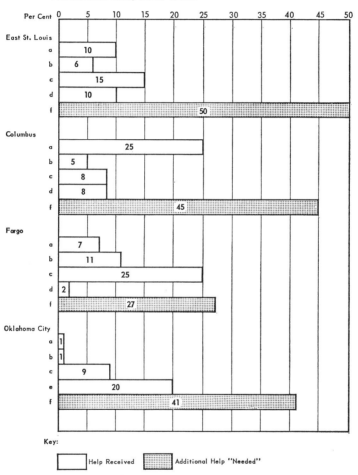

Key:

☐ Help Received   ▨ Additional Help "Needed"

a. Company helped find jobs or made recommendations.

b. Union helped find jobs or made recommendations.

c. State Employment Service made referrals or gave other help.

d. Others helped-- churches, friends or relatives, chamber of commerce, other meatpacking companies, N A A C P, Urban League.

e. Armour Automation Fund Committee--financial aid for training, ability test, "trying to help."

f. Additional help "needed"--help in finding job or in getting training.

Source: Personal interview data.

ployment service in finding jobs than the men in the other cities, but in Fargo those under 45 reported twice as much help from this source as those who were 45 or over.[8]

For the sample as a whole and for all subgroups, assistance from agencies other than the union, company, or employment service was distinctly minor.

East St. Louis men and women, particularly Negroes, expressed a *need* for additional help after the layoff in significantly greater numbers than the workers in either Fargo or Columbus. The very high rate of unemployment among the East St. Louis Negroes and the low pay on many of the jobs they did find explain this result. As might be expected, the long-term unemployed were more likely to express the need for additional help. A majority of those with less than three months out of work in East St. Louis said they did not need additional help, while four out of five of those with three months or more of unemployment said they could have used additional help. If white workers alone are considered, those in Columbus and East St. Louis reported need for assistance about equally, but Fargo workers reported less need for help in finding jobs.

For the three cities combined, women reported greater need for job-hunting assistance than men. Differences between older and younger workers, however, are small. Unmarried workers, in particular, needed help in finding jobs. The higher proportions of Negroes and older workers among the unmarried provide the major explanation.

Oklahoma City. When asked about help from the Automation Fund Committee, a large majority of those interviewed (78 per cent) reported they had received no help of any kind, although some mentioned the letter about the possibility of a job in Kansas City. Among the 111 individuals, 16 (14 per cent) reported financial aid for retraining or schooling and two others (2 per cent) said they had been offered training courses.

---

8. It should be noted that these data are based on the workers' perceptions of help received. They may have failed to give weight to indirect assistance in locating jobs, such as suggestions made by an employment service interviewer.

As for specific help from the company or union, virtually all of the interview respondents (99 per cent) said they had no help at all, although three persons said they heard about their first post-layoff jobs through the company. The respondents were also asked if any other agency or group had helped them find jobs; again the response was almost entirely negative. Two individuals (one white, one Negro) said they were helped by friends, and two Negroes said they were helped by the Urban League. In general, help actually received was far below what was anticipated from employment service, company, and union.

When the Armour plant was closed in Oklahoma City, the Armour Automation Fund Committee arranged to send a consultant, Professor Edwin Young of the University of Wisconsin, to the area for a month to help the workers find new jobs. In an attempt to "rationalize" the job-seeking process, he organized and supervised a program which included contacting other firms in the community, counseling of workers, testing and additional counseling by the Oklahoma Employment Service, and arranging for special training classes for displaced workers.

Evaluation of the program is complicated by the fact that the job market was shrinking at the time and, as a result, only a limited number of new jobs were located for displaced workers. Nevertheless, Professor Young recommended that a permanent person be found and attached to the Automation Committee who would be available to move into each new situation as soon as possible to assist workers displaced either by plant closings or by permanent reductions in a work force. In his view, such a person could give the workers much more help in finding new employment if he were given enough time before they were separated from their former jobs.[9]

As in the three cities, large numbers indicated they could have used various types of assistance, and only 36 per cent said they had not needed any help at all. Twenty-five per cent said they could have used assistance in finding work; 16 per cent mentioned assistance in getting training; and 16 per cent mentioned the need for

9. Unpublished "Final Report" from Edwin Young to the Armour Automation Committee.

financial help. Most of the remainder remarked that a longer notice of the shutdown would have been helpful.

These data on help needed reflect the unemployment and lowered incomes of the displaced workers. Older white men were above average in saying they could have used job-finding assistance. Younger white men and older Negroes were above average in mentioning training. Women were much more likely than men to say they needed financial help.

INFLUENCE OF SEVERANCE PAY AND UNEMPLOYMENT
INSURANCE ON JOB SEARCH

Both severance pay and unemployment insurance are intended, among other things, to allow the worker some time in which to look for suitable work and to provide funds which he can use to cover the cost of job search and possibly relocation. In the plant-shutdown situations studied, however, large numbers of workers became job seekers simultaneously at a time when there were inadequate job opportunities for them in the local community. As a result, these purposes of compensation tended to lose their relevance. Time to look doesn't mean much if few jobs are available. Further, since even the combined compensation was less than half the workers' previous earnings and since most of them were primary breadwinners with families to support, the pressure to seek and accept almost any type of work became quite strong. Thus, it is not surprising to find that most of the displaced workers felt that neither unemployment insurance nor severance pay had much, if any, influence on how and where they looked for work or on whether they accepted jobs.

Armour studies. The Armour workers were asked whether severance pay helped them in any way in looking for work. Only in Oklahoma City did a substantial proportion believe that the severance pay was of some help in job search. However, while 52 per cent thought it was of some help, if we eliminate such general reasons as "it just helped" and "it paid bills," this leaves only 25 per cent who gave relevant reasons. The latter figure compares with 14 per cent in the three other Armour cities. The higher proportion in Oklahoma City may be due to the fact that the average amount of severance pay was greater than in the other cities and it was the only major source of income for many until they qualified for unemployment insurance. Of the minority who thought severance pay of some help in job search, most mentioned either the greater time it allowed or its assistance in paying transportation costs.

A majority of the Armour workers, however, saw no direct connection between severance pay and job search. The severance pay was used to pay debts and to help cover everyday living expenses. Even when it was not all used immediately to pay debts, it seemed to disappear very fast. The limited duration and amount of the severance pay, together with the fact that there appeared to be little likelihood of any improvement in job opportunities, meant that the great majority of the displaced workers, and particularly the men, tried to obtain jobs as quickly as possible and could not afford to turn down less-than-satisfactory jobs in the hope that more suitable work would turn up.

For the most part, therefore, the laid-off workers related severance pay to immediate financial problems and not to more extensive job search or to waiting for a "better job." While the severance pay eased the financial burden of joblessness, most of the workers seemed to believe that their methods of job hunting and the intensity of job hunting were unaffected. Breadwinners, particularly, felt they had to find jobs right away, even though most confined their job search to a commuting radius. On the other hand, the severance pay undoubtedly kept some workers from considering the lowest levels of jobs.

ABC study. In Peoria, those interviewed who had ten or more weeks of unemployment insurance benefits were asked whether the benefits had in any way affected how they went about looking for work. The results are comparable to those on the severance-pay question in the Armour studies. Only 15 per cent thought that unemployment compensation affected their job search, with the major reason being that it gave them more time to find a better job. Those who took the position that there was no relationship did so primarily on the ground that, with or without unemployment insurance, they needed to find a job as soon as possible.

Comment. The conclusion suggested by these findings is that in plant-shutdown situations that lead to a considerable amount of long-term unemployment, neither unemployment insurance nor severance pay will enable many workers to maintain their standards of pay and working conditions by holding out for suitable work comparable, at least in pay, to their previous employment.[10] When jobs are scarce and unemployment insurance is well below the initial goal of covering half the worker's usual wages, the typical manual worker tends to find it necessary to take the first job he can find, regardless of pay or other conditions of employment.

The primary effect of severance pay seemed to be an easing of the financial burden in the period immediately following the plant closing. Workers with substantial short-term debts were helped out of a hole, but whether the allowance was used up quickly or spread out over a number of months, it was nevertheless of major importance to the workers and their families. Severance pay, however, has recently been criticized as not having a very positive effect in providing the displaced workers with "a new start" since so little of it is used for the purpose of obtaining retraining, finding better jobs, or, in appropriate cases, establishing self-employment. The significance of this criticism is that it would be unrealistic to expect severance pay to accomplish any more than unemployment insurance. Most industrial workers, because of limitations in income and savings, cannot be expected to manage and finance their own retraining programs.

Summary

The job search of the Armour and ABC workers was for the most part purposeful rather than random, but was seriously hampered both by a general lack of detailed job information and by the relative scarcity of jobs for workers with their qualifications. Because of the short notice of the plant shutdowns, little job search occurred prior to layoff, and very few had jobs lined up when they left Armour or ABC.

Those who were unsuccessful in their job search and who be-

---

10. This conclusion was also reached in a study by Harold W. Hansen on "The Role of Unemployment Compensation in a Depressed Area After a Major Plant Shutdown," unpublished Master of Arts thesis (Urbana, Ill.: Institute of Labor and Industrial Relations, University of Illinois, 1961).

came long-term unemployed attributed their joblessness primarily to the scarcity of jobs, but significant proportions of the middle-aged and older workers spoke of their age as a distinct handicap. These reasons predominated in the workers' own explanations for their long-term unemployment. Race, sex, level of education, and the nature of work experience were factors that influenced the success of job search but were mentioned by only a few of the workers in relation to long-term joblessness.

The state of the local labor market and the industrial and occupational composition of the community influenced the scope and nature as well as the relative success of job search. In all of the cities, job search was largely informal—"plant-gate" application and informal recommendations from relatives, friends, and neighbors—but the extent of active job search, including the number of applications to employers, varied with the degree of industrial diversification and the number of large employers in the several communities. In the cities where unemployment was high, job search slacked off more quickly than it did where job opportunities were more numerous.

In general, the workers received little help from public employment service, company, or union, although there may have been a tendency not to report assistance that did not directly result in jobs. The workers in Oklahoma City and Peoria, who were interviewed prior to the shutdown, anticipated before the layoffs much more help from employment service, company, and union than they subsequently received. Even in Oklahoma City, where the Armour Automation Committee made special efforts to assist the workers, only about one in five of those interviewed reported any kind of help from this source.

Unemployment insurance and severance pay are often thought of as providing financial assistance to workers in seeking new jobs and allowing them time to find suitable work. Because of the levels of income from these sources and the general scarcity of jobs, most of the respondents felt that they had to find jobs as quickly as possible and that neither unemployment insurance nor severance pay had any particular influence on the extent or timing of their job search.

The major influence on job search seemed, instead, to be the number of suitable job opportunities. Where jobs were scarce, as they were in most of the cities where the Armour plants had been, the workers felt they could not afford to pick and choose among jobs. Only 12 to 14 per cent of the ex-Armour workers turned down any jobs during the year, and four out of five, when asked why they took their first job, answered in terms of economic necessity (needed a job, needed the money, had bills to pay, best could get because of age). In Peoria, on the other hand, where job opportunities were more plentiful and the work force younger, 65 per cent gave reasons for taking the first job that reflected greater choice—job was attractive, convenient, or steady, or the worker had had previous experience. Half of the Peoria workers who found jobs, for example, said the new jobs were in types of work they liked.

Few workers in any of the cities thought that job opportunities were better elsewhere and as a result only 10 to 20 per cent looked for out-of-area jobs. However, in spite of a preference for local-area jobs (more than nine out of ten), sizable proportions of the workers expressed willingness to transfer to other plants of Armour or the parent company of ABC. In the three cities, approximately two out of three expressed interest in a job at some other Armour plant and, in Oklahoma City, about half said they would take a job in Kansas City, even they would start as new employees with respect to layoffs. Of particular interest is that two out of three in Oklahoma City who had indicated lack of interest in an out-of-area meatpacking job *prior to the layoff* subsequently said they would accept a job offer in Kansas City. The change in view can be attributed to unemployment and to dissatisfaction with the pay or other conditions of post-Armour employment.

Worker willingness to transfer—and presumably, more generally, to relocate in other areas—may be greater than often supposed. If specific jobs are available and known to the worker, he will prefer to relocate rather than remain unemployed or in a low-paying job. If the pay differential is small, however, most will prefer the lower pay in the home community. Certainty about a job would appear to be more important than assistance in relocation costs. In cases of transfer, retention of seniority significantly increases willingness to move.

6

The Jobs Found

To COMPLETE OUR PICTURE of the labor market experience of the displaced workers, we need to examine the kinds of jobs found by those whose job search was successful. What occupational and industrial job shifts occurred, and how did the new jobs compare in pay and skill level with the jobs the workers held before the layoffs? Consideration of these questions is necessarily a part of the evaluation of the effectiveness of market adjustments to large-scale permanent layoffs.

Who Found Jobs and How

JOB MOBILITY AFTER THE SHUTDOWNS

Displaced workers had varying degrees of success in finding new jobs in the five cities. At one extreme, only about half of the former Armour employees in East St. Louis worked on any regular job during the year after the shutdown. In Peoria, on the other hand, about 90 per cent of those who were laid off by ABC worked on at least one job for a month or more during the year. Of those who had worked at all, a large majority, ranging from 59 per cent in Peoria to 76 per cent in East St. Louis, had only one job. About two-thirds of those employed a year after the shutdowns had had no work other than the jobs they held at that time.

Most of the workers who had found jobs and subsequently left them had done so involuntarily. Of those who were no longer on their first jobs, about three-fourths in the three cities, three-fifths in Oklahoma City, and half in Peoria were laid off or in a few cases discharged. In Peoria and Columbus, however, where job opportunities were more plentiful, the number who quit first post-layoff jobs voluntarily almost matched the number laid off. Many of those who quit were young workers who left to accept better jobs. In the three cities, more than one-third of the younger workers who left their first jobs did so voluntarily, compared with only one-tenth of the older workers. Sex and race differences in this respect are small.

Thus, first jobs after the shutdowns were of considerable importance. Most of the workers remained in the first jobs they found, not because they were necessarily satisfied with them, but presumably because they felt they could do no better.

Our analysis of jobs found by the displaced workers, however, will be confined for the most part to jobs held at the time of the mail questionnaire surveys. We made this decision because the results are very similar to those obtained from an analysis of first jobs only and because most of the workers were still on their first job at the time of the survey. These jobs appear to represent the "best" the displaced workers could get, and they provide a good picture of employment adjustment as of a year after the shutdowns.[1]

HOW THE JOBS WERE FOUND

In each of the five cities, most of the displaced workers who found employment first heard about their new jobs either by making applications at company gates or through leads supplied by relatives, friends, or acquaintances (see Figure 14). These methods

---

1. In Oklahoma City, the mail questionnaires were returned about five months after the shutdown. The Peoria data are for the "longest job held after the shutdown," but for 93 per cent of job holders the "longest" job was also the job held at the time of the questionnaire survey.

Figure 14. PERCENTAGE DISTRIBUTION OF THOSE WITH JOBS BY HOW HEARD
ABOUT THE JOBS, FIVE CITIES

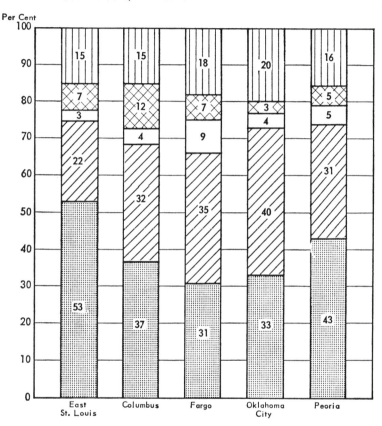

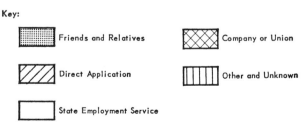

Key:

▓ Friends and Relatives   ⊠ Company or Union

▨ Direct Application   ⫿ Other and Unknown

☐ State Employment Service

Source: Mail questionnaire data.

were used by about two-thirds of the workers in Columbus and Fargo and about three-fourths of the workers in the other cities. Only small proportions of workers obtained jobs through more formal channels such as the state employment service (3 to 9 per cent) or help-wanted advertisements (3 to 7 per cent). Even fewer received any information from former employers or unions.

Men and women, white and Negro, young and old, all had to rely for job information primarily on their own efforts and the assistance of relatives and friends. In each of the cities, however, Negroes depended more heavily than whites on relatives and friends for job leads. In general, there was little difference between the long-term and short-term unemployed in the methods used to find jobs.

These findings are similar to those of other plant-shutdown and labor market studies—that the majority of manual job-seekers hear about jobs from acquaintance or through random application at plants and that only a few line up jobs through the state employment service or other formal channels. Also, neither the companies nor the unions turned up many jobs.

The methods used by the displaced workers in finding new jobs reflect to a considerable extent the hiring practices of employers. When labor is not in short supply, employers rely heavily for new hires on recommendations of their present employees and on persons making applications at the gate. Only when these methods prove unsatisfactory do they go to public or private employment agencies or use newspaper advertisements to recruit workers.

The fact that both employers and employees rely heavily on these informal methods, however, does not necessarily mean that nothing can be done to aid workers in their job search. Advising displaced workers of labor market conditions and the most probable employment opportunities—through public employment offices, through special programs like those recommended by Professor Young,[2] or through companies and unions—might often be more efficient than leaving each worker almost entirely on his own in the labor market.

---

2. See discussion in Chapter 5.

Industry and Occupational Shifts

Most of the displaced workers had spent all of their working lives in factories and considered themselves to be factory manual workers. And most of them hoped to find new jobs similar to the ones they had left. Their interests and preferences are indicated in a number of ways.

One of the questions in the in-plant surveys in Peoria and Oklahoma City was: "What type of work or occupation do you consider your regular or usual line of work?" Nearly 90 per cent of the ABC workers mentioned some kind of factory manual work. Similarly, about 85 per cent of the Oklahoma City workers mentioned skilled, semiskilled, or unskilled manual occupations. The Armour workers differed from the ABC workers, however, in the number whose regular occupation was peculiar to one industry. Almost 60 per cent of the Oklahoma City workers gave as their regular line of work an occupation that was strictly a meatpacking job.

Prior to the shutdown, the Peoria and Oklahoma City workers were also asked to give their judgment as to the best companies to work for in their areas. Of the ABC workers who expressed a judgment, over 80 per cent named a company in the durable goods manufacturing industry as their first choice. Of employers named by the Oklahoma City workers, on the other hand, 35 per cent were meatpacking plants and 51 per cent were government establishments.

Applications for jobs in each city were influenced by the industrial composition of the community, but they also reflect worker preferences for particular industries, types of work, and establishments. Among ABC workers who had any unemployment after the shutdown, 90 per cent of their first two applications for work were with firms in the durable goods industry. In Oklahoma City, about one-third of the workers' first two applications were in manufacturing, with most of these at meatpacking firms. Almost as many, 25 per cent, were made with government establishments. Thus, over half of the first two applications were with meatpacking firms or government establishments. In the three cities, 70 per cent of the employment applications were in manufacturing—39 per cent in nondurable goods and 31 per cent in durable goods manufacturing. All of these proportions are much larger than the proportions of community employment covered by these industry groups.

Each of these factors—what the workers considered their regular work to be, the firms in the area they considered to be the best to work for, and the places at which they applied for work—shows a preference on the part of a majority of the workers to find new jobs similar to the ones they had left.

While most of the displaced workers preferred and were looking for factory work similar to their old jobs, not many were able to find jobs either in the same industry or in the same occupation. In the four Armour cities, about 13 per cent obtained jobs in meatpacking; in Peoria, only 2 per cent secured jobs in the electrical machinery industry. Most of these were in the same occupations. In addition, 10 per cent in the three cities and 20 per cent in both Oklahoma City and Peoria stayed in the same occupation in their new jobs but changed industries.[3]

In all of the cities, a large majority of the workers who found jobs changed both industry and occupation. Three out of four in the three cities and two out of three in Oklahoma City made such complex shifts. In Peoria, 79 per cent changed both industry and occupation, with 28 per cent going to different occupations in other durable goods manufacturing and 51 per cent going to different occupations outside of durable goods.

The over-all complexity of the job shifts vividly demonstrates the extent to which the layoffs meant a sharp change in the employment experience of the displaced workers.

CHANGES IN INDUSTRY

Other than in Peoria, the majority of displaced workers who found employment were working in nonfactory jobs. In each city,

---

3. Change of industry means a move to any industry other than meatpacking (Armour workers) or electrical machinery (ABC). Change of occupation means a shift from one three-digit code to another in the U.S. Bureau of the Census occupational classification. These data on industry and occupational shifts are from the personal interviews.

however, manufacturing claimed a larger proportion than any other industry group. Other concentrations were found in trade and in service industries—about 15 per cent in each. The manufacturing, trade, and service industry groups together accounted for at least two-thirds of the employment except in Fargo, where it was half. In Peoria, over 80 per cent were working in these industries (see Table 13).

Table 13
Industry of Job, by City[a]
(in Per Cent)

	East St. Louis (N = 462)	Columbus (N = 199)	Fargo (N =203)	Okla. City (N = 100)	Peoria (N = 419)
Agriculture	1	1	10	—	4
Construction and mining	8	5	22	3	3
Manufacturing	35	45	23	30	59
Transportation, communication, and utilities	11	15	6	6	2
Trade—wholesale and retail	17	11	13	19	12
Finance, insurance, and real estate	4	—	4	4	2
Services	16	15	13	19	12
Government	8	8	10	19	6

Source: Mail questionnaire data.
a Unknown cases omitted from computation of percentages in this and the following tables and charts in this chapter.

The major deviations from the general industry distribution occurred in Fargo and Oklahoma City. In Fargo, which is located in a rural setting, almost one-third of those working were employed either in agriculture (10 per cent) or construction (22 per cent). The availability of agricultural employment in the area and a large road-building program during the period following the layoffs explain the prevalence of employment in these two industry groups. Many of these jobs were of a temporary nature.

In Oklahoma City, two to three times as many workers as in the other cities were employed by some unit of government, reflecting the unusually high proportion of governmental wage and salary jobs in that city. The government jobs obtained by the ex-Armour workers were primarily manual jobs, such as janitors and street repair and park maintenance laborers.

Although more workers in each city found jobs in manufacturing than in any other industry group, there was a great difference between the ABC and Armour workers in the types of firms they worked for within manufacturing. The proportions working in durable goods industries, for example, were roughly reversed between the two groups. While 77 per cent of the former ABC workers with jobs in manufacturing were working in durable goods industries, almost as many of the former Armour workers, 68 per cent, were working in nondurable goods industries.

Of the Armour workers in nondurable goods industries, about three-fourths were employed in the food products industry group. Further, about half of the Armour workers in manufacturing, or 13 per cent of all those working, had jobs in the meat products industry.

Outside of manufacturing, the Armour workers were in a wide variety of industries. In the three cities, for example, 69 persons were working for utilities, all but two in trucking or warehousing. Of those in service industries, 10 were working in hotels or motels, 10 in laundry and drycleaning establishments, 16 in miscellaneous business services, 10 in amusement and recreation services, 18 in hospitals, and 23 were employed by colleges and universities. In wholesale and retail trade, the largest numbers of workers found jobs in grocery stores (28), gasoline service stations (10), and eating and drinking places (29).

Whereas the Armour workers in manufacturing were concentrated in the food products industry, the ABC workers found jobs to a large extent in the nonelectrical machinery industry, particularly in firms producing construction equipment. One hundred sixteen workers had jobs in the machinery industry, a number equal to over one-fourth (28 per cent) of the post-shutdown jobs. Further, 68 persons, or 16 per cent of all workers with jobs, were employed by one firm in this industry.

In industries other than manufacturing, the ABC workers were widely dispersed. In trade, 11 persons were working in grocery stores and 7 in eating and drinking places. And in services, 9 worked in hospitals and 7 for schools or colleges. Otherwise, there were no concentrations of workers in specific industries.

The personal characteristics of the displaced workers are significantly related to the industries in which they found jobs. The women who found work, for example, were more likely than men to be in retail and wholesale trade, in the service industries, and in certain manufacturing industries. At least three-fourths of the women in each of the cities who found jobs were employed in manufacturing, trade, or service industries.

Age was a decided factor in the industrial distribution of jobs. In each city, higher proportions of workers under the age of 45 found employment in manufacturing, while higher proportions of older workers accepted employment in the lower paying service industries (see Figure 15). In East St. Louis, Columbus, and Oklahoma City, the proportions of younger workers employed in factories were almost twice those of older workers. Further, in all five cities, the proportion of workers 45 and over employed in the service industries was two to four times higher than that of younger workers. The age differences in other industries were not as great, although in each city a higher proportion of older workers were working for governmental establishments, generally in low-paying, manual jobs.

Thus, the older workers were often relegated to less desirable jobs in low-paying industries and occupations. Not only did they experience longer unemployment, but in order to find work at all they often had to make more drastic and unfavorable shifts in industry.[4]

A similar pattern emerges in the industry distribution of whites and Negroes, although the differences are not as pronounced (see Figure 16). In general, the Negroes were more frequently employed in service industries, demonstrating the more limited success of Negroes in finding factory employment comparable to their former jobs.

Skilled workers (that is, those who were in skilled jobs at Armour or ABC) found employment in manufacturing in somewhat greater proportions than other workers, particularly in Columbus

---

4. Other studies have also found that when older workers seek new jobs they, more often than younger workers, find it necessary to shift to service industries. See, for example, U.S. Department of Labor, Bureau of Employment Security, *Older Worker Adjustments to Labor Market Practices,* BES Bulletin No. R 151 (Washington, D.C.: U.S. Government Printing Office, September, 1956).

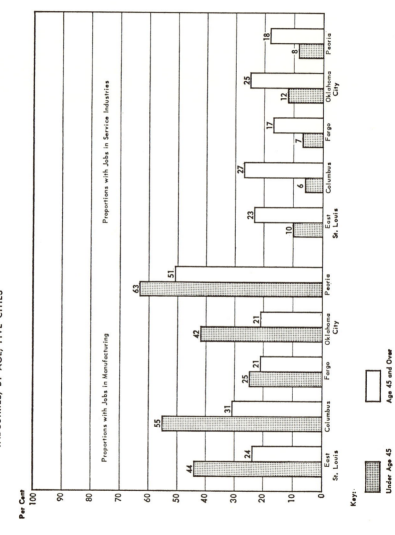

Figure 15. PROPORTIONS OF EMPLOYED DISPLACED WORKERS IN MANUFACTURING AND SERVICE INDUSTRIES, BY AGE, FIVE CITIES

Source: Mail questionnaire data.

Figure 16. PROPORTIONS OF EMPLOYED DISPLACED WORKERS IN MANUFACTUR-
ING AND SERVICE INDUSTRIES, BY RACE, FIVE CITIES

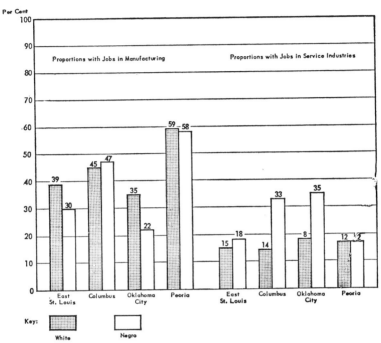

Source: Mail questionnaire data.

and Peoria. In Peoria, for example, 71 per cent of the employed
skilled workers as compared with a little over half of the laborers
and slightly over 60 per cent of the semiskilled operatives were
working in manufacturing industries.

The data on the industry distribution of the post-shutdown jobs
held by the displaced workers suggest the following conclusions.

First, the jobs obtained reflect to some extent the interests, preferences, and experience of the workers themselves. The tendency
for Armour workers to obtain jobs in nondurable goods industries
and the ABC workers in durable goods reflects both the experience
and the preferences of the two groups. Nevertheless, only a minority found work in industries of their first choice.

Second, the ABC workers were more successful in finding jobs in industries comparable to the electrical machinery industry than the Armour workers were in finding jobs in meatpacking or allied industries. This seems to reflect a greater transferability of skills from one durable goods industry to another than from meatpacking into other industries. A large number of ABC workers were able to transfer into other manufacturing firms, but the Armour workers were required to a much greater extent to seek and accept nonmanufacturing jobs. In Fargo and Oklahoma City, this can be partly explained by the relatively scarce opportunities in manufacturing generally. Both East St. Louis and Columbus, however, have extensive and diversified manufacturing industries, but of those with jobs, only one out of three workers in East St. Louis and less than half in Columbus were employed in manufacturing.[5]

Finally, the industrial distribution of various groupings of workers exhibits a pattern similar to that of unemployment. Just as women, older workers, Negroes, and the lower-skilled workers experienced the greatest unemployment, these same groups of workers had more difficulty than others obtaining factory jobs comparable with those they had held prior to the shutdowns.

CHANGES IN OCCUPATION

Most of the former Armour workers were working in other than meatpacking occupations at the time of the mail surveys. Only about 11 per cent of the three-city workers and 14 per cent of those in Oklahoma City had obtained jobs identified as meat-cutting or packing.

A very large majority of both Armour and ABC workers who had obtained new jobs, however, were still doing manual work. At least three-fourths of the workers in each of the five cities were employed as semiskilled operatives, unskilled laborers, or service workers (see Figure 17). The proportion is somewhat smaller in Fargo. If, however, the farmers and farm managers are included as

5. The results of the Packard study tend to confirm the conclusion that the ABC workers were more easily able to tranfer to other manufacturing jobs because of their experience in the durable goods industry. Of the Packard workers who obtained new jobs, about three-fourths were working in manufacturing. See H. L. Sheppard, L. A. Ferman, and S. Faber, *Too Old to Work—To Young to Retire* (Washington, D.C.: Special Committee on Unemployment Problems, Committee Print, December, 1959), p. 29.

Figure 17. PERCENTAGE DISTRIBUTION OF DISPLACED WORKERS BY OCCUPA-
TION[a] ON POST-LAYOFF JOB, FIVE CITIES

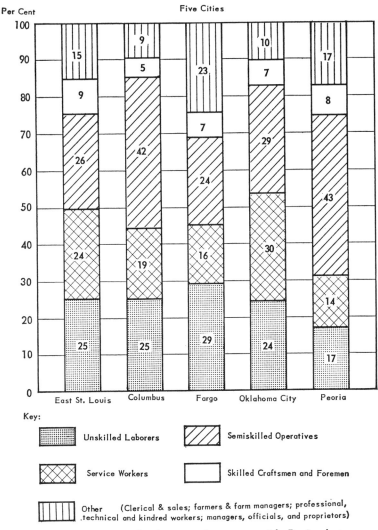

Key:

▦	Unskilled Laborers	▨	Semiskilled Operatives
▨	Service Workers	☐	Skilled Craftsmen and Foremen
▥	Other	(Clerical & sales; farmers & farm managers; professional, technical and kindred workers; managers, officials, and proprietors)

a. Occupation is at time of mail questionnaire survey except for Peoria, where ·
occupation is for longest post-ABC job.

Source: Mail questionnaire data.

manual workers, the figure is comparable to the other cities. The major differences among the cities were the larger proportions in Columbus and Peoria who had obtained work as semiskilled operatives (reflecting the greater proportion of displaced workers in those cities who found manufacturing jobs) and the relatively greater number of workers in Fargo who had jobs as farmers or farm hands.

Although the large majority were working on manual jobs, the specific jobs they held were for the most part far different from their old jobs, particularly for the Armour workers. In the three cities, for example, where more than two-thirds of the workers had been employed on exclusively meatpacking jobs such as slicers, packers, and boners, only about 11 per cent had similar post-layoff jobs.

Among the many manual occupations, just five accounted for 25 per cent of the post-Armour jobs in the three cities: truck and taxi drivers; machine operators (semiskilled); watchmen and guards; janitors, custodians, and porters; and waiters, waitresses, and cooks. Janitors and custodians alone comprised over 10 per cent of the post-Armour jobs in the three cities. In Oklahoma City, these same five occupations accounted for 35 per cent of the post-Armour jobs. In fact, over 20 per cent of those with jobs in that city were working as janitors, custodians, or porters.

The new jobs of the ABC workers were more varied. Nevertheless, 10 per cent of those with jobs were working as janitors or charwomen. On the other hand, jobs such as machinist, assembler, packer and shipper, grinder, welder—jobs comparable to ABC jobs —accounted for a substantial number of the post-ABC jobs.

The occupational patterns for various groups of workers were very similar in the five cities. Women, as would be expected, were more likely to have clerical, sales, and service jobs than men and less often were working as operatives and laborers. Exceptions occurred in Columbus and Peoria, where proportionately as many women as men were working as semiskilled operatives. In general, Negroes were more likely than whites to have jobs in unskilled and service occupations and less likely to be semiskilled operatives and skilled craftsmen. In each city, much smaller proportions of the older men obtained jobs as operatives in factories and much larger proportions were employed in service jobs such as janitors and guards. The relegation of the older workers to service jobs was particularly pronounced. In Peoria, for example, 35 per cent of those aged 55 and over, compared with only 8 per cent of those under age 35, were working in service occupations. The pattern was the same in the other four cities.

These occupational patterns support the conclusions reached in the analysis of industry changes: the same groups that experienced the longest unemployment also found it necessary to accept lower-level, less desirable jobs in order to find work at all.

Thus, a great amount of shifting of both industries and occupations was required as the aftermath of the shutdowns. Changes in skill *level,* however, are more difficult to measure, because within occupational groups there are wide differences in the skill content of jobs. For most of the Armour occupations there were no equivalents in other industries.

Comparison of pre- and post-shutdown jobs as measured by the Census occupational classifications indicates, however, that both upward and downward shifts in skill occurred. Over half of the skilled craftsmen were working in less-skilled clerical, semiskilled, service, and unskilled occupations. Most of the semiskilled operatives who were not employed at the same level had moved down to service and unskilled jobs. In general, more workers had been downgraded in skill level on their new jobs than had moved up.

This conclusion is supported by a comparison of pre- and post-shutdown occupations of each jobholder who responded to the mail questionnaire in Oklahoma City and Peoria. Table 14 shows the occupational shifts for these individuals.

The data indicate that of those individuals who were in different occupational groups on their post-shutdown jobs, many more had shifted to lower skill levels than had been upgraded. Also, relatively few were doing precisely the same kind of work as they had done at Armour and ABC, and few had obtained jobs of their first choice or jobs they "liked best."[6]

---

6. Data on first occupational choice and jobs "liked best" were obtained in the pre-shutdown surveys. Workers were also asked what job they felt "best qualified" for. For the most part, these were the same as the jobs they "liked best."

Table 14

Comparison of Present Occupation[a] with Pre-shutdown Occupation, Oklahoma City and Peoria
(in Per Cent)

| CITY | PRESENT OCCUPATION COMPARED WITH PRE-SHUTDOWN OCCUPATION | | | | | | PRESENT OCCUPATION | |
| | | Different But Same Group[b] | DIFFERENT GROUP[b] | | | | Occupation of First Choice | Occupation Likes Best |
	Same		Same Level[c]	Higher Level	Lower Level			
Oklahoma City (N = 98)	7	26	19	7	41		9	5
Peoria (N = 405)	5	42	7	13	32		6	3

Source: In-plant and mail questionnaire data.

[a] "Longest" job in Peoria.

[b] Same occupational group means first digit of Census occupational classification remained the same—semiskilled operatives on both jobs, for example. Different occupational group means the first digit changed—from unskilled laborer to semiskilled operative, for example.

[c] Same level means first digit of occupational classification changed but the skill level was approximately the same. An example would be a change from unskilled laborer to service worker.

Further, many of the employed Armour workers felt that they were not making much use of their previous skills and experience. A majority of the Armour interviewees, varying from 40 per cent in Columbus to 65 per cent in Fargo, described their jobs as being entirely different from their work at Armour, although about one in four said they were using the same skills. The ABC workers were not asked to comment on the degree to which they were utilizing previous skills or experience.

Negroes and older workers, in general, were less successful than others in finding jobs that utilized past skills. In East St. Louis, for example, only 5 per cent of the employed Negroes compared with 31 per cent of the employed whites found jobs they considered comparable in skill to their Armour work. Workers 55 and over in all of the Armour cities were generally unable to find jobs in occupations they had held at Armour. Only 7 per cent in that age group found a job in which they used the same skill as at Armour.

To sum up, the industry and occupational shifts were extensive, and the evidence is that most of the new jobs were at a lower skill level and very different from the old jobs. Many of these job shifts were not made by choice, since most of the workers preferred jobs similar to those they had been working on. That they accepted the jobs they did is indicative of the limited choices that most of them had. They accepted what was available and, at that, were much more fortunate than many of their fellow workers who found no work at all.

Pay and Hours of Work

PAY COMPARISONS

Along with their extensive industry and occupational shifts, many of the workers experienced drastic pay cuts. Average hourly straight-time earnings of the Armour workers in the three cities had been about $2.20 per hour and in Oklahoma City about $2.33 per hour. The Peoria workers had averaged about $2.22 per hour on their ABC jobs. Average pay on the new jobs was lower for the displaced workers in each city, and in East St. Louis, Fargo, and Oklahoma City the reduction was very substantial. Median hourly rates of pay on the post-layoff jobs are as follows: Columbus, $2.00; Peoria, $1.97; East St. Louis, $1.86; Fargo, $1.70; and Oklahoma City, $1.37. The smallest average cut in pay was in Columbus (9 per cent); the largest was in Oklahoma City (41 per cent).

Pay for many of the workers was very low on their new jobs. A small percentage of workers in all of the cities were earning less than $1.00 per hour. In Oklahoma City, this was the case for 14 per cent. About one in three workers in East St. Louis, Fargo, and Peoria had earnings of less than $1.50 per hour, and in Oklahoma City 60 per cent were in this group. Only 17 per cent of the Columbus workers, however, had earnings this low.

The very drastic wage reductions experienced by the Oklahoma City and Fargo workers are due in part to the fact that wage levels in those areas were generally lower than those that had prevailed in the Armour plants. Generally lower wages received by Negroes also reduced the average in East St. Louis, as did the lower pay of women and Negroes in Oklahoma City.

In all five cities there were substantial differences in wages received by different groups, but the patterns are very similar (see Figure 18). The median wage in each city was far lower for women than for men and was also lower for older workers than for younger, for Negroes than for whites,[7] and for the less-skilled than for the more highly skilled workers. In terms of former pay, women suffered the greatest reduction in wages, although pay cuts also were large for older workers and for most Negroes.

Although the average wage on the new jobs was less for workers in each Armour and ABC wage category, higher-paid skilled workers from both companies not only tended to be paid more on their new jobs but also suffered smaller average reductions in pay than did other groups. In the three cities, for example, the median wage rate on the new jobs was $2.55 for those who had been earning over $2.64 per hour at Armour; for those whose pay at Armour was between $2.08 and $2.19, average pay on the post-layoff job was only $1.64 per hour. This relationship held in all of the cities.

7. An exception is Peoria. There appear to be two reasons: The median for Negroes is based on a relatively small number of cases (33) so that the difference that appears may not be significant. Also, a substantial number of Negro males were hired by one manufacturing firm which happened to be increasing its work force at the time of the shutdown, and these workers benefited from the relatively good wages paid by this firm.

Figure 18. MEDIAN HOURLY RATES OF PAY ON POST-LAYOFF JOB, BY SEX, AGE,
RACE, AND SKILL LEVEL AT ARMOUR OR ABC, FIVE CITIES

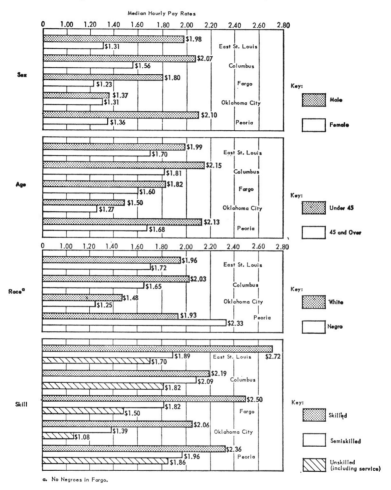

a. No Negroes in Fargo.

Source: Mail questionnaire data.

Workers who had had some kind of special occupational training also benefited through higher wages on their new jobs. Among
ABC workers, those who had completed an apprenticeship program
averaged $2.42 per hour on their new jobs, compared with $2.11
per hour for those who had training of less than an apprenticeship

level and $1.90 for those who had no special occupational train-
ing at all. The pattern was similar in Oklahoma City, although the
wages across the board were lower; the median wage there was
$1.56 for those who had some training and $1.32 for those who
did not.

HOURS OF WORK

Sizable minorities of the displaced workers who found jobs were
working more than 40 hours a week. The long hours were generally in industries and occupations where long hours and low
hourly pay are common. In both Oklahoma City and Fargo, where
wages on post-layoff jobs were the lowest, about 45 per cent of
those with jobs were working more than 40 hours per week. The
corresponding figures for the other cities are: East St. Louis, 21
per cent; Columbus, 32 per cent; and Peoria, 20 per cent. The
long hours made it more feasible for breadwinners to accept low-
paying jobs.

Most of those in each city not working over 40 hours were working 40-hour weeks. Only small minorities were working less than
full time (under 35 hours per week), varying from 2 per cent in
Columbus to 7 per cent in East St. Louis. Women were working
on part-time jobs more often than men. Moonlighting (that is, a
regular job plus a second job) was not common. In both Oklahoma
City and Peoria, for example, only 4 per cent of those who found
full-time jobs held second jobs.

Size of Firm

The ABC workers who found jobs in private establishments were
classified by the size of firm they worked for in their longest post-
layoff jobs. There were sizable variations according to the sex, race,
and age of the workers.

Most of the former ABC women were employed in small firms.
Eighty-six per cent of the women compared with 32 per cent of the
men worked for firms with less than 100 employees. Conversely,
while only 18 per cent of the women were employed by large firms
—those with over 1,000 employees—this was the case for 51 per
cent of the men. A partial explanation is that many of the large

firms in Peoria are in heavy industry, where employment of women is relatively rare.

Negroes were more likely than whites to be employed in large firms. Seventy per cent of the Negroes (all men) but only 51 per cent of the white men worked for large firms. This may have resulted from the hiring policies of one or a few firms at the time, particularly since the number of Negroes with jobs (34) was small. Larger firms, however, are also more likely to have nondiscriminatory hiring practices.

The age distribution of former ABC workers in firms of various sizes exhibits a clear pattern. Many more younger than older workers were employed in large firms (see Figure 19). Seventy-six per cent of those under the age of 25 were working in firms with over 1,000 employees compared with only 6 per cent of those who were age 55 and over. Conversely, only 12 per cent of the youngest age group worked for small firms compared with 70 per cent of those aged 55 and over.

This age pattern appears to result from at least three factors. First, small firms generally have less-structured personnel policies. For example, strict seniority provisions requiring promotion from within are less prevalent among small firms. The absence of such provisions tends to make it easier to hire older workers because they can be hired at other than the lowest skill levels.

Secondly, fewer small firms have pension plans that, rightly or wrongly, tend to stand in the way of hiring older workers.[8]

Finally, older workers tended more than younger to find jobs in service and trade establishments, which are typically small. The work in these establishments may be more suitable to the utilization of older workers, but more importantly the demand for younger workers by the larger (and better paying) firms tends to leave many small firms with no alternative but to hire some older workers.

A combination of factors appears to be responsible for the re-

8. See Margaret S. Gordon, "The Older Worker and Hiring Practices," *Monthly Labor Review,* November, 1959, pp. 1198–1205. The pension plan and promotion-from-within policies were among the more prevalent reasons given by employers studied in this survey for not hiring older workers. The study also found that only a negligible proportion of smaller firms had pension plans. Also, upper age limits in hiring were less likely to apply to all job openings.

Figure 19. PROPORTIONS OF EMPLOYED FORMER ABC WORKERS WORKING IN
FIRMS WITH OVER 1,000 AND UNDER 100 EMPLOYEES, BY AGE, PEORIA

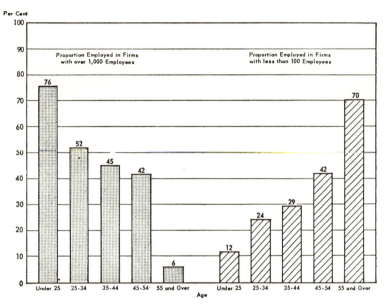

Source: Mail questionnaire data.

luctance of larger firms to hire older workers. The result, however, is that older workers are precluded access to a significant proportion of the job opportunities in the community.

Location of Jobs

Nearly all of the workers who had jobs at the time of the mail survey were working in or near the local areas of the five cities. Only 5 to 15 per cent of those with jobs were employed in locations outside the five local labor market areas. Migration was much less than these figures suggest, however, because many of those working outside the "official" local labor market areas still maintained their original residences and were working in nearby cities and towns. In the three cities, for example, only about 4 per cent of the displaced workers had moved to a location outside a 100-mile radius of the local areas. Out-migration from Oklahoma City and Peoria was also slight within the first year. The greatest amount of migration occurred among the Fargo workers, a number of whom moved out of state to accept other meatpacking jobs.

A number of explanations of the small amount of out-migration are possible, but the major one appears to be that in one year the situation did not become desperate enough to cause many workers to make a permanent move. For the Armour workers particularly, unemployment insurance and severance pay made it possible to get by for the first year. The evidence from our 1962 resurvey indicates that migration increased substantially after the first year, presumably because of the persistence of unemployment.

The results of the special questionnaire sent to the migrants in East St. Louis, Columbus, and Fargo indicate that in most respects the migrants did not differ greatly from their fellow workers at Armour. Compared with the mail respondents generally, the three-city migrants included somewhat larger proportions of men, younger workers, and workers with large families (three or more children)—groups with the greatest economic responsibilities.

Three-fourths of the three-city migrants who responded to the special questionnaire gave as their major reason for moving the fact that they had been unemployed and could not find work in the local area. Of the 30 people who couldn't find local work and migrated, only 4 were responding to specific offers in other communities. In contrast, of the 8 individuals who gave a reason for moving other than lack of local-area jobs, 5 moved to accept job offers.

The migrants obtained better jobs, for the most part, than the displaced workers who remained in the three cities. Almost twice as many migrants, proportionately, secured jobs in manufacturing (61 per cent compared with 35 per cent of the total mail respondents). All but a few of the remainder worked in construction or wholesale and retail trade. Almost 80 per cent were working in manual occupations as semiskilled operatives (55 per cent) and unskilled laborers (23 per cent). Almost all of the rest were in clerical or sales work. Thus, semiskilled-operative jobs were held by twice the proportion of migrants as of three-city workers generally. And whereas many of the three-city workers were required to accept low-level service jobs, few of the migrants did so.

The migrants who responded to the special questionnaire were also better paid than were the total group of mail respondents in the three cities. Their median hourly pay rate was $2.36, compared with the $1.86 per hour received by all those with jobs. Only one-third of the migrants were paid less than $2.25 per hour, while two-thirds of all those with jobs were paid less than this amount.

In spite of their more favorable experience, three-fourths of the migrants said they would prefer to work in the three-city area they came from rather than where they were living at the time of the survey. Further, all but two who said they preferred one of the three-city areas also said they would go back for the same wage they were receiving at Armour.

Most of the migrants moved, not because they wanted to, but because they thought their chances of finding satisfactory jobs would be better elsewhere. It appears that their more favorable experience can be attributed to the extra effort and sacrifice involved in relocation. The major advantage probably accrued from removing themselves from a market glutted with workers with the same skills and experience as theirs.

The Workers' Evaluation of Their Jobs

The extent of industrial and occupational shifting and the reductions in pay on post-shutdown jobs would lead one to expect that the workers, particularly the former Armour employees, would rate their new jobs below their pre-shutdown jobs. The following question was asked on the mail questionnaire: "In general, compared to your job at Armour (ABC), would you rate this job better, worse, or about the same?" The results are shown in Figure 20.

The evaluations correspond closely to the extent of job shifts and pay cuts in the various cities. The Oklahoma City workers rated their new jobs the lowest; Peoria workers the highest. In all of the cities women, older workers, and Negroes to a much greater extent than others rated their new jobs as worse.

The Oklahoma City and Peoria workers were asked in the pre-shutdown survey to estimate "what their new jobs would be like." The Peoria workers were more optimistic about their future jobs and their expectations were more fully realized. Table 15 compares

Figure 20. PERCENTAGE DISTRIBUTION OF EMPLOYED DISPLACED WORKERS BY THEIR COMPARISONS OF "PRESENT" JOB WITH ARMOUR OR ABC JOB, FIVE CITIES

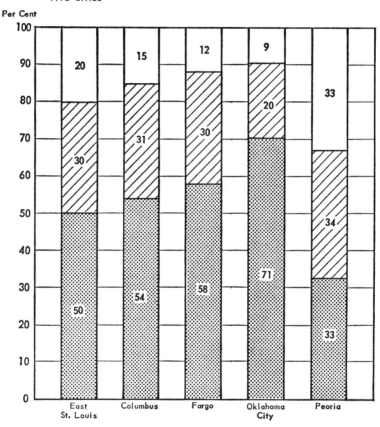

Key: "Present Job Is -- "

 Worse

About the Same

Better

Source: Mail questionnaire data.

Table 15
Predicted Versus Actual Pay on New Job
(in Per Cent)

	Predicted Better or Same; Was Better or Same	Predicted Worse; Was Worse	Predicted Better or Same; Was Worse	Predicted Worse; Was Better or Same
Oklahoma City	3	58	39	—
Peoria	60	9	23	7

predicted pay with actual pay on the new job for those who obtained work.

About two-thirds of the Peoria workers realized or exceeded their pay expectations on their new jobs. In contrast, almost 40 per cent of the Oklahoma City workers found things worse than they expected, while most of the remainder predicted correctly that they would have to work for less pay. For both cities, the data suggest a considerable awareness by the workers of labor market conditions and their opportunities for employment, although the Oklahoma City workers found things even worse than they had anticipated.

Table 16 shows for Oklahoma City and Peoria the workers' ratings of a number of factors in their new jobs compared with the old. The data were obtained by personal interview and are based on worker ratings of their Armour and ABC jobs in the pre-shutdown survey compared with their ratings of the same factors on their new jobs a year after the shutdowns.

The major cause for dissatisfaction with the new jobs among the Oklahoma City workers was pay, on which a large majority rated their present jobs as worse than their Armour jobs. Substantial minorities also rated as less satisfactory the retirement plan, supervision, and whether the work was interesting. Causes for dissatisfaction among the ABC workers are more evenly distributed among the various job factors, although again pay was mentioned most often. Other than pay, the interesting work factor was the greatest cause for dissatisfaction. In both studies, more workers thought working conditions were better on their new jobs than the reverse.

Table 16

Comparison of Job Ratings: Armour or ABC Job and Post-shutdown Job,[a] Oklahoma City and Peoria
(in Per Cent)

JOB RATING FACTOR	NUMBER[b]		HIGH SATISFACTION[c]		LOW SATISFACTION[d]		LESS SATISFACTION ON NEW JOB[e]		MORE SATISFACTION ON NEW JOB[f]	
	Okla. City	Peoria	Okla. City	Peoria	Okla. City	Peoria	Okla. City	Peoria	Okla. City	Peoria
Pay (wage or salary)	42	385	24%	21%	—	34%	74%	28%	2%	17%
Interesting work	41	382	49	39	5%	20	32	26	14	15
Impression of people you work with	38	383	74	77	—	2	13	12	13	9
Immediate supervision	42	373	36	50	7	10	38	17	19	23
Working conditions	43	385	46	29	9	21	12	16	21	34
The company as a place to work	41	373	63	48	12	12	15	15	10	25
Retirement plan	27	297	15	13	37	39	48	18	—	29

Source: In-plant questionnaire and personal interview data.
a "Present" job.
b Responses of "don't know" and nonresponses on the factors not included in the computations.
c Very good or good on both.
d Fair or poor on both.
e Very good or good on Armour or ABC job; fair or poor on new job.
f Fair or poor on Armour or ABC job; very good or good on new job.

In the three-city study, where there was no opportunity to have the workers rate their Armour jobs before the shutdowns, no comparable comparison of job factors on pre- and post-shutdown jobs is available. Data from the personal interviews conducted in the three cities suggest, however, that again lower wages constituted the most important factor in the low ratings of the post-shutdown jobs. Of those with jobs, 71 per cent rated their pay worse than at Armour, while only 39 per cent rated the "job itself" as worse and 34 per cent rated the "company as a place to work" as worse.

The findings suggest that for a majority of the workers at the skill and occupational levels of most of the workers in these studies "a job is a job" if the pay is satisfactory. Apparently the workers found it much easier to adapt to different kinds of work and different employers than to cuts in pay.

Perception of Chances in the Labor Market

How did the workers feel about their chances of getting jobs more to their satisfaction? Those who were working were asked a series of questions in the personal interviews that were designed to reveal whether they thought their chances were good of improving their occupational status. Their responses are shown in Figure 21.

Most of the workers were not anticipating a change in jobs; they thought their chances were good of staying with their present employers permanently. The percentages who thought they would remain permanently probably would have been even higher had the questions been asked so as to eliminate the possibility of layoff from consideration. In Fargo, for example, a relatively large proportion thought their chances only fair or poor of remaining with their current employer permanently. This result is probably due primarily to the large number who were working on temporary or seasonal jobs and thus anticipating layoff.

In view of the large number of workers who were dissatisfied with their jobs, the high proportion who were inclined to consider their jobs permanent appears to result from the workers' judgment that they would not be able to find better jobs. This conclusion is supported by the workers' pessimism that they would obtain jobs more to their liking in the future. The majority thought their

Figure 21. MOBILITY PROPENSITIES OF EMPLOYED DISPLACED WORKERS, FIVE CITIES (IN PER CENTS)

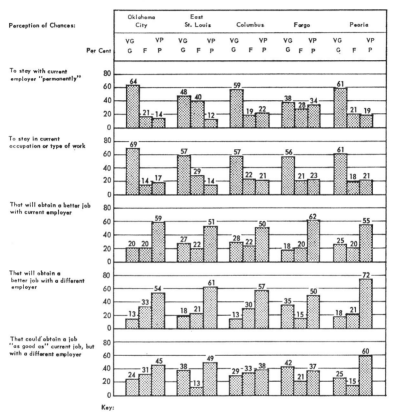

Key:
VG = very good; G = good; F = fair; P = poor; VP = very poor.
Numbers in bars equal percentages in each category.

Source: Personal interview data.

chances were poor of getting into another kind of work or getting a better job, either with their present employer or with another one. Further, only a minority thought the chances were good that they *could* get another job as good as the one they had. The majority thought their chances, if they were forced back on the labor market, would be only fair or worse of duplicating what they now had.

These perceptions of poor chances in the local labor market, together with the extensive unemployment and dissatisfaction with their jobs, help explain the degree of interest in transferring to other locations for jobs comparable to those at Armour and ABC. They also explain the eagerness of the workers to change jobs in their own communities. When asked whether they would take the same job they now had with another employer *if* the pay were 30 cents an hour more, about two-thirds of the workers in each of the five cities said they would, and a few others thought they might do so.

Among the minority who said they would not move, the ABC workers differed from the former Armour workers in the reasons they gave. A majority of the ABC workers (57 per cent) who said they would not move indicated they were satisfied with their present jobs or liked their present employers. Only one in four cited the importance of retaining the security they had obtained on their present jobs.[9] In contrast, the Armour workers who would not move for increased pay usually gave as their reason their desire to keep what security they had on their present jobs. Only about one in four said it was because they were satisfied with their present job.

In spite of their willingness to change jobs, many of the displaced workers were aware of the value of the job they had. The ABC workers employed at the time of the personal interviews were asked:

What would you do if you are laid off and find exactly the same type of work with the same pay at another company. Your present company calls you back after one month (year). Would you go back?

Fifty-nine per cent said they would return after one month and 9 per cent said they might. Of those who would return, 58 per cent cited either the importance of sticking with one job or the security and seniority that had accrued on their present jobs. Thirty-five per cent said they would return because they liked their jobs or their employers.

---

9. On the other hand, a substantially lower proportion of those who had been working the entire period since the shutdown (50 per cent) said they would move for the increased pay than was the case for those who had worked only part of the time (70 per cent). This suggests that seniority was an element in deciding how to answer the question.

Only 20 per cent said they would return to their jobs if called back after a year (10 per cent said "maybe"), indicating that most of the workers felt that after a year whatever advantages went with their present employment would be lost or outweighed by the benefits of a new job. Of the 20 per cent who would still go back, the majority again cited the security of the job, while a much smaller number would go back because they liked the employers or the jobs.

Thus, some former ABC workers liked their present employment well enough that they would return to it even after a year's layoff. And there were many others who felt, even after a relatively short time on their post-layoff jobs, that they had a sufficient investment in their jobs that it would be advantageous to hold on to them even when alternative employment was available.

Summary

The post-shutdown employment experiences of the displaced workers demonstrate how difficult it is for workers who have lost their jobs to find new ones that fit their skills, experience, and training. Relatively few of them were able, in the year following the shutdowns, to find jobs of their preference or jobs they felt best qualified for. The typical experience of those who found jobs was a change in both industry and occupation. Further, extensive downgrading, both of skill level and remuneration, occurred, particularly among older workers, Negroes, and women.

Most of the workers found new jobs through their own endeavors or with the help of relatives and friends. Only small minorities heard about their post-shutdown job from their former company or union or the public employment service.

In view of the extent of industry and occupational shifting, the downgrading of skill levels, and the reductions in pay that the new jobs entailed, it is not surprising that many of the workers held a low opinion of their new jobs. In general, the workers regarded their new jobs as worse than those they had left. The major reason for these low evaluations was the substantially lower pay.

In spite of the general dissatisfaction with the new jobs, relatively few workers thought they either would or could obtain better ones. Most viewed the new jobs they had as permanent. This pessimistic view of their prospects for better jobs suggests that the workers felt they had done about as well as they could. If better jobs did become available, either in their own community or elsewhere, a majority indicated that they would be willing to accept them.

These findings indicate that when a plant shutdown occurs, throwing substantial numbers of workers into the labor market at one time, it is not likely that the normal operation of the labor market will provide either jobs for all who want them or jobs which are reasonably commensurate with former employment. The experiences of the three-city migrants show that relocation can result in a substantially more favorable post-shutdown adjustment. The migrants found better jobs and jobs more comparable with those they had left than did those who remained in their home communities.

Even under relatively favorable circumstances, such as existed in Peoria, it can be anticipated that many displaced workers will be either unemployed or seriously underemployed following a shutdown. This results both from the workers' being stranded where there is not sufficient demand for their particular qualifications and from the economic and technological changes which make the skills and experiences they do have unwanted. In addition, many must face the barriers of prejudice based on sex, race, or age.

The result is unsatisfactory not only to the displaced workers but also in terms of the effective utilization of manpower. It is apparent that the problems resulting from permanent displacement of large numbers of workers cannot be more than partially solved through the normal functioning of the labor market.

7

Summary
and Conclusions

In EACH of our five case studies of the impact of plant shutdowns on the workers permanently laid off, we found that the displaced workers experienced a great deal of unemployment and that the jobs they found were almost invariably at substantially lower wage rates. In our analysis of the data, we have tried to explain the reasons for the high levels and long duration of the joblessness and why some groups had more unemployment than others. We have also examined the problems the workers faced when they were without work for long periods of time, the process of their job search, and their degree of success in regaining a productive role in society. Finally, we have critically evaluated the efforts of company, union, and governmental agencies in assisting the displaced workers in finding jobs.

The Extent and Causes of Unemployment

In four of the five cities, about half of the displaced workers were unable to find jobs during the first three months after layoff. The job-seeking workers in East St. Louis were even less successful; in that city, 83 per cent could not locate regular jobs within three months. In Fargo and Peoria, 45 per cent were in this category of long-term unemployment; in Columbus, it was 50 per cent; and, in Oklahoma City, 57 per cent. The others, who had either no unemployment or short-term unemployment, are not our major concern inasmuch as some unemployment can be expected when there are permanent layoffs, and unemployment insurance and severance pay provide a reasonable level of income for a short period of time. Instead, we have concentrated our attention on the long-term unemployed who either took three months or more to find a job or found no job at all.

Once in the ranks of the long-term unemployed, the workers found it increasingly difficult to locate jobs. A large majority of those out of work more than two months were still unemployed at the end of six months and many remained jobless a year after layoff and even two and one-half years after layoff. In the three cities of East St. Louis, Columbus, and Fargo, for example, 28 per cent secured jobs in less than three months, only 10 per cent found them between three and six months after layoff, 23 per cent took six months or more to find work and 40 per cent had not found any after a year. In East St. Louis, 30 per cent had still not found any work two and one-half years after the plant closed. Even in Peoria, where job opportunities were relatively the most numerous, almost twice as many took six months or more to find work as took three to six months. These very long-term unemployed (six months or more to the first job) ranged from 30 per cent among the former ABC workers to 74 per cent among the ex-Armour workers in East St. Louis.

Even when jobs were found, they were often temporary. In the three cities, a third of those who found jobs were no longer in them at the end of the year; and the proportion in Peoria was one in four. As new employees, they had little seniority protection.

Perhaps the most dramatic index of the extent of unemployment among the displaced workers is a comparison between their rates of unemployment a year after layoff and the prevailing unemployment rates in the local labor market areas. In East St. Louis, the displaced meatpacking workers had an unemployment rate 12 times as high as the community rate. In Columbus, it was eight times the community rate; in Fargo, nine times; and, in Peoria, six times. In Oklahoma City, the displaced workers' rate seven to eight months after the shutdown was 13 times higher than the community average. Although general unemployment was serious only in East St. Louis and none of these areas was technically one of chronic labor surplus, the unemployment of the displaced workers was well above even depressed-area levels in all of the cities and far above any tolerable level. Since unemployment rates for these workers were still abnormally high two and one-half years after the shutdowns and had fallen appreciably only in Columbus and Oklahoma City, it seems clear that displaced workers with their characteristics require special help as well as a general increase in job opportunities.

THE CAUSES OF LONG-TERM UNEMPLOYMENT—DEMAND

The general level of labor demand in the five cities was one of the important determinants of the displaced-worker unemployment. Thus, one reason the ABC workers had a more favorable experience than the Armour workers in the year following layoff is that labor demand in Peoria was higher than in the other cities and was rising during much of the post-shutdown year. Not explained by this factor, however, is the fact that after a year the unemployment rate for the ex-ABC workers was six times above the local-area average and after three years the rate was still almost as high.

The unemployment rates of the displaced workers, nevertheless, are clearly related to the level of economic activity. The lowest unemployment rate (after a year) and the closest relationship to the community rate were found in Peoria, where economic activity was strongest; the highest rate and the widest margin over the community rate were found in East St. Louis, which had experienced considerable economic contraction.

Another determinant of unemployment is the type of demand for labor, that is, the specific occupational and industrial distribution of available job opportunities. This factor seems to have had less effect than the demand level on the amount of post-shutdown unemployment. The workers in Fargo did benefit from the availability of laborers' jobs in agriculture and construction, although many of these jobs were temporary and seasonal. The ex-Armour workers

in Columbus and Oklahoma City did somewhat better than those
in East St. Louis and Fargo in obtaining meatpacking and meat-
cutting employment. A number of the ABC workers found that
their work experience helped them get jobs in durable goods industries in Peoria at a time when there was some expansion in
employment. Thus, in each of the cities, the particular composition
of employment in the local market clearly had some influence on
the types of jobs that were found. Nevertheless, differences or
similarities in industrial composition appear to have little relationship to the *level* of unemployment. Columbus and East St. Louis
are similar in proportions of diversified durable goods industries,
but unemployment was much higher in East St. Louis.

The most important conclusion is a negative one. Even though
none of the five areas was depressed (although the City of East St.
Louis might merit that label) and all have been expanding in population and economic activity in recent years, none was able to
absorb effectively into its economy the workers displaced from a
single plant. Data from other studies, although not strictly comparable in time periods and methods of measurement, indicate that
our results are typical. In addition to the meatpacking and electrical
machinery workers we have covered in this book, workers displaced in other cities and from other manufacturing industries—
textiles, automobiles, farm equipment, and freight cars—have also
experienced extensive unemployment after plant shutdowns. Case
studies thus far suggest, therefore, that long-term unemployment
can normally be expected when plant shutdowns occur, in or out
of depressed areas.

THE CAUSES OF LONG-TERM UNEMPLOYMENT—SUPPLY

If a fully satisfactory explanation of extended unemployment
for displaced workers cannot be found in an analysis of the demand
for labor, we must look at the characteristics of the displaced
workers and their qualifications for available jobs. Here we find
significant differences between the long-term unemployed and those
who found jobs fairly quickly. Among the long-term unemployed
there were above-average proportions of women, Negroes, older
workers, the lowest educated, the least skilled, and those whose

skills were not transferable to other industries. Also important is the large proportion of the displaced workers having more than one of these characteristics that are often handicaps in the search for work.

About one-fifth of the displaced workers were women. Those who stayed in the labor force had more than their share of unemployment. The major reason is that in each of the cities factory jobs open to women were relatively scarce. In each city where the displaced workers included Negroes, the Negroes were unemployed for longer periods than the whites. In East St. Louis and Columbus, for example, twice as many Negroes as whites were unemployed the entire year after the plant closings. This was a major influence on the unemployment rate in East St. Louis, where three-fifths of the work force was Negro. Since in both age distribution and years of schooling the women were comparable to the men and the Negroes comparable to the whites, it seems clear that the substantially higher unemployment of both women and Negroes resulted from their limited job opportunities and discrimination.

More than half of the workers studied were 45 years old and over, and this group had both higher rates of unemployment and unemployment of longer duration than younger workers. In Columbus, Fargo, and Peoria, very long-term unemployment of more than six months was 50 per cent higher among older workers. Some of the excess of unemployment for older workers, as compared with younger, can be attributed to a somewhat higher degree of poor health, physical disability, inadequate education, and obsolete work experience, but there seems little doubt that discrimination was also a factor. One piece of evidence is that long-term unemployment was as high for older workers with better-than-grade-school education as it was for those who had less education, whereas among the younger workers those with some high school had substantially *less* long-term unemployment than those with eight or fewer years in school.

Worth special note is the fact that among the long-term unemployed the handicap of age was by far the greatest shock to these workers. Few women and few Negroes mentioned their sex or race as the major reason for long-term joblessness. Age, however, ranked with job scarcity as a major cause in the workers' own view. Where jobs were more scarce, as in East St. Louis and Fargo, scarcity of jobs was mentioned most frequently. But in the other three cities, half or more of the long-term unemployed attributed their unemployment to the age barrier.

As for skill levels achieved in the lost jobs, these had relatively little effect on success in finding new jobs. Those who had vocational training or craft skills that are used in a number of industries had less unemployment than others, but only small proportions of the workers could be classified as skilled.

The low level and lack of transferability of Armour skills seems to be one explanation for the relative failure of the retraining experiment of the Armour Automation Committee in Oklahoma City. The experiment was a failure in that those who took vocational courses had a higher rate of unemployment in the spring of 1962 than those who did not receive retraining. The limited scope of this retraining, the "crash" nature of the planning for it, the personal and work-experience characteristics of those in the program, and the general scarcity of jobs in the local area make it impossible to generalize about the potential effectiveness of retraining for displaced manual workers. The experiment was useful, however, in pointing up some of the hazards and difficulties of retraining programs.

The Personal Impact of Unemployment

Long-term unemployment was particularly serious for those men and women who were the breadwinners in their families. Virtually all of the men and a sizable proportion of the women who were jobless or had lengthy periods out of work were breadwinners. What were the economic, social, and psychological effects on these workers and their families?

EFFECTS OF REDUCED INCOME

Almost all of the displaced workers suffered reduced income, either because of unemployment or because of lower pay on new jobs. Unemployment insurance and severance pay enabled most of the families with unemployed breadwinners to get along at least for a year without drastic reductions in living standards or going on relief. To this degree, their self-respect was preserved. Most, however, had to curtail spending on both luxuries and necessities, use savings, cancel vacation trips, and, in general, operate at a lower standard of living. At the time of the spring, 1962, resurvey, however, a third or more of the unemployed in Columbus and East St. Louis were on relief, as were approximately 10 per cent in the other cities.

For the first year after the shutdowns, unemployment insurance and severance pay meant, on the average, an income up to one-half of what they had received at Armour or ABC. The income was not spread throughout the year, however, and severance pay particularly was in many cases quickly used up to pay accumulated debts and to meet everyday living expenses. Also, about half of all the displaced Armour workers in the three cities exhausted unemployment insurance benefits during the first post-shutdown year. Few of the displaced workers had any other nonwage sources of income, although almost half of the men had working wives who supplemented the family income.

As of the spring of 1962, five out of six who were unemployed at that time (with the exception of those in Oklahoma City) had no income from unemployment insurance. Two out of three of the unemployed, however, had some income from unemployment insurance, or wages of others in the family, or public relief, or some combination of these.

Although unemployment insurance and severance pay were of major financial assistance to the long-term unemployed, at least in the first year after the shutdowns, few of the workers felt that these sources of income had any significant bearing on their search for work. In the three cities, only 14 per cent, and in Oklahoma City, 25 per cent, thought that severance pay was of some help in job search, mostly in allowing more time to look and in covering transportation costs. Since, in addition, only about 12 per cent turned down any jobs, it seems evident that for most of these workers unemployment insurance and severance pay did not serve as important factors in maintaining standards of work and pay. Nor were they significant factors in facilitating the matching of workers and jobs. Only in Peoria were there substantial numbers who felt they had much choice as to the jobs they accepted.

The major impact of reduced income was in the enforced lower standards of living. The lower income would not have been too serious if of short duration. For the very long-term unemployed, however, exhaustion of unemployment insurance and severance pay meant that many had few or no sources of income. In the second year larger proportions were going on relief, and undoubtedly many others would have been on relief were it not for restrictions in eligibility for able-bodied unemployed. Available sources of financial support were clearly not sufficient to maintain many of the long-term jobless and their families at even a minimally acceptable standard of living.

SOCIAL AND PSYCHOLOGICAL EFFECTS

Perhaps the most serious impact of the shutdowns, particularly for many of the long-term unemployed, was a loss of confidence and a feeling of uselessness. The loss of a long-tenure job was in itself a traumatic shock. Many discovered that they had become "old" in the eyes of potential employers. As unemployment lengthened, a number of the unwanted workers quite understandably felt bitter about those they felt were responsible for their plight and about the system that seemed to deny them jobs. The interviewers reported a whole range of human emotion—bewilderment, resentment, anger, frustration, and, for a few lucky ones, pleasure that they ended up in better jobs. The general picture for the long-term unemployed is a tragic one, both for the individuals involved and for the economy that fails to utilize its human resources.

The Barriers to Re-employment

The abnormally high unemployment rates of the displaced workers had two basic and interrelated causes—(1) the relative scarcity in their communities of job openings for which they were qualified and (2) various personal handicaps and barriers to re-employment which faced the individual workers. The former we have already summarized. The latter may be broken down into a number of factors: (1) the imperfections in the labor market that make it difficult for a worker to find a suitable job opening even when one exists—his lack of job market information and the relative failure of public and private agencies in the task of matching unemployed workers and available jobs; (2) the barrier of geographic immobility caused by the desire to remain in the home town and by the costs and uncertainties of migration; (3) the personal characteristics and qualifications that limit the job opportunities of individuals—age, sex, race, level of education, and types of work skills and experience.

IMPERFECTIONS IN THE LABOR MARKET

Although the displaced workers were aware of their limited knowledge of the labor market when they started looking for work, they tended to be overly optimistic about both job prospects and the amount of help they might receive in locating jobs. The workers in Oklahoma City seemed to have the most specific knowledge about individual occupations and industries or firms in the local market. We attribute this in part to the existence of a number of large establishments, particularly in government. In the other large cities, all of which are more diversified in industry, more of the workers were vague about the nature of job opportunities.

Optimism about the amount and kind of help they would receive in job search also illustrates a lack of knowledge about the functioning of the labor market. The ABC workers, who, on the average, had had experience with more employers and had more recently been in the labor market, were less optimistic about job-hunting assistance than were the Armour workers. In the two pre-shutdown surveys, the ABC workers expected significantly less help from the public employment service, the company, and the union than did the Oklahoma City workers.

The expectations of help were, to a large degree, not realized. In Oklahoma City, three out of four expected help from the employment service and only one in ten said they received any; more than half expected help from either company or union and only 1 per cent received it. In all of the cities, job-seeking help actually received and the workers' estimates of help needed were far apart. For the most part, those who found jobs fell back upon the traditional methods of manual workers—"plant-gate" application and leads from friends, relatives or acquaintances.

The extent to which the workers were on their own is illustrated by the fact that among the former Armour workers in the four cities only 6 per cent reported specific help from the union, 9 per cent from the company, and 13 per cent from the state employment service. Particularly unfortunate in cases such as these is the limited ability of the public employment service to locate jobs for displaced workers. In Columbus and Oklahoma City, fewer than 10 per cent of the men reported referrals or other help from the employment service. In East St. Louis it was 15 per cent and in Fargo, 25 per cent, but many of the Fargo referrals were to temporary jobs. Indirect help may have been somewhat greater than these figures suggest. The problems faced by the employment service in filling employer demands and meeting employer preferences are shown by the fact that younger workers, whites, and skilled workers reported more help than other groups.

In interpreting the data on expectations of help, we have concluded that these expectations were not necessarily strong and might more accurately be described as *hopes*. Few seemed to think that any agency—company, union, or public employment service—had a strict obligation to find jobs for them. The displaced workers for the most part accepted as a matter of course that they were largely on their own. Nonetheless, they would have welcomed more job information, recommendations, and referrals, with large proportions saying they could have used additional help.

We cannot be sure that any amount of job-seeking assistance would have found jobs for some of the displaced workers. It is certain, however, that many would have benefited from some preparation in job-seeking techniques and more effective assistance in locating jobs that were available. Some of the problems in improving and developing programs to assist workers involved in mass layoffs are discussed in Chapter 9.

GEOGRAPHIC IMMOBILITY

Virtually all of the displaced workers preferred employment within commuting distance of their established homes, and in each city from 80 to 90 per cent of the job seekers confined their search to the local labor market area. Few thought the grass was greener elsewhere and most of those who sought work in other areas also looked locally. Nevertheless, in spite of the strong preference for area jobs, substantial numbers in each of the cities indicated an interest in transferring to other plants of their former companies, if the opportunity were given them. The degree of this interest is a good measure of their unfavorable employment experience in their home communities.

In East St. Louis, Columbus, and Fargo, where there was little realistic hope of transfer, 72 per cent of the men and 49 per cent of the women said they thought they would accept transfer to another Armour plant at their previous pay level. Only a small minority of these specified retention of seniority as a necessary condition. In Oklahoma City, where the workers received a letter from the Armour Automation Fund Committee about the possibility of both preferential hiring at the Kansas City plant and coverage of moving costs, 57 per cent of the men and 36 per cent of the women who were interviewed believed they would accept a job offer.

Of particular interest in Oklahoma City is the fact that there was a substantial shift of interest in transfer before and after the shutdown. The proportion in the pre-shutdown survey showing an interest in out-of-area jobs at the Armour pay scale and with moving costs was about the same as the proportion who later thought they would accept transfer to Kansas City. Two out of three in the latter group, however, had earlier expressed little interest in transfer but had apparently changed their minds because of unemployment or dissatisfaction with their post-Armour employment.

Even in Peoria where local job opportunities were better, interest in transfer increased after exposure to the rigors of the labor market. Among the men, interest in transfer increased from 16 per cent before the shutdown to 34 per cent who, over a year later, said they would transfer to obtain similar work and wages and another 23 per cent who would transfer if they could regain their seniority rights or have their moving costs paid.

Home ownership as a barrier to migration was important in each of the cities. Home owners were less interested in transfer than those who rented their homes. In Peoria, home ownership seemed to be at least as important as age in reducing the interest of older workers in transfer.

Since there had been only a handful of transfers at the time of the post-shutdown surveys, out-migration was very slight. Data from the resurvey, however, indicate that out-migration did increase in the second year after the shutdowns.

In the three-city study, a special questionnaire was sent to those who had migrated. These migrants included an above-average proportion of younger breadwinners with large families who had difficulty finding local jobs. The results suggest that those with heavy family responsibilities were more willing to go elsewhere for jobs or would migrate more quickly than others. The migrants, as a group, had less unemployment and more frequently found better-paying manufacturing jobs than did the nonmigrants. As has been found in other studies, however, a majority of the migrants who had been long-time residents expressed the desire to return to their home communities.

Interest in transfer to another plant of the same company is limited by home ownership and other ties to the local community and also by the costs of moving. Migration to new jobs with other companies is limited not only by the same factors but also by the lack of job information and by the cost of job hunting in out-of-town and out-of-state areas. These barriers to migration seriously limit geographic mobility as a partial solution to the problem of long-term unemployment.

PERSONAL CHARACTERISTICS

Market imperfections in matching jobs and workers and the obstacles that limit geographic relocation were major barriers to re-employment. Of far greater importance, however, were the personal characteristics and qualifications of the displaced workers. These factors greatly influenced both the numbers who found jobs and the types of jobs found.

The job opportunities for the displaced women were more restricted than those for men; as a result, not only did fewer women find jobs, but these jobs were in a more narrow range of industries and occupations. In each of the cities, at least three-fourths of the women who located jobs found them in trade, services, or manufacturing. The manufacturing jobs located were in only a few industries.

Similarly, older workers found jobs less frequently than did younger workers and in a more restricted list of industries and occupations. Older workers more often had to accept jobs in the lower-paying service industries and occupations or in lower-level occupations in government. Most of the older workers sought manufacturing jobs but experienced a considerable amount of rejection on the basis of age.

Negroes, also, had a more-than-average shift out of factory employment into service jobs. Unlike women and older workers, however, who more often found jobs in small firms than large, Negroes more frequently located jobs in large firms. To some degree at least, this results from a differential pattern in job discrimination. Larger firms are more likely to have nondiscriminatory hiring practices with respect to race and religion, but at the same time are more likely to reject older applicants. In large firms, seniority practices, promotion-from-within, and the greater prevalence of pension plans and compulsory retirement militate against the employment of older workers.

Differences in previous skill level and work experience, and differences in level of education, had less influence on the number and types of jobs found than did sex, race, and age. The reason, in part, is that a large proportion of the workers we studied did not differ greatly from one another in prior skill level and educational attainment. Nevertheless, it is apparent that among workers with relatively equal work experience and years in school those who were white, male, and under 45 had a better chance in the labor market. An above-average proportion of those who were skilled workers at Armour and ABC were white men, and their more favorable, post-shutdown employment experience can be explained both by their work skills and by their personal characteristics.

The labor market difficulties of women, older workers, and Negroes stem to a large degree from two factors. (1) For a variety of reasons they have, on the average, lower job qualifications than other groups. (2) They are the victims of prejudices and habits that often exclude them from jobs on grounds other than their qualifications. Improvement in their job opportunities requires retraining and re-education as well as fairer employment practices.

Evaluation of Employment Experience

For those who found jobs, the typical experience was a change in both industry and occupation, with the new job being somewhat lower-skilled and at a substantially lower pay level.

TYPES OF JOB SHIFTS

Among the former Armour workers who found work, 87 per cent changed industries and 77 per cent changed both industry and occupation. Among the ex-ABC workers, almost all changed industries and 79 per cent changed both industry and occupation. In both groups, one in five of the successful job hunters found a job in his old occupation. Since most of the workers would have preferred the same occupations they had at Armour and ABC, these data illustrate the extent of the employment adjustment required.

Although changes in skill level are difficult to measure, it is clear that downward shifts in skill far outnumbered upward shifts. Using job titles, we have judged that about as many stayed at approximately the same skill level as moved downward. A majority of the workers themselves felt that they were not making much use of their previous skills and experience.

REDUCTION IN PAY LEVEL

The most drastic difference between the new jobs and the Armour or ABC jobs was in level of pay. In Columbus and Peoria, the average difference in pay between the former jobs and subsequent employment was about 10 per cent, but in the other three cities it was much greater. Women, Negroes, and older workers suffered the largest pay cuts. Those who had held the higher-skilled and higher-paid jobs at Armour and ABC lost less in average earnings on their new jobs than did those who had held lower-skilled jobs. In each of the cities except Columbus, a third or more of those with jobs were earning less than $1.50 per hour.

The lower hourly pay was associated with longer hours of work, and presumably many of the breadwinners could accept lower-paying jobs because of the longer hours. In Oklahoma City and Fargo, where post-shutdown wages were lowest, almost half of those who had found jobs were working more than 40 hours per week. In all of the cities, most of the employed had full-time jobs.

INTERCITY DIFFERENCES

The number who found jobs varied with the general level of economic activity in each city, and the types of jobs found were influenced by differences in industrial and occupational composition. Thus, in Fargo, more of the new jobs were in agriculture and construction than in the other cities. In Oklahoma City, a much higher proportion took government jobs than in the other areas.

In all of the cities, more jobs were found in manufacturing than in any other industry group. Since all of the displaced workers had been factory workers, this result is not surprising. The former ABC workers tended to find jobs in durable goods manufacturing, while the former Armour workers more frequently found jobs in non-durable goods industries, particularly in food products. The ABC workers in Peoria came closer than the ex-Armour workers in the other cities to obtaining the types of jobs they preferred.

The ABC workers were also more successful than the Armour workers in finding jobs that were comparable to the ones from which they were displaced. Several factors account for this: more of them had skills that could be transferred to other manufacturing industries; the job market was generally more favorable, with a rising level of employment; and more had personal characteristics that employers prefer. Among the ex-Armour workers, those in Columbus did best in finding jobs somewhat comparable to the ones they lost, because of both the diversity of manufacturing industry in Columbus and a fairly high level of economic activity. Employment in East St. Louis, in comparison, was relatively depressed, while Fargo and Oklahoma City have relatively low concentrations of manufacturing industries.

THE WORKERS' OWN EVALUATION

The displaced workers who had jobs were asked to rate them in comparison with their former jobs. In general, they rated the new jobs as worse, with the Oklahoma City workers having the lowest opinion of the new jobs and the Peoria workers the highest. A majority of all of the employed ex-Armour workers rated their new jobs as worse. The major reason for these low ratings seems to be the substantially lower pay. Data on specific job factors in two of the studies suggest that adjustment to the change in pay was far more difficult than adjustment to any of the other differences.

Although there was considerable dissatisfaction with the new jobs, only a small minority of the workers thought they either would or could obtain better jobs. Most of those with jobs apparently thought they had done about as well as possible under the circumstances. In fact, a majority felt they had found their jobs primarily through luck, and only a few credited their diligent job search. The generally pessimistic view of job prospects is further evidenced by the fact that even in Peoria, where employment opportunities were best, only one in four thought he could get another job as good as the one he had found. Further, few expected much advancement with their present employers.

The responses on chances of better jobs do not seem to be the result of a mere reluctance to change jobs. The strong interest of many in transfer to other communities for jobs comparable to those at Armour or ABC and the two-thirds in each of the cities who would move to another employer for higher pay suggest that most of these workers would respond to a clear-cut economic incentive. They wanted job security but also decent wages.

Acceptance of jobs at low levels of pay and skill suggests considerable willingness on the part of these displaced manual workers to adjust to the realities of the labor market. In order to obtain work, many had to give up or subordinate job goals that they considered very important. Some were working at wage rates that provided little more income than was available to them through unemployment insurance. Also, many of those who failed to find jobs expressed a readiness, even if reluctant, to make rather drastic changes in their living patterns for the sake of finding work—willingness, for example, to give up homes and friends and relocate in distant places. The evidence of willingness to adjust suggests that the attitudes of the unemployed are not likely to be a major obstacle to efforts to reduce long-term joblessness.

The Case Studies as Illustrations of Larger Problems

Additional case studies would provide further variation in the possible patterns of unemployment and employment resulting from large-scale permanent layoffs. As the ABC experience suggests, for example, a work force with higher-skilled and better-educated workers would tend to have more success in the labor market than did the Armour work forces. Nevertheless, we believe that these five case studies present a sufficient array of types and sizes of communities, differing labor market conditions, and differing characteristics among the displaced workers to show that plant shutdowns or other permanent layoffs in sizable groups are very likely to create a substantial amount of long-term unemployment as well as a downgrading in skills and pay for those who find new jobs.

Our case studies show that even in communities with high and rising levels of employment, displaced workers suffer much more unemployment than the community labor force in general. A major reason is that ordinarily a labor market area is not equipped to absorb a sudden influx of job-seekers, particularly if many of them are below-average in education and above-average in age. Further, groups who traditionally face limited job opportunities—such as Negroes, women, and older workers—will fare worse than others because there are fewer jobs for which they can or are allowed to compete.

Higher rates of economic growth and job creation are a basic but not a complete solution to the problem. In our view, policies of economic growth must be supplemented by special efforts both to relieve more effectively the burdens of long-term unemployment and to reduce long-term unemployment among specific groups and in specific areas. In the final part of the book, we turn to an analysis of these special efforts—those that have been tried, those that have been proposed, and those that we recommend.

PART THREE

▶ PUBLIC AND

▶ PRIVATE MEASURES

▶ TO REDUCE

▶ LONG-TERM

▶ UNEMPLOYMENT

▶ AND RELIEVE

▶ ITS BURDENS

Relieving the Burden
of Long-Term
Unemployment

T WO APPROACHES CAN BE TAKEN to meet the problems of permanently displaced workers who have difficulty finding new jobs.
One is to reduce the financial hardships of lengthy unemployment
through income maintenance and service programs. In this chapter
we look at existing public and private programs and evaluate their
usefulness in reducing some of the hardships of long-term unemployment. Our point of view is that persons who are able and willing to work should not suffer drastic financial hardship when the
economy does not provide jobs.

Providing income over long periods of time for those who are
not producing goods and services, however, is clearly not the most
desirable solution to the problems of long-term unemployment. In
Chapter 9 we shall consider the second approach—the steps that
business, labor, and government can take to prevent or reduce the
displacement of experienced workers and to speed the placement
in new jobs of those who do become unemployed. Without minimizing the importance of fiscal and monetary policy in stimulating

economic growth, we emphasize those measures that will improve utilization of the work force and the functioning of the labor market.

In Chapter 10, we examine the relationship of long-term unemployment and economic growth. We ask the questions: will a more satisfactory rate of economic growth solve the problem of long-term unemployment? or is the cause of this unemployment primarily a malfunctioning of the labor market with growing numbers of workers lacking the qualifications for available jobs? Finally, we shall try to assess the responsibilities of business, labor, and government in a coordinated public and private attack on long-term unemployment that would be consistent with national goals of full employment and price stability.

Unemployment Insurance—The Basic Program

Unemployment insurance in the United States was originally designed as a first line of defense against dire want and dependency for those workers who lose their jobs through no fault of their own. It was never intended to provide benefits for all of the unemployed. Nor was it intended to afford complete protection, either in dollars or in length of time, to those who are eligible for benefits. Thus, in all of the states, benefits have always been limited in both amount and duration and have been restricted to persons who have had a previous substantial attachment to the labor market.

Because of these limitations, unemployment insurance is of greatest value to workers who normally have fairly steady employment and who, when unemployed, have a reasonably good chance for early re-employment. Such workers compose the great majority of the American labor force, and for them unemployment insurance has played a very vital, if not entirely satisfactory, role.

Unemployment is not always limited, however, to short periods of time. Ample evidence for this is found in the experiences of the displaced Armour and ABC workers and in the post-World War II national trend of increasing long-term unemployment. Both in good times and bad, substantial numbers of workers exhaust their rights to unemployment insurance and thus undergo periods of joblessness without protection.

What is the appropriate role for unemployment insurance in

meeting the risk of long-term joblessness? Edwin E. Witte quotes Sir William Beveridge as arguing,

Unemployment insurance is an appropriate remedy so long as the unemployed worker has a good prospect of re-employment. But it is no longer appropriate when the unemployed man has no real prospect of returning to the type of work he is fitted to do.[1]

Many of the workers in our case studies are of this type; that is, they have little prospect of re-employment in their usual occupation or type of work. In commenting on the Beveridge viewpoint, Witte notes, "For such workers, unemployment insurance must be supplemented by training programs, assisted migration, emergency work programs, and the development of industrial opportunities."[2]

In the context of the periodic postwar recessions and the higher unemployment in "prosperity" periods, unemployment insurance has come under severe attack because of its failure to meet adequately the needs of the unemployed. Certainly a good deal of the criticism is valid, but some of it appears to arise because too much is expected of unemployment insurance and because other methods for meeting some of the hazards of unemployment have failed to expand or develop.

On the other hand, our changing and dynamic economy requires changing and dynamic social institutions. Changes in the nature of the labor force and in types of unemployment perhaps require some shift in emphasis in unemployment compensation objectives. It is assumed in the discussion that follows, however, that the basic insurance nature of the program should be maintained.

In this section we attempt to evaluate the role of unemployment insurance in meeting the needs of the long-term unemployed. We consider only the issues directly related to meeting these needs; other more general issues, such as financing, adequacy of coverage, and experience rating, are deliberately omitted from the discussion.[3]

1. Edwin E. Witte, *Five Lectures on Social Security* (Rio Piedras, Puerto Rico: Labor Relations Institute, College of Social Sciences, University of Puerto Rico, 1951), p. 55.
2. *Ibid.,* p. 55.
3. See Wilbur J. Cohen, "Some Major Policy Issues in Unemployment Insurance and General Assistance," *Studies in Unemployment,* prepared for the Special Committee on Unemployment Problems, United States Senate (Washington, D.C.: U.S. Government Printing Office, 1960), pp. 311–341, for a summary of unemployment insurance issues.

THE ADEQUACY OF BENEFITS

The amount of weekly benefit is of paramount importance to the unemployed worker, whether his unemployment be short or long. In some respects, however, it is of greater concern to the long-term unemployed than to others. Although the unemployed worker may be able to postpone certain usual expenditures, such as purchase of shoes for children, for a month or two, eventually the time will come when he will have to make the purchase. And although his creditors might be willing to "carry" him for a short period of time, their interest in his "on-the-cuff" business is likely to wane after a few months. Thus, the financial burden of joblessness becomes progressively worse the longer the duration of unemployment.

Unemployment insurance laws have never recognized this differentiated need among the unemployed. In all of the states, the basic criterion for assessing need is past wages, and benefits are computed on the basis of an earnings record.

The rationale in basing benefit formulas on wages has been the assumption that workers whose wages were high in the base period need and deserve a higher benefit than those whose wages were low. The establishment of maximum benefits by all states and the weighting of benefit formulas in favor of low wage earners in many, however, mitigates the effect of the wage-related benefit. In recent years as many as one-half to three-fourths of the beneficiaries have been receiving maximum benefits, thus to a large extent negating the wage-related concept.

If the objective is to provide adequate benefits for the majority, what standard of adequacy is to be used? Witte has emphasized that

social security seeks merely to insure necessary *minimum* income on the occurrence of the personal hazards of life. It does not aim to provide comforts and luxuries, nor relieve people, able to do so, of the need for working and saving. . . . [But] even our great nation, the wealthiest on earth, cannot afford to guarantee more than a minimum income sufficient for a decent existence to all its people in all contingencies of life. Nor is the objective of social security more than that. For more than a necessary minimum, people will have to depend on their own industry and thrift.[4]

Not everyone agrees, however, as to what the primary objective of unemployment insurance should be with respect to the level of benefits. Further, judging the adequacy of benefit levels is complicated by large variations in the circumstances of the unemployed. Such factors as marital status, number of dependents, breadwinning status, length of unemployment, and attachment to the labor force substantially influence the degree of need and deprivation resulting from unemployment.

Assessment of the adequacy of the benefit amount in unemployment insurance should be based on a comparison of average benefits and average base-period net pay of beneficiaries. The resulting ratio then must be judged against some acceptable standard. Unfortunately, statistics are generally not available on net wages of beneficiaries, and it therefore becomes necessary to compare benefits with average wages of all workers in covered employment. Wages of covered workers are likely to be higher than those of unemployed beneficiaries.

A common standard for assessing unemployment insurance benefits, and one incorporated in many state benefit formulas, is 50 per cent of the claimant's weekly earnings. The assumption made in this standard is that benefits at this level would be sufficient to meet nondeferrable expenditures, such as food and housing.[5]

The average benefit for total unemployment in the calendar year 1960 was about $33 per week for the nation as a whole. This amount represented only about 36 per cent of average weekly wages in covered employment in 1959. Benefits in only a few states average 50 per cent of claimants' earnings, and in 1960 no state had average benefits as much as 50 per cent of average wages in covered employment.[6]

4. Witte, *op. cit.,* p. 11.
5. Recent studies of adequacy by the Bureau of Employment Security included food, housing and utilities, clothing, and medical care in the definition. See Joseph M. Becker, *The Adequacy of the Benefit Amount in Unemployment Insurance* (Kalamazoo, Mich.: The W. E. Upjohn Institute for Employment Research, May, 1961), p. 43.
6. Bureau of Employment Security, U.S. Department of Labor, *Unemployment Insurance: State Laws and Experience* (Washington, D.C.: April, 1961), Table 9.

Although benefits have increased substantially since unemployment compensation laws were first enacted, they have not increased rapidly enough to result in any improvement in the proportion of wages recouped through unemployment insurance. In 1938, the average weekly benefit amount was about 43 per cent of average weekly wages;[7] in 1948, it was about 35 per cent;[8] in 1960, it was only slightly higher. On the other hand, decreases in waiting periods and increases in duration have resulted in substantial improvement in the real protection afforded the unemployed; these improvements are not fully reflected in benefit statistics. Similarly, since 1938 the federal income tax provisions have tended to increase the value of tax-free unemployment insurance benefits.

In a survey of benefits in six states conducted between 1954 and 1958, Becker found that benefits were adequate for the average beneficiary without dependents and were inadequate for the average beneficiary with dependents. Among the norms used in these studies were whether benefits replaced half of the net wage loss and whether they were adequate to meet nondeferrable expenditures.[9] Based on his finding that benefits for primary beneficiaries (heads of families) were inadequate, Becker concluded that

since the benefits received by the primary beneficiaries nearly equaled 50 per cent of net wages and yet were inadequate, . . . benefits for the average primary beneficiary should certainly equal at least 50 per cent of net wages and perhaps should equal a higher percentage.

Yet, the difficulty of assessing unemployment insurance benefits was recognized by noting that "benefits were adequate by some criteria but not by others, and were adequate for some classes of beneficiaries but not for others."

It is also difficult to assess how adequately unemployment insurance met the minimum needs of the displaced workers of our case studies, partly because most of them also received a sub-

---

7. Margaret S. Gordon and Ralph W. Amerson, *Unemployment Insurance* (Berkeley: Institute of Industrial Relations, University of California, 1957), p. 49.

8. U.S. Advisory Council on Social Security, *Recommendations for Social Security Legislation*, a report to the Senate Committee on Finance from the Advisory Council on Social Security (Washington, D.C.: U.S. Government Printing Office, 1949), pp. 138–139.

9. Becker, *op. cit.*, pp. 48–54.

stantial separation allowance. It was clear, however, that most of them were adversely affected by the relatively low ceilings on benefits. Nearly all of the displaced workers received the maximum amount allowed under the state law and, on the average, benefits replaced only about one-third of pre-shutdown gross wages.

Although evaluation of the adequacy of unemployment insurance benefits is difficult, benefit levels for breadwinners who are family heads are quite clearly inadequate. Further, the inadequacy has a cumulative effect, so that the long-term unemployed worker is likely to have no reserves to fall back on and/or substantial debts at the time he exhausts his benefits.

Many proposals have been made for improving unemployment insurance benefits. President Eisenhower recommended

that the States increase maximum benefits so that the great majority of the covered workers will be eligible for payments equal to at least half their regular earnings, and that States which have not already done so lengthen the maximum term of benefits to 26 weeks for every person who qualified for any benefit and who remains unemployed that long.[10]

Although there has been some response from the states to this plea, particularly with respect to duration provisions, the great majority of workers do not yet qualify for benefits equivalent to half their regular pay. The slow action of the states has led many to urge such measures as minimum federal benefit standards, federal sharing of the costs of benefits, and a federal reinsurance fund.

In June, 1961, President Kennedy submitted to Congress a legislative draft, the Employment Security Amendments of 1961, the provisions of which were incorporated in H.R. 7640 and S. 2084. The bills provided for additional federal benefits to certain workers who have exhausted their state benefits and for automatic increases in duration of benefits during recessions; equalization grants to states hard hit by unemployment; expansion of coverage; an increase in both the base and rate of the Federal Unemployment Tax; federal requirements for the weekly benefit amount; and a federal standard prohibiting a state from denying benefits to a

---

10. Economic Report of the President, Transmitted to the Congress, January 20, 1958, p. 65.

claimant undergoing training or retraining approved by the state employment security agency.[11]

The provision in the Kennedy proposals for a federal benefit standard would require that in order to receive the full tax offset each state must raise its maximum weekly benefit to 50 per cent of the statewide average weekly wage in 1964–65, to 60 per cent in 1966–67, and to 66⅔ per cent thereafter.

Unless and until the Kennedy proposal for higher benefit standards is adopted, the inadequacy of benefits, particularly for family heads, will continue to have important consequences for the long-term unemployed.[12] After long periods without work, they are likely to have exhausted their own resources and are in a poor position to continue postponement of "deferrable" items. Perhaps of even more concern to the long-term jobless, however, are the limits in the duration of unemployment insurance benefits.

DURATION OF BENEFITS

None of the original state laws had a maximum duration of more than 16 weeks. Further, except in Ohio, the duration for each individual worker was governed by a formula which limited the total amount any worker could draw during his benefit year to a fraction of his base-period earnings. Thus, duration of benefits varied with base-period earnings. As early as 1939, however, two states raised their maxima above 16 weeks, and in the same year Ohio was the first state to provide a uniform duration of 16 weeks. Under a uniform duration provision, all eligible claimants qualify for the same number of potential weeks of benefits.

The upward trend in benefit duration continued throughout the

---

11. Training allowances under the Manpower Development and Training Act of 1962 and their relation to unemployment compensation are discussed later in this chapter.

12. Our views on public policy with respect to benefit adequacy and uniform standards are given in Chapter 10. For elaborate expositions of the positions of both proponents and opponents of federal standards, see the testimony before the House Ways and Means Committee on H.R. 3547, introduced in the House in early 1959, in *Unemployment Compensation*. Hearings before the Committee on Ways and Means, House of Representatives, Eighty-sixth Congress, First Session (Washington, D.C.: U.S. Government Printing Office, 1959), 1167 pp. In the same Hearings (p. 850) there is a list of 21 noted economists and students of social security who issued a statement in support of Congressional action along the lines of H.R. 3547.

1940's and 1950's. In 1945, four states increased the maximum duration to 26 weeks and New York became the first state to provide for a 26-week uniform duration. Wisconsin was first to break the 26-week limit when in 1949 it established 26½ weeks as the maximum. In 1955, Pennsylvania was the first state to establish a uniform duration of 30 weeks for all eligible workers.

The 1958 recession provided a severe test of the adequacy of duration provisions in the unemployment insurance system and resulted in some significant developments. During the recession, exhaustions under the state programs reached an unprecedented level. Congress reacted with the establishment of the Temporary Unemployment Compensation program (TUC), under which interest-free loans were made to the states for the purpose of paying exhaustees additional benefits equal to one-half of their state benefit amount. In most cases this provided up to an additional 13 weeks of benefits.

For the first time, the federal government took emergency action to encourage the improvement of benefits in a recession period. Seventeen states participated in the program which was in effect for approximately one year, terminating at the end of June, 1959. In addition, five states operated similar programs of their own without the assistance of federal loans. About 70 per cent of the unemployed who exhausted benefits during the period lived in these 22 states.[13]

The 1958 recession also had an impact on state action. By the end of 1960, eight states had joined Pennsylvania in providing regular maximum durations of more than 26 weeks (28 to 39 weeks) on a permanent basis; six additional states had enacted permanent automatic provisions which extend benefit duration temporarily when unemployment rates (and exhaustions in one state) exceed specified levels. Under state laws in force at the end of 1961 as many as ten states could be paying benefits for over 30 weeks in a recession period. In six states the potential duration is 39 weeks.

The 1960 recession resulted in a further expansion of the role of the federal government in the unemployment insurance program. The Temporary Extended Unemployment Compensation Act of

13. "Changing Views on the Duration of Unemployment Benefits," *The Labor Market and Employment Security*, August, 1961, p. 7.

1961 (TEC) provided, as had TUC in 1958, for federal advances to the states to enable them to extend by 50 per cent the duration of benefits to any jobless worker who exhausted his state unemployment insurance benefits. The provisions of the law were in effect for workers who exhausted benefits between June 30, 1960, and March 31, 1962. The special benefits were limited to 13 weeks and the total of all benefits (including regular UC) to 39 weeks.

Rather than requiring each state to repay the exact amount of its advance, as was required under TUC, the 1961 Act provided for repayment by increasing from 0.4 per cent to 0.8 per cent the net federal unemployment tax levied on employers for calendar years 1962–63. Thus, the costs of the extended benefits were financed by imposing the same tax on employers in all states, regardless of differences in state unemployment rates. The result was that states with heavy unemployment were relieved of some of the burden they would otherwise have carried and which they did carry during the 1958 recession.

Another consequence of the financial provisions was that all states were, in effect, required to participate in the program. Not to do so would have meant that employers in a nonparticipating state would be taxed but no additional benefits would be paid to the state's unemployed workers.

At the close of the one-year TEC program on June 30, 1962, nearly 2.8 million long-term jobless workers had received $769 million in additional benefits after exhausting their regular state benefits.[14] At the peak load in mid-June, 1961, TEC beneficiaries represented 34 per cent of insured unemployment under regular state programs.

The experience of the last two recessions has demonstrated that the duration provisions of state laws are inadequate to deal satisfactorily with recession unemployment. This is the case in spite of continued improvement in state laws over the years. In two consecutive recessions the duration problem has been met primarily with temporary action on the part of the federal government.

Our case studies show that extensive long-term unemployment can also occur among some groups of workers in periods of relative

14. *The Labor Market and Employment Security,* August, 1962, p. 1.

prosperity. About half the displaced Armour workers exhausted their unemployment insurance benefits during the first year following the shutdowns.

The question of how to meet the problem of long-term unemployment, however, remains, not because of lack of ideas or proposals, but because of disagreement as to the proper assignment of responsibility and questions as to the proper role of unemployment insurance in meeting the problem.

One plan was contained in the Employment Security Amendments of 1961, proposed to the Congress by President Kennedy. The bills incorporating the President's recommendations were introduced in June, but no hearings were held and no action was taken during the year. The bills, which provided for permanent federal benefits to the long-term jobless in addition to the regular benefits available under the state laws, were designed to assign the responsibility for meeting the needs of short-term unemployment to the states and the responsibility for meeting the needs of longer duration unemployment to the federal government. The unemployed worker who exhausts his state benefits would receive additional benefits. The extra benefits would be equal in amount to his regular state benefits and would run for half the duration of his state benefits up to a maximum of 13 additional weeks. The program would be financed by retaining indefinitely the temporary increase in the Federal Unemployment Tax from 3.1 per cent to 3.5 per cent of taxable payrolls in effect in 1962 and 1963. The extended benefits would be paid only to workers who could demonstrate a lengthy period of unemployment and a substantial attachment to the labor force. Workers would be required to satisfy two tests:

1. They must exhaust their state benefits and have weeks of state benefits plus weeks of unemployment totaling 26 weeks during the preceding year.

2. They must have 78 weeks of covered employment in the last 156 weeks, including 13 weeks of employment in each 52-week period. These benefits would be available at all times, regardless of economic conditions.

To meet the special problem of recessions, the requirement of 78 weeks of employment would be waived and state qualifying requirements, which are less severe, would govern during such periods. Recession periods would be proclaimed by the President when the Secretary of Labor found insured unemployment was 5 per cent or more for three consecutive months and for the same three months the total number exhausting regular benefits exceeded 1 per cent of those covered by state unemployment compensation. The recession would be considered over when exhaustions were less than 1 per cent of covered employment in any three-month period.

Thus, the bills provided for improved benefits for the long-term unemployed both in "normal" times and in times of recession. Other than during recessions, extended benefits would go only to workers with a substantial history of employment. Eligibility requirements during recessions would be relaxed, in recognition of the scarcity of jobs and the difficulty in maintaining a current employment record.

In keeping with the traditional nature of unemployment insurance, however, the length of benefits would be limited. Both in good times and bad, no worker could collect benefits for longer than 39 weeks. Since extended benefits are based on the duration of benefits under the regular state programs, the extended benefits would also be variable in duration in states where regular benefits are variable in length.

The provisions of these bills were introduced again in 1962, but, again, no action taken. Further, in spite of the continuing high level of unemployment during 1962, Congress failed to respond to the Administration's request for an extension of the Temporary Emergency Unemployment Compensation Act of 1961, which lapsed at the end of June, 1962.

Some groups, particularly labor unions, believe that benefits should be available for as long as a worker is unemployed. This point of view and the arguments supporting it were included in the report of the Special Collective Bargaining Convention of the UAW, AFL-CIO in 1961:

The increasing extent of long-term unemployment and the possibility of increasing displacement under the impact of automation require that we provide for a duration of benefits which accords with the realities of economic life in the 1960's. . . . Such situations must be remedied but even the most effective of remedies will take time and, in the meantime, the human needs of those without jobs and without any immediate hope of jobs must be met. For men and women in this situation, there is no realistic method of placing a limit on the duration of their benefits.

The unemployed and their families must continue to eat and to obtain clothing and shelter no matter how long their unemployment lasts. If their needs are not met as a matter of right through an adequate system of unemployment insurance, society will nevertheless carry the costs—through the pauper's oath mechanism of public welfare. It is much sounder to meet those costs through the insurance method that preserves the dignity and morale of the unemployed. Under the Employment Act of 1946, our government has assumed the responsibility for providing adequate employment opportunities. Periodic or continued failures to meet that responsibility are not the fault of the unemployed and they and their families should not be made to suffer in consequence of such failures by government. Their unemployment insurance benefits should continue until suitable jobs become available for them.

Such extension of duration should be a responsibility of the federal government and, since defective public policy rather than the individual employer is responsible for long-term unemployment, the extension should be financed out of general revenues instead of payroll taxes.[15]

Although it is not likely that, in the foreseeable future, the time limit will be removed from unemployment compensation, the maximum duration of benefits provided under the law may be liberalized and the federal government may assume more of the responsibility for meeting the needs of the long-term unemployed. The major problem is that of determining an appropriate maximum duration of benefits. Using Beveridge's criterion that unemployment insurance is an appropriate remedy for unemployment only when the unemployed worker has a good prospect of re-employment, our case studies of displaced workers suggest that one year might be an appropriate maximum. Most of the displaced workers who found jobs obtained them within a year of their layoff. Most of those

---

15. United Automobile Workers, Special Collective Bargaining Convention, *Workers' Problems Are Democracy's Problems*, April, 1961, pp. 86–87.

who found no work during this first year were still jobless two and one-half to three years after the shutdowns. At least in nonrecession periods, a duration period of one year would probably cover most workers who have any reasonable chance of re-employment. This might not be the case, of course, in a recession.

Whatever maximum limits are established, some workers will still be unemployed when their eligibility for unemployment compensation runs out. Although it seems clear enough that a majority of the states do not provide for maximum durations of benefits that are realistic in view of recent trends in long-term unemployment and that the duration of benefits should be improved, it is equally apparent that companion measures are required in order to meet the growing problem of long-term unemployment.[16]

UNEMPLOYMENT INSURANCE AND RETRAINING

Retraining is one of the companion measures that offers considerable hope for reducing long-term unemployment. To the individual it promises increased opportunities for employment and a higher standard of living. To the economy it promises increased productivity and reduction in the welfare burden.

Development of retraining programs has been limited because of a number of obstacles; these must be removed if retraining is to become a significant aspect of any program to reduce long-term unemployment. Most important of the barriers to retraining are: (1) cost to the trainee; (2) lack of training facilities; (3) no assurance of prospective employment; and (4) other institutional factors that discourage the unemployed from seeking retraining opportunities. These barriers together with efforts and proposals for removing them are discussed in Chapter 9. One, however, is closely related to unemployment insurance provisions.

A basic aspect of the unemployment insurance concept is that benefits should go only to persons who are available for work and willing to accept suitable employment. Most states do not allow the payment of unemployment compensation benefits to individuals enrolled in a training program; such persons are considered unavailable for work during the period of their retraining. Thirteen

---

16. Our recommendations are given in Chapter 10.

states and the District of Columbia (seven of them in 1961) have amended their unemployment insurance laws to allow workers attending vocational or retraining courses which have been approved by the appropriate state agency to receive benefits if they are otherwise eligible.[17]

The purpose of the amendments is to remove the restriction on benefits—a restriction which acts as a deterrent to seeking or accepting retraining—for workers trying to improve their skills and job prospects. The Employment Security Amendments of 1961 proposed by President Kennedy were designed to speed up state action by including a federal standard for state unemployment insurance laws that would prohibit the denial of benefits to an otherwise eligible claimant who was enrolled in a retraining program.

The Manpower Development and Training Act of 1962 in effect removed the restrictions on receipt of unemployment insurance for those who qualify for retraining allowances under the Act. Unemployed workers receiving weekly training allowances under this Act receive a payment equal to at least the average unemployment insurance benefit in their state. States in which unemployment insurance is paid to workers in approved training programs are reimbursed by the federal government for the benefits paid. Beginning in July, 1964, the states shall pay 50 per cent of these benefits. Thus, the only workers at present who are denied unemployment insurance or its equivalent because they are in training programs are those who are in courses not approved under the Manpower Act or whose training exceeds the 52-week limit of the Act. The Act also provides for transportation expenses and subsistence expenses not to exceed $35 per week for those who take training courses in places beyond normal commuting distance. Retraining allowances for unemployed workers thus can be viewed as a new form of social security meeting the risk of loss of skills due to technological change. Benefits are not paid as a matter of right, however, out of a trust fund established for the purpose. And

---

17. The 13 states are California, Idaho, Illinois, Massachusetts, Michigan, Missouri, Nebraska, New York, North Dakota, Ohio, Rhode Island, Utah, and West Virginia.

the question remains of whether it would be desirable to integrate retraining allowances and unemployment insurance.[18]

Suggestions have also been made for integrating unemployment insurance with other programs for assisting workers to find jobs. The UAW in its 1961 convention, for example, noted that "other programs to help get the unemployed back to work, such as financing the cost of moving and relocating for workers and their families, should be closely coordinated with the unemployment compensation program."[19] The form of integration in this proposal was not specified, but presumably the worker would be assured that if he relocated for the purpose of accepting or seeking a job, he would continue to receive benefits until he was re-employed.

RELATED PROBLEMS IN UNEMPLOYMENT INSURANCE[20]

Changes in the composition of the labor force, in the nature and causes of unemployment, and in the characteristics of the unemployed have raised other questions with respect to the role of unemployment compensation in meeting the problem of long-term unemployment.

Increasingly during the last two decades, the labor force has been characterized by a high degree of partial and shifting attachment; that is, many persons move into jobs for relatively brief periods of time and then out again, and many others work only at part-time jobs. In 1959, for example, 30 per cent of the 78 million different persons who worked at some time during the year worked at part-time jobs or at full-time jobs for only one to 26 weeks. During the 1940's and 1950's, workers with only partial or intermittent attachment to the labor market became an increasing proportion of the labor force.

This increase in what might be called "secondary" attachment to work has been associated with important changes in the composi-

---

18. See Chapter 9 for further discussion of the provisions of the Manpower Act.

19. United Automobile Workers, *op. cit.,* p. 87.

20. This section draws heavily on data presented in Richard A. Lester, "Implications of Labor Force Developments for Unemployment Benefits," *The Quarterly Review of Economics and Business,* Vol. 1, No. 2 (May, 1961), pp. 47–56.

tion of the labor force. A growing percentage of employed persons are students who combine school with part-time or summer employment, housewives who work when the children are in school, and pensioners aged 65 and over who work on a part-time or occasional basis. In the two-decade period from 1940 to 1960, for example, the proportion of married women in the labor force nearly doubled, increasing from 14.7 per cent to 28.5 per cent. Between 1950 and 1960, part-time employment increased 40 per cent, while full-time employment increased only 8 per cent. Much of the increase in part-time employment is the result of the large influx of women, students, and semiretired persons into the labor force. The result is that in May, 1960, about 18.5 per cent of those working in nonfarm jobs were working only part-time, compared with 15 per cent in 1950.

These changes in the labor force have resulted in a significant shift in the distribution of unemployment insurance benefits to various groups. Larger proportions of the increasing total benefit payments are used for seasonal rather than cyclical unemployment and are dispersed to other than primary breadwinners.

In a number of states, for example, the total amount of unemployment insurance payments in prosperous years is at least two-thirds of the amount paid out in recession years. One of the explanations is the pattern of unemployment among persons with sporadic attachment to the labor force. Married women, for example, have relatively high unemployment rates in "good" times. While women constitute less than a third of the labor force, they have comprised 40 per cent or more of unemployment insurance beneficiaries in relatively prosperous years such as 1952, 1953, 1955, and 1956. In recession years, such as 1958 and 1960, the proportion drops to about 33 per cent. In some states the proportion of beneficiaries who are women has been as high as 50 to 60 per cent. And women also are a disproportionately high percentage of workers receiving partial benefits for underemployment or partial unemployment.

The changing nature of unemployment and the trends in the distribution of benefit payments among various groups have resulted in a number of problems for the unemployment insurance system. The tendency for a large part of a state's fund to be used for seasonal unemployment and the large amounts paid out by some states in normal times to workers with only partial or intermittent attachment to the labor force, for example, make it more difficult to improve benefit levels and durations for workers with a more permanent attachment to the labor force.

To overcome these difficulties, some suggestions for change have been made that would put more emphasis on meeting the problem of recessionary and long-term unemployment. One suggestion, which would tend to shift benefits in favor of "regular" workers, is to tighten eligibility by requiring the unemployed to have more employment or greater wages in the base year in order to qualify for benefits. This would have the effect of excluding some persons who worked only part-time or intermittently in the base year.

A variation of this proposal would relate the duration of benefits to the amount of employment the beneficiary had had extending over a two- or three-year base period. A version of this idea is incorporated in the proposed Employment Security Amendments of 1961. Under this provision, eligibility requirements for regular benefits would not be tightened, but additional federal benefits would be available to workers with longer and more consistent work records.

Relating the duration of benefits to length of employment and amount of contributions would be consistent with the general principles of social insurance.[21] It would be particularly beneficial for permanently displaced workers who have had a long record of continuous employment—the displaced Armour and ABC workers, for example.

A way of reducing the outflow of unemployment insurance benefits to seasonal workers is to classify some industries as seasonal and either provide benefits for workers in those industries only during the seasonal period or limit benefits during the off-season periods. Problems of administration, however—determining the season for each industry, defining and identifying the seasonal

21. See, however, Harry Malisoff, *The Insurance Character of Unemployment Insurance* (Kalamazoo, Mich.: The W. E. Upjohn Institute for Employment Research, December, 1961), pp. 32–36, for a discussion of the implications of extended benefits on the insurance character of unemployment insurance.

worker, obtaining and keeping records—are very difficult. Some of the 18 states with these provisions in their laws do not enforce them.

The use of a dependency allowance, in effect in 12 states, is a way of favoring the regular as opposed to the irregular or secondary worker. Male workers aged 25–64, most of whom are heads of families, generally work or seek work on a full-time basis. Most of them would receive increased benefits from dependents' allowances while many of the part-time or intermittently employed secondary workers would not. Much the same effect could be obtained by varying the maximum benefit with the number of dependents.

The use of dependents' allowances has been objected to because of its departure from the social insurance principle of compensation for wage loss. This principle, however, has also been modified in other social insurance programs, including workmen's compensation and OASDI.

Another proposal that would have the result of redistributing benefits in favor of regular workers is to have a dual-eligibility system. Requirements would be more rigid for workers without dependents than for those with dependents. Dual eligibility requirements are also a departure from insurance principles. A 1959 amendment to the Iowa law included a version of this idea. Under this provision, a claimant could qualify for extra benefits by meeting three conditions: (1) wages in the base period above the usual qualifying wages, (2) having one or more dependent children under age 18, and (3) having a nonworking spouse. Administrative difficulties have been reported, however, particularly in determining whether there is a working spouse.[22]

The objective of these and other proposals is to reallocate unemployment insurance benefits to take account of changes in the nature of unemployment and changes in the labor force. All of them would have the effect of either directing a larger proportion of benefits to the long-term unemployed or directing them away from members of the labor force who are judged less needy or who

---

22. See "UI Claims Experience and the Iowa Dependency Provisions," *Employment Security Review,* July, 1961, pp. 17–18.

have questionable attachment to the labor force when they are out of work.

Many of the proposals deserve serious study. Unemployment insurance proved inadequate for many of the displaced Armour and ABC workers. With the increases in total and long-term unemployment rates, it is important that unemployment insurance and other programs designed to relieve the burdens of unemployment be reconsidered and re-evaluated, taking into account the total problem to be met and the alternatives available for meeting the need.

Efforts to Supplement the Basic Program

Unemployment insurance never has met and was not designed to meet the total problem of income loss resulting from unemployment. Workers in some occupations and industries or in small firms are not covered. For many covered workers, the benefits are not adequate, particularly for workers with large families or with unusual expenses. And much unemployment outlasts the duration of benefits. Lester estimates that the regular programs replace only about 20 per cent of wage loss from total unemployment.[23]

None of the supplementary programs discussed below has been of major importance when measured by the number of unemployed persons eligible to benefit from them. All, however, deserve attention as possible ways of helping to relieve the burdens of unemployment.

GENERAL ASSISTANCE

General assistance is theoretically available to needy people who cannot qualify for the special forms of public assistance—old age assistance, aid to the blind, aid to the disabled, aid to dependent children, or medical assistance to the aged. In practice, however, this is not always the case. In many jurisdictions, the eligibility requirements are so strict that many needy persons, and particularly the unemployed, are excluded from aid.

23. Richard A. Lester, *The Economics of Unemployment Compensation* (Princeton, N.J.: Industrial Relations Section, Princeton University, 1962), p. 38.

The federal government does not participate, financially or otherwise, in general assistance as it does in the special public assistance programs. Not only does the entire burden of financing general assistance fall on state and local governments, but there are no general standards that the states are required to meet. Thus, administration, coverage, eligibility, and benefits vary greatly among the state and local governments. In 17 states the only source of funds for general assistance is the local government, and in another ten the state government contributes less than half the cost of the program. All but 14 states specify a minimum residence requirement for benefit eligibility.[24]

Perhaps more important, public assistance in many states and localities is limited to persons who are not employable. In 17 states no person can receive benefits if any member of his family is employable. In four additional states, employability restrictions are applied to couples and nonfamily persons although not to families. General assistance payments average about $70 per month per case, but, again, the variation among the states is very large. In eight states in 1959, for example, benefits averaged less than $30 per month.

General assistance has not been an important source of support for unemployed workers. Benefit standards are generally low, eligibility requirements are very strict, and in many cases employable persons are not eligible for assistance under any circumstances. Strict eligibility requirements and low payments have led some fathers to leave or pretend to leave their families in order to permit the family to receive benefits under aid to dependent children (ADC) programs. The temporary program during the 1961 recession which provided federal grants for extension of ADC to children of unemployed workers made this practice unnecessary. In July, 1962, President Kennedy signed the bill extending the program for five years. The program, of course, aids only the long-term unemployed who have dependent children.

---

24. See Special Committee on Unemployment Problems, United States Senate, *Characteristics of General Assistance in the United States* (Washington, D.C.: The Committee, Eighty-sixth Congress, First Session, U.S. Government Printing Office, 1959), pp. 7–13, for a summary of characteristics of general assistance programs.

Our resurvey in the five communities early in 1962 showed a substantial increase in the number of long-term unemployed who were receiving assistance in one form or another. Relief payments were most common in Columbus and East St. Louis (more than one-third of the unemployed); and in East St. Louis, particularly, many had children receiving ADC.[25]

Many persons and groups argue that the federal government should participate in general assistance programs much as it does in the special programs. Wilbur Cohen, before he became Assistant Secretary of Health, Education and Welfare, stated the argument as follows:

The Federal Government should share financial responsibility with the states and localities for all groups of needy people instead of only the needy aged, blind, some dependent children, and the permanently and totally disabled. The national interest extends to all needy people regardless of the reason for, or the circumstances of, their needs. Because of gaps and inequities of coverage, considerable numbers of needy unemployed people cannot and do not receive public assistance.[26]

Opponents of federal participation in the financing of general assistance generally argue that: (1) The proper growth of the social insurance programs is thwarted by increased federal aid to public assistance. (2) General assistance case loads are unpredictable. Costs of the program increase greatly in a prolonged recession, and recession needs could be met more efficiently by special emergency measures. (3) General assistance weakens economic incentives, and many people dependent on it would be self-supporting were it not for the availability of assistance.[27]

The case for limiting responsibility for general assistance to the

---

25. A special survey of The Survey Research Center, University of Michigan, showed that the proportion of unemployed on relief increases substantially with the duration of unemployment. William Haber, Fedele F. Fauri, and Wilbur J. Cohen, "Significant Findings on the Impact of the 1957–58 Recession in Relation to Unemployment Insurance," *Studies in Unemployment, loc. cit.,* p. 1406.

26. Cohen, *op. cit.,* p. 330.

27. See Hilary M. Leyendecker, *Problems and Policy in Public Assistance* (New York: Harper & Brothers, 1955), pp. 123–124.

state and local governments does not appear to be strong. These governments are already very hard pressed for revenues and in many cases their tax structures are highly regressive. Thus the burden of supporting those who need general assistance falls most heavily on those least able to pay. The result has been an inadequate program of general assistance and the absence of any comprehensive underpinning of the unemployment insurance program to meet either emergency unemployment needs during a depression or the needs of the long-term unemployed during prosperity. In view of the relatively high rates of long-term unemployment in the past few years, deficiences in general assistance must be judged a serious gap in the nation's social security system.

COLLECTIVELY BARGAINED SUPPLEMENTS

Supplemental Unemployment Benefits. Since World War II, labor unions have given increased attention in collective bargaining to programs that reduce the insecurities faced by workers in an industrial economy. Private plans to supplement social security programs have been developed rapidly to meet the contingencies of old age, death, accident, disability, unemployment, and the costs of medical care. Perhaps the most dramatic development in collective bargaining emanating from these efforts has been the expansion of industrial pensions. The pension movement has been built on the base provided by our legislated social security system.

Collective-bargaining attempts to provide supplementary financial protection during periods of unemployment have not had the success of the pension drive, however. In the mid-1950's, a number of unions began to push hard for some kind of guaranteed annual wage for production workers. This drive was generally unsuccessful, but a number of unions did obtain agreements providing supplemental unemployment benefits (SUB).

The SUB plan negotiated by the United Automobile Workers with the Ford Motor Company in June, 1955, became a pattern for other firms and industries. Similar arrangements have been negotiated in steel, rubber, maritime, and a few other industries. SUB plans, however, have not spread rapidly. In 1956, an estimated two million wage and salary workers or about 4 per cent of the total were covered; by 1959, however, both the total number and proportion covered had declined.[28]

SUB payments are usually tied to unemployment insurance in two ways: (1) to be eligible a worker must also be eligible for unemployment compensation; and (2) the benefit to which the worker is entitled under the plan is reduced by any unemployment insurance payments he receives.

The most usual type of SUB plan has provided a weekly benefit that equals about 65 per cent of weekly take-home pay, including any unemployment compensation. Some plans provide an additional allowance for dependents, usually about $2 per week for each dependent up to a maximum of four. Most plans also stipulate a minimum and maximum amount that can be paid out of the reserve funds, and many limit benefits to workers with at least one or two years of seniority.

Generally, the plans also specify the duration for which benefits are available. The most common maximum duration has been 26 weeks, although a number of industries, including auto and steel, now provide up to 52 weeks of benefits. Some plans provide that SUB benefits should be of the same duration as unemployment compensation in states where duration of benefits is longer than 26 weeks. The duration of benefits commonly varies with "credits" earned by the unemployed worker. One credit, for example, might be earned for each two weeks of work, and the value of the credit might vary with seniority and the status of the reserve fund.[29]

While the number of SUB plans in American industry has not increased, those plans in existence have been improved. In 1961 negotiations with companies in the auto industry, for example, the United Automobile Workers, in addition to obtaining a number of improvements in existing provisions, negotiated two new provisions: SUB payments alone are paid after unemployment in-

---

28. Alfred M. Skolnick, "Trends in Employee-Benefit Plans, 1954–59: Part I," *Social Security Bulletin,* April, 1961, pp. 6–7.

29. See Bureau of National Affairs, *Collective Bargaining Negotiations and Contracts* (53:1-7, Dec. 9, 1962), for a summary of provisions in 49 collectively bargained SUB plans. In the glass industry, SUB plans differ from the usual pattern in that employer contributions are credited to the accounts of individual workers. Benefits to a worker are limited to what is in his account and are not tied to unemployment compensation benefits.

surance benefits are exhausted, and benefits are paid for short workweeks scheduled by the companies. Similar improvements were negotiated for the steel industry in the 1962 agreement. In addition, a moving allowance is provided from the SUB fund for laid-off employees who accept jobs at other plants under a new interregional preferential hiring program.

A variation of SUB was worked out in 1961 negotiations with Armour and Company in the meat industry. Workers below age 60 with five or more years of seniority who are permanently displaced by a departmental or plant shutdown are eligible to choose either severance pay or technological adjustment pay (TAP). TAP benefits are available only to those who request transfer to another Armour plant and are waiting for the arrangements for transfer to be made. Transfers are made as openings in other plants occur. If a worker who applied for transfer turns down a job in another Armour plant, he will receive severance pay but with his TAP and other company-paid benefits deducted.

The TAP is $65 per week, less any unemployment compensation or wages received while eligible and waiting for transfer. The number of weeks of TAP, however, is limited, ranging from 26 weeks for those with 5 to 15 years of service to 39 weeks for those with more than 25 years.

In principle, TAP does not differ from SUB except that it is limited to workers permanently displaced from their regular jobs. The TAP is tied in with transfer rights also negotiated in the contract and tides the worker over part or all of the period required to arrange a transfer.

SUB programs were proposed by labor unions when they were frustrated in their attempts to obtain improvements in unemployment insurance. The benefits are obviously of great value to unemployed workers covered by SUB plans. The value of the plans is severely limited, however, by the relatively small numbers of workers covered. Finally, SUB, in its usual form, has made only a minor contribution in meeting the problem of long-term unemployment. Benefits under most plans have been limited in duration to about the same length of time as unemployment insurance. There are now some important exceptions. SUB, therefore, will be somewhat more important in the future in meeting some of the financial problems of long-term unemployment.

Severance Pay. SUB is, for the most part, directed at the problem of providing support for workers temporarily separated from their jobs. Severance pay is designed to cushion the shock of permanent separation from a job.

Severance-pay arrangements have experienced a steady growth during the last two decades. A 1944 analysis of collective bargaining contracts found separation-pay provisions in only 5 per cent of the agreements. Similar surveys at later dates reported 8 per cent in 1949 and 16 per cent in 1955–56.[30] The plans in effect in 1955–56 covered about 1¾ million employees.

Some plans are negotiated in collective bargaining, but apparently a large number are established unilaterally by management. The National Industrial Conference Board estimates on the basis of 1958 surveys made in manufacturing companies, gas and electric utilities, and financial institutions that between 32 and 73 per cent of the surveyed firms in various categories had some type of severance-pay plan.[31] The inclusion in the Conference Board surveys of nonnegotiated plans and of a disproportionate sampling of large firms accounts, at least in part, for figures much higher than in the BLS surveys.

Severance-pay arrangements tend to be concentrated in certain industries. Three industries—communications, primary metals, and electrical machinery—accounted for half of all severance-pay clauses reported by the BLS in 1955–56. There is evidence, however, that the plans are rapidly expanding in other industries. In the 1958 negotiations in the automobile industry, a severance-pay plan was integrated with SUB. In the same year the International Ladies' Garment Workers Union succeeded in obtaining widespread acceptance of severance-pay programs in its industry. The

30. U.S. Bureau of Labor Statistics, *Dismissal Pay Provisions in Union Agreements,* Bulletin No. 808; *Labor-Management Contract Provisions,* 1949–50, Bulletin No. 1022; *Collective Bargaining Clauses: Dismissal Pay,* 1955–56, Bulletin No. 1216 (Washington, D.C.: The Bureau, various dates).

31. National Industrial Conference Board, *Severance Pay Patterns in Manufacturing,* Studies in Personnel Policy, No. 174; *Severance Pay Patterns in Nonmanufacturing,* Studies in Personnel Policy, No. 178 (New York: The Board, 1959, 1960).

Oil Workers' Union has had some success in negotiating plans in the oil and chemical industry, and in 1959 the International Union of Electrical Workers negotiated an agreement with the Philco Company integrating severance pay with the pension plan.[32] The AFL-CIO estimated that as of October, 1959, about "25 per cent of agreements contain severance-pay provisions and that these agreements cover at least 35 per cent of all workers under union agreements."[33]

Severance pay is receiving more and more attention from labor unions, in part because of the rise in job displacement growing out of the many plant relocations and company mergers of recent years. The basic purpose of severance pay, in the view of unions, is to compensate the permanently displaced worker to some degree for the loss of rights he has built up on the job. It is also viewed as compensation for disruption of living patterns resulting from job loss and, of course, as a financial aid to the displaced worker in the event that extended unemployment follows his separation. Finally, unions also view severance pay as a form of job protection. If severance payments are substantial, there might be some incentive for the employer to adjust to changes in operating or other conditions by methods other than layoff.

Employers, too, often see advantages in severance-pay arrangements. They can be viewed as a method of obtaining better employee relations, decreasing resistance to technological changes, and improving community relations.

The benefits payable under severance-pay arrangements vary considerably. Typically, however, the benefit is based on length of service and is computed on the basis of so many weeks' pay for each year of service. One week's pay might be provided for each year of service up to ten. For service beyond ten years, the payment might be proportionately greater.[34]

---

32. Sumner H. Slichter, James J. Healy, and E. Robert Livernash, *The Impact of Collective Bargaining on Management* (Washington, D.C.: The Brookings Institution, 1960), pp. 468–469.
33. AFL-CIO, *Collective Bargaining Report*, Vol. 4, No. 10 (October, 1959), p. 58.
34. For a somewhat more detailed presentation of typical eligibility requirements as well as other characteristics of severance pay arrangements, see *ibid.*, pp. 57–62.

Severance pay is generally viewed as a desirable form of compensation for workers who are displaced from their jobs. The question has been raised, however, of whether there might be better ways of protecting workers in the event of permanent layoff. The experience of the Armour workers might be interpreted as a failure of severance pay to fulfill its function, since so many of the displaced employees used the money to satisfy previously incurred debts and to meet current expenses rather than for more positive purposes—to finance retraining, to tide the worker over while he looked for a better job, or to start a business of his own.

Perhaps the severance pay received by the Armour workers could have been used for more productive purposes than it typically was. But it should be recognized in interpreting the Armour experience that the displaced workers were given little help or guidance. Other than in Oklahoma City, no major effort was made to advise them of employment opportunities and training possibilities and facilities, or to counsel or test them on their job aptitudes. It seems unrealistic to expect that workers attached to one company and occupation over a long period of time would be aware of the opportunities and facilities available to them or able in most cases to finance their own retraining.

On the other hand, it is possible that if the objective of severance pay is something more "positive" than that of meeting current living expenses, severance-pay arrangements could be administered to encourage alternative uses. Job counseling services, for example, could be included to complement the severance-pay arrangements. Or retraining allowances could be an alternative or supplementary element in the severance-pay plan. Even without these "extras," however, the conclusion seems warranted from the Armour experience that severance pay can be of major, if not crucial, importance to displaced workers and their families.

Other Supplements. Other provisions for meeting the economic needs of displaced and unemployed workers have been devised, although little information is available on their prevalence. In a number of recent cases, for instance, fringe benefits have been extended to laid-off or permanently displaced workers. When the American Viscose Corporation closed its plant in Roanoke, Virginia, in 1958, the separation agreement negotiated by the Textile

Workers Union included an extension of health and welfare benefit coverage for a period of time to workers unable to find other employment. Paid-up life insurance policies financed by the company were also provided for workers who were 55 years of age or older.[35] While these provisions were arranged for on an *ad hoc* basis, similar terms have been negotiated elsewhere and may become more common.

Extension of group insurance coverage to workers on layoff and to retired workers is of value, even if the workers are required to pay all or part of the cost. Otherwise the protection would be available to them only on an individual and much more costly basis. Provisions of this type for retired workers seem to be spreading, and it is likely that they will be increasingly extended to unemployed and displaced workers.

Other programs, both private and public, will undoubtedly be developed in the future to supplement the basic protection to the unemployed available in unemployment insurance.[36] As the pace of technological change and automation quickens, unions will almost certainly put increased pressure on both employers and legislatures to cushion the burdens placed on the workers affected.

Other Types of Assistance to Displaced Workers

Programs to assist workers in their economic adjustment to loss of jobs often include types of aid other than direct payments.

ADVANCE NOTICE

In cases of temporary layoff, a common practice under collective bargaining agreements has been to provide advance notice of one week. When layoffs are permanent, however, brief advance notice is likely to be unsatisfactory to both worker and company. This is particularly true when a large department or an entire plant is being closed. As a result, many unions and companies have devised special programs for advance notice in cases of permanent

35. *Ibid.,* pp. 59–60.
36. See discussion of interplant transfers and relocation allowances in Chapter 9.

reduction of force. These programs include the following objectives:[37] (1) To avert the dissemination of rumors concerning impending plant shutdowns which may have adverse effects on morale and productivity. (2) To give employees who will be displaced by the plant shutdown the opportunity to seek employment with other firms in the labor market. (3) To provide sufficient time for employees to choose among such alternatives as early retirement, severance pay, retraining, or transfer to other company plants when such options are available. (4) To minimize the net displacement of permanent employees subject to layoff as a result of the plant or departmental shutdown. The reduction in force is obtained gradually through the attrition process, and the short-run employment opportunities of permanent workers can be maximized during the advance notice period by offering overtime and deferring various forms of compensated time off as ways of meeting current manpower needs. (5) To prepare the community in which the plant is located for the economic dislocations expected to arise from the plant shutdown, particularly when the closing plant is an important element in the community's economy.

From the viewpoint of the displaced workers, the value of advance notice is that it gives them time to make and embark on plans for new work careers and to arrange their financial and personal affairs. One of the complaints of the displaced Armour workers was that the short notice of the shutdown caught them with heavy financial commitments which they would not have assumed had they known earlier that they were to lose their jobs.

Weber found a number of cases of plant shutdowns in which *ad hoc* arrangements of advance notice were worked out. The length of notice given in the various situations he studied (31 cases of plant shutdowns) varied from three weeks to 29 months. The median notice was about ten months. The length of advance notice appears to be related to (1) technical factors that limit the speed at which a plant can be closed down or new facilities constructed; (2) concern over customer relations, fluctuations in

37. The material on advance notice is largely based on the unpublished report of Arnold R. Weber, "Advance Notice of Plant Shutdown," April, 1961 (mimeographed), prepared for the Armour Automation Fund Committee.

market demand, and production requirements; and (3) the objectives of the advance notice program.

The major management concern about advance notice provisions has been that they might result in substantial additional operating costs because of reduced work force efficiency and complications in the orderly shutdown of the plant. Weber reports, however, that in the cases he studied few problems arose from advance notice. Fears that employees will become apathetic about their work or engage in mischief in protest to the shutdown do not appear to be well founded. Further, he found no evidence that advance notice resulted in any crippling reduction in the work force as a result of excessive quits. In the ABC shutdown in Peoria, as an example, the advance notice was about three months. After the strike over terms of the settlement, productivity increased and there were relatively few early quits.

Unions have begun to press more frequently for advance notice provisions in their collective bargaining agreements. A good example of such a provision is the 90-day notice of planned plant or department shutdowns agreed to by both Swift and Armour in the 1961 meatpacking agreements. Union demands for advance notice in other types of layoff situations will probably increase.[38]

EMPLOYEE ADJUSTMENT SERVICES

Advance notice by itself can be of only minor help to workers in their adjustment to displacement. The effectiveness of advance notice can be enhanced, however by supplementary services.

Weber indicates that most of the companies that followed "model" advance notice procedures coupled them with an effort to describe the various benefits and opportunities that would be available to workers after their separation. Such services include information on benefits such as separation pay, early retirement, and continuation of insurance policies available under existing plans, discussion of any "extra" measures formulated to meet the

38. See, for example, *AFL-CIO News,* September 9, 1961, p. 1, for statement of G. E. Leighty, Chairman of the Railway Labor Executives Association, supporting demands of nonoperating railroad unions for a new work rule requiring six months' advance notice of layoff.

special problems of the situation, and assistance in locating new jobs.

Information and counseling on benefits available can be of special importance to displaced workers. Workers aged 58 and over in the closed Armour plants, for example, could choose between severance pay and early retirement. There is some indication that many of the workers chose severance pay even when it was probable that the pensions would have provided them with substantially greater income over the long run. In such cases, full information concerning the rights to which they are entitled and the implications of choosing various alternatives might make a significant contribution to the workers' welfare.

In the area of helping workers find jobs, a number of opportunities are available to a company, among them the following:

1. Early notice of layoffs gives the workers time to look for other jobs before the layoff takes place.

2. Permission for workers to leave early allows them to accept other jobs without jeopardizing any separation rights.

3. Personal calls to personnel directors and employment managers of other companies may open up jobs.

4. Assignment of personnel department staff to prepare letters of recommendation, answer inquiries, seek job leads, and supply information to the public employment service will help many workers.

5. Counseling in the techniques of job seeking is frequently needed.

Although many companies have taken one or more of these steps, few have developed any policy in advance of layoff situations. When no policy exists, management's concern with the immediate problems associated with production cutbacks tends to relegate the workers' problems to the background. The result is that the laid-off workers receive little or no assistance from their former employer in locating new jobs.

Most of the steps open to a company are also available to a trade union when its members become unemployed. The union cannot, of course, grant early notice and permission to leave early, but it can seek through collective bargaining to persuade the company to grant them. The union can also assign staff who will counsel the members on job-seeking techniques, call or visit employment departments, and provide other informational and counseling services. One problem is that unions often find it difficult to spare staff for such purposes.

When Republic Aviation closed two plants in 1957 and severed 4,000 workers from the payroll, local lodges of the International Association of Machinists were mobilized throughout the country to help find jobs for the laid-off workers. More than 5,000 job openings around the country were located and reported. Through its newspaper, the union kept the workers informed on how to apply for jobs at the local IAM office; how layoffs affected pensions, life insurance, health insurance, and the company's obligation to prorate vacation pay; and how members could protect their IAM membership while unemployed.[39]

Company-union cooperation in assisting laid-off workers is generally limited to agreements on what steps will be taken by the company with respect to benefits, benefit rights counseling, and job-seeking assistance. These services might in some cases be provided more effectively by an "outside" party. Young, in fact, has suggested that the job might be assigned to a person experienced and "expert" with displacement situations. He therefore suggested attaching a person permanently to the Armour Automation Committee who would handle all kinds of services for the workers in event of plant or departmental shutdowns.[40]

EARLY RETIREMENT AND PUBLIC WORKS PROGRAMS

The direct payments and services discussed thus far are the major types of assistance that can be made available to displaced and unemployed workers. Other, less direct alternatives, such as early retirement and public works programs, are additional possibilities.

---

39. *The Machinist,* April 11, 1957.
40. Unpublished "Final Report" from Edwin Young to Armour Automation Committee.

Since the passage of the Social Security Act in 1935, age 65 has come to be thought of as the "normal" retirement age. Because old age insurance payments have been available to many workers at age 65, retirement from paid employment and the labor force usually becomes a realistic option at that age.

In many instances, however, retirement before age 65 might be beneficial both to the worker and to the economy. This is clearly the case for a worker who is in ill health. Such early retirement might also be beneficial to the worker who has difficulty finding employment because of advanced age, lack of education, or obsolete skills. In time of high unemployment, it might be argued, it may be of advantage to the economy if older workers can be encouraged to leave the labor force in order to lessen the competition for scarce jobs.

The first departure from the established retirement age of 65 in the Social Security Act occurred in the 1956 amendments to the Act. The change made it possible for widows to receive full benefits and for retired women and wives of beneficiaries to receive actuarially reduced pensions as early as age 62. The same privilege was accorded men in the 1961 amendments to the Act.

The age 62 provision introduces a desirable element of flexibility into the Act and is likely to be of substantial benefit to older unemployed workers. In a special tally of claims for benefits by men aged 62 through 64 made by the Department of Health, Education and Welfare four weeks after the 1961 amendments went into effect, it was found that 33 per cent of the applicants were unemployed, 40 per cent were already retired, 25 per cent were employed but at wages so low that they were entitled to some or all of their benefits without quitting their jobs, and only 2 per cent would have to quit work or reduce their earnings to be eligible for benefits. Among the applicants who were unemployed, two-thirds had been out of work for more than six months and half for more than a year.[41]

Clearly, the long-term unemployed were taking advantage of the new provision, at least in the early months of the program. Be-

---

41. "Social Security Shows Third of Early-benefit Applicants Jobless," BNA, *Daily Labor Report,* September 18, 1961, p. A-12.

tween August, 1961, and February, 1962, about 360,000 men aged 62 to 64 were awarded reduced pensions.[42]

Most privately negotiated pension plans include provisions that allow retirement before the normal retirement age of 65. Because a private pension is usually cut almost in half for retirement at age 60 and social security is not available as a supplement, early retirement is not financially very attractive unless the pension is thought of only as supplementary income to part-time employment.[43]

A number of unions, however, have recently succeeded in improving early retirement benefits in their negotiated pension plans. In the auto industry, for example, a double pension is provided until age 65 when early retirement occurs under "mutually satisfactory" conditions. In the 1961 agreements between the auto companies and the UAW, it was agreed that there would be no deduction in the double pension even if a worker decides to take reduced social security benefits before age 65.

The double-pension idea appears with increasing frequency in collective bargaining agreements, and early-retirement benefits generally appear to be improving. In the 1961 agreement between Armour and the meatpacking unions, for example, the parties agreed to a provision that employees aged 55 or over with 20 years of service, who are separated from their jobs and eligible for severance pay, may choose instead a pension equal to 1½ times their normal pension until age 62. The agreement reached by the same unions with Swift in 1961 includes a provision for optional retirement on full pension between the ages of 55 and 60 in cases of either plant and department shutdowns or layoffs which last more than two years. Under the same circumstances, retirement on full pension is mandatory for workers 60 years of age or older.

---

42. U.S. Department of Labor, *Monthly Report on the Labor Force,* March, 1962, p. 14.

43. Margaret Gordon points out that there has been hardly any research on the extent to which people who retire early take other employment. See her Chapter, "Work and Patterns of Retirement," in Robert W. Kleemeier, ed., *Aging and Leisure* (New York: Oxford University Press, 1961), pp. 40–42.

The 1962 steel agreement liberalized pension rights for victims of either shutdowns and long layoffs or disability by providing early retirees with a pension more nearly approximating the retirement income of normal retirees who receive both company pension and social security. Also, a provision was adopted to encourage retirement by reducing the new "pension-vacation" plan benefits by 10 per cent per quarter for the period a worker stays on the job beyond age 65.[44]

Early-retirement benefits are particularly helpful in cases of plant or department shutdowns. When, for example, Ford closed its Chester, Pa., assembly plant in March, 1961, the parties agreed to apply the double-pension provision of their agreement for workers between the ages of 60 and 65 if they were not able to transfer to other Ford plants.

Financing the early withdrawal of workers from the labor force benefits one group of workers among whom long-term unemployment is particularly high. The burden of unemployment for other groups of workers might be relieved by providing employment through public works and related programs. Although other methods of expanding employment opportunities for the unemployed are discussed in Chapter 9, public works is discussed here because of its "welfare" connotations.

The WPA, the CCC, and similar programs of the New Deal were attempts to fill the shortage of private jobs with public employment during the depression. Most of these programs were unpopular, both with the general public and with the workers who participated in them. Attached to employment in these programs was the "welfare-case" stigma.

The argument has been made, however, that in dealing with the problem of long-term unemployment public works might be preferable to further lengthening of the duration of unemployment compensation benefits. Long-term unemployment, much more than unemployment of short duration, is likely to depress and demoralize the individual and to result in loss of skill. These

---

44. The "pension-vacation" plan, financed by a company contribution of three cents an hour, features an extra week's retirement pay for each five years of service.

problems presumably would be greatly reduced through public works programs that provide jobs for the unemployed.

Because of the postwar rise in unemployment rates, there has been a revived interest in the possibilities of increasing private job opportunities through public works programs. Senator Clark introduced a bill in the 1961 session of Congress—the Emergency Employment Acceleration Bill (5986)—which would have provided one billion dollars in federal grants to state and local governments for needed public projects. Matching funds would have been required and priority was to be given to projects which could be started in 90 days and completed within 15 months. No grants were to be authorized after the unemployment rate fell to 4 per cent.

Hearings were held on the bill; it was supported by the AFL-CIO and opposed by the U.S. Chamber of Commerce. President Kennedy did not support the bill because of the projected budget deficit for fiscal 1962, but in his 1962 economic message he asked the Congress for authority to make expenditures under certain conditions to bolster the economy and provide jobs. He asked for a two billion dollar stand-by program under which public works expenditures would be "triggered" when economic indicators signaled a coming recession.

In response to this request, Senators McCarthy and Humphrey and Congressman Blatnik introduced bills providing for the creation of an Office of Public Works Coordination and Acceleration, which would be authorized to expend up to two billion dollars both in the form of direct federal expenditures for projects previously authorized by law and in matching grants and loans to states and local governments for capital improvements. The Office would be empowered to act when the unemployment rate increased by 0.5 percentage points or more in three out of the four most recent months or when the unemployment rate was 5.0 per cent or more in four of the preceding six months.

Although the House blocked the request for standby authority that would permit the President to institute public works expenditures as needed, Congress did in September, 1962, approve a bill authorizing 900 million dollars of emergency public works spending in areas of chronic unemployment. This represents some acceptance of the reasoning that job-creating public works are needed to supplement such indirect methods as general tax reductions or increased welfare expenditures.

Summary

Unemployment compensation, supplemental unemployment benefits, severance pay, savings, short-term credit—these and other resources make it possible for most unemployed workers to get by for relatively short periods without really serious hardship. When unemployment is extended, however, the unemployed deplete their resources and are no longer protected from economic and social deprivation. In this chapter, we have discussed the major public and collective bargaining issues related to the problem of meeting the economic needs of the long-term unemployed.

UNEMPLOYMENT INSURANCE

In any consideration of resources available to the unemployed, the starting point is the federal-state system of unemployment insurance. In the quarter-century of its operation, unemployment insurance has been the major and first line of defense against the economic ravages of unemployment. Although it has been of very great value to the individual unemployed worker, his dependents, and to the general public, the system has built-in limitations and shortcomings. The most serious of these shortcomings involve the level and duration of benefits.

Although benefits have increased substantially over the years, they replace no larger proportion of the wage loss resulting from unemployment than in the early years of the program. Further, the level of benefits varies considerably among the states. Although there are no precise standards for measuring adequacy of benefits and there is considerable difference of opinion on what tests of adequacy are appropriate, the available evidence is that benefits are not sufficient to cover nondeferrable expenditures, particularly for "primary" wage earners.

Increases in part-time and intermittent employment have resulted in the use of a large part of unemployment insurance funds for the short-term and seasonally unemployed. This has led to a number of proposals that would result in greater benefits to primary breadwinners and the long-term unemployed, possibly at the expense of other groups of beneficiaries.

A major question is where the major responsibility lies in improving and in standardizing benefits among the states. There are those who argue that improvements should be left to the states. Others, however, believe that adequate benefits can be obtained only if the federal government establishes minimum standards and participates to a greater extent in financing the benefits than it has in the past. The proposed Employment Security Amendments of 1961 included both minimum federal standards and greater federal participation in financing.

High exhaustion rates among unemployment insurance beneficiaries in the 1958 and 1960 recessions focused attention on the question of the adequacy of duration provisions in the state laws. In both recessions, temporary emergency action was taken by the federal government to provide extended benefits to those out of work for long periods of time.

Should the problem of long-term unemployment persist, either because of frequent or serious recessions or because of a continuation of the rise of long-term unemployment in "prosperity" periods, there will be increased pressure to lengthen the duration of benefits and for the federal government to take increased responsibility for the problem. Although the Kennedy proposals for federal standards and for financing extended unemployment insurance benefits for the long-term unemployed during both recession and prosperity were not acted on by Congress in either 1961 or 1962, they will surely be considered again unless unemployment is materially reduced.

Unemployment insurance, of course, should not be considered as the only or even the major weapon against long-term unemployment. It would be preferable to get the long-term unemployed back to work. Retraining and the upgrading of the skills of the unemployed would be a step in this direction. In most states, restrictions on unemployment compensation payments have been a potential barrier to getting the unemployed into training programs, because payment of benefits may be denied to persons enrolled in retraining courses. The Manpower and Development Act of 1962, however, provides for retraining allowances equivalent in amount to unemployment insurance for unemployed workers taking approved training.

Unemployment insurance could be used in other ways to implement efforts to increase the employability and mobility of unemployed workers. Supplemental allowances or extended benefits, for example, might be made available to workers willing to relocate in areas where employment opportunities are more favorable.

Regardless of the improvements that might be made in the unemployment insurance program in the future, it will not meet all needs arising from long-term unemployment. Even much higher benefits would be insufficient in some cases and could destroy the insurance character of the system. Also, unless duration is made equivalent to the length of unemployment, some workers will exhaust their benefits. For these situations and others, supplementary programs are required.

SUPPLEMENTARY PROGRAMS

Theoretically, general assistance could be a second line of defense against the risk of unemployment; in practice, it is somewhat of an "orphan" program. It is the only public assistance program in which the federal government does not participate, either financially or in setting program standards. Instead, it is the responsibility of state and local governments, many of which have had great difficulty in financing adequate programs, Another major problem is that, in many states, employable persons are not eligible for public assistance.

We see no convincing arguments against the federal government's sharing in the responsibility for the program much as it does in the special public assistance programs. As long as public assistance is exclusively a state and local responsibility, there is little possibility that it will become an effective public program to supplement unemployment compensation.

Recent years have seen the growth of a number of private arrangements for meeting the risk of unemployment. The most noteworthy of these are the collectively bargained supplemental unemployment benefits. They have made only a modest contribution in meeting the needs of the long-term unemployed, although recently negotiated improvements seem to indicate that benefits might be extended substantially. The major limitation of supplemental unemployment benefits is the relatively small number of workers covered.

Severance pay, a program usually associated with the displacement of workers resulting from plant or department shutdowns, is potentially of considerable help to a worker with lengthy unemployment. If his other resources are limited, however, he is likely to use his severance pay for current expenses and the payment of previously incurred debts. If severance pay is to serve the "positive" role of giving him a start in a new career, it should be supplemented with information and counseling and, preferably, with a program of retraining and relocation.

A displaced worker often loses more than his wages. Among his losses are valuable "fringe" benefits. Some fringe benefits, such as group life insurance and hospital insurance, are in some cases extended to workers on layoff, and even to permanently separated workers. Such extensions are particularly valuable because they provide protection that is not likely to be obtained otherwise by a worker out of a job.

OTHER TYPES OF PROGRAMS

Advance notice, various employee adjustment services, early retirement, and public works programs are other devices of some importance in attempting to reduce the burdens of long-term unemployment. Of these, early retirement and public works are likely to be of most benefit to the greatest number of workers. Greater flexibility has been introduced into both public and private pension programs, making early retirement a realistic option for many workers of advanced age who have difficulty finding employment. Emergency public works programs can be an effective instrument for attacking both total and long-term unemployment during periods of recession or when economic growth is inadequate to provide full employment.

Since the passage of the Social Security Act in 1935, we have tended in this country to rely almost exclusively on unemployment insurance to relieve the burdens of unemployment. The increasing incidence of long-term unemployment, in both recession and prosperity periods, has forced not only a re-evaluation of the adequacy of the unemployment insurance system but a consideration of other methods of attacking the financial burden of long-term joblessness. This chapter has surveyed the major approaches to the problem that have been attempted and proposed. In the next chapter, we shall consider approaches, other than general monetary and fiscal measures, that might be used to increase the employment opportunities of the long-term unemployed.

9

Efforts to Reduce Long-Term Unemployment

W E HAVE SAID IN CHAPTER 1 that the solution to the problem of long-term unemployment must embrace both a higher rate of economic growth and specific public and private measures to combat unemployment more directly. Although we favor measures that would accelerate economic growth, including fiscal and monetary policies that would stimulate growth without being unduly inflationary, an analysis of these policies is beyond the scope of the book.[1]

We recognize, however, that many of the specific measures discussed here will have relatively little effect unless they are taken in the context of an expanding economy. For example, retraining

1. An analysis of the requirements for a more rapid rate of economic growth is contained in Edward F. Denison, *The Sources of Economic Growth in the United States and the Alternatives Before Us* (New York: Committee for Economic Development, Supplementary Paper No. 13, 1962), 297 pp.

for nonexistent jobs would have little point. For these reasons, when we discuss direct action to reduce unemployment, we do so with the understanding that the basic requirement is to strengthen and stimulate the demand for labor.

In the previous chapter this caution did not apply because income maintenance measures have, on the whole, greater impact and usefulness when labor demand is weak or declining. Measures to maintain jobs or to prepare workers for jobs, however, have greater impact and are more likely to be effective when labor demand is strong or rising.

Shorter Hours, Work Sharing, and Job Security

The traditional form of job security in the United States has been seniority. Seniority has always been emphasized by the American labor movement because neither legal nor cultural sanctions have ever prevented employers from making constant adjustments in the size of their work forces through hiring and layoff. Except as modified through collective bargaining, the employment contract in the United States traditionally permits almost instant layoff.[2]

Seniority has been the major restriction on employer freedom to lay off workers, providing protection for the long-service worker and generally putting the burden of job shifts on younger workers. This system works fairly well in expanding industries and when times are good. It does not work well, however, when plants are closed down completely (whatever the reason) and when there is considerable unemployment. As our case studies show, when high-seniority workers are thrown on the labor market by plant shutdowns many are likely to be disadvantaged by age and obsolescent skills.

The pace and nature of technological change has made necessary

---

2. In many countries, layoff is not so simple. In Japan, most workers with regular full-time jobs continue to work for the same employer indefinitely. See James G. Abegglen, *The Japanese Factory: Aspects of Its Social Organization* (New York: The Free Press, 1958), Chap. 2. In a number of European countries there are various legal or customary restrictions in layoffs. See Gladys L. Palmer, "Contrasts in Labor Market Behavior in Northern Europe and the United States," *Industrial and Labor Relations Review*, Vol. 13, No. 4 (July, 1960), pp. 522–524.

a thorough re-evaluation of job security questions. The job security issues we are interested in here are those which offer some possibility of preventing or reducing unemployment—work sharing through shorter hours, permanent reductions in hours, reduction of work forces through attrition, and guaranteed employment. Later in the chapter we shall examine attempts to expand the concept of job security in multiplant firms and in cases of plant relocation.

TEMPORARY SHARING OF WORK THROUGH
SHORTER HOURS

Work sharing normally means that a group of workers (and the company) temporarily share the burden resulting from the reduction in labor demand. In an analysis of labor-management agreements, the Bureau of National Affairs found that 20 per cent of the contracts provided for work sharing, either by shortening the work week or by rotation of work.[3] The most common provision, found in about half the contracts with work-sharing clauses, was to limit the number of weeks in which a work-sharing rule could apply at any one time. The most usual limit was four weeks, or it might be a total of 10 or 12 weeks in the course of a year. The reduction in hours was also limited. The minimum of hours varied from 24 to 36 hours per week, with 32 hours being the most common.

One-fourth of the provisions in the Bureau of National Affairs analysis stipulated that work sharing was to go into effect before any regular employees were laid off. Further, about one in six provided for the layoff of some regular employees—either an agreed-upon number or those with less than so many years of service.

Work sharing is basically a compromise between maintaining a full work week for senior employees and sharing the work so that fewer workers will be laid off. The limits of work sharing are typically set by the views of a majority of the union members. The

3. Bureau of National Affairs, *Collective Bargaining Negotiations and Contracts* (Washington, D.C.: The Bureau, 1961), 60:301–303. Historically, work sharing has been most common in industries with sharp seasonal swings, such as ladies' garments, millinery, and costume jewelry.

pattern found in contracts suggests that workers find it reasonable to accept modest cuts in hours (down to 32 hours a week) for short periods of time (around four weeks) but that bigger cuts for longer periods are not reasonable. The conclusion, as reflected in the contract clauses, is that when work goes below that level it is preferable to have some of the workers go on unemployment insurance and perhaps find new jobs.

Some genuine sharing, based on altruistic motives, is evident, but the limits found in most contracts indicate that temporary work-sharing devices make only a very modest contribution to reducing unemployment. They can be used effectively for only a short period of time.[4] Developments with far greater potential are the demands of a number of the major industrial unions for either a permanent reduction in the hours of work or a flexible workweek with hours reductions when unemployment exceeds a given level.

PERMANENT REDUCTION IN THE HOURS OF WORK

Organized labor in the United States has always attached great importance to the question of the hours of work. In the early days of unionism, the shorter-hour movement based its arguments on the importance of the workingman's having time to be with his family, to improve himself culturally, and to participate in community affairs. This battle has long since been won; the basic argument for shorter hours in recent decades has been the necessity of providing work for more people. Samuel Gompers once stated the extreme of labor's case by saying "so long as there is one man who seeks employment and cannot obtain it, the hours of labor are too long." Walter Reuther, who has sought shorter hours in the automobile industry and in other industries in which the United Automobile Workers has contracts, has said that the objective is not more leisure. Instead, ". . . we are fighting for more

---

4. An unusual example of sharing was that of 450 women employees of Parke, Davis who voluntarily gave up one to two weeks of employment so that the company could rehire 24 laid-off men for a minimum of five months. The cost per woman ranged from $94 to $196 in lost wages. *The Wall Street Journal,* July 19, 1961, p. 5. A subsequent poll showed a much weaker interest in work sharing. *Business Week,* Sept. 23, 1961, p. 121.

jobs. And if we can't provide full employment at 40 hours, then we ought to cut the work to that level where we can have full employment." The AFL-CIO, while stressing the dangers of both excessive reductions in weekly hours and "moonlighting" or the holding of two jobs, has urged its affiliated unions to press for a permanently shorter workweek.

Since the passage of the Fair Labor Standards Act in 1938, the "standard" workday has been eight hours and the "standard" workweek forty hours. Although hours were longer during World War II (with overtime), working hours have changed relatively little for a quarter of a century. A number of American unions concluded that the time had come for another basic change and began working for it during the 1960–1961 recession both in collective bargaining and in pressing for amendments to federal legislation.

The demand for hours less than eight in a day and forty in a week is, of course, not new. In the 1930's, shorter hours were tried in bituminous coal, rubber, ladies' garments, printing, and other industries, and since World War II there have been shorter hours in parts of many industries, including ladies' garments, printing, construction, rubber, brewing, and baking.[5] Some of the postwar developments may be attributed to attempts to increase pay through overtime premiums, but the recent demands for shorter hours have the same cause as the demands in the 1930's—large-scale displacement of workers. While the economy has not been threatened with a general depression, the rising trend in long-term unemployment described in Chapter 1 has given considerable impetus to a revival of the shorter-hour movement.

The union case for shorter hours is illustrated by a document prepared for the United Automobile Workers' "Special Collective Bargaining Convention" in April, 1961. It made no specific demands; rather, the UAW position was that industries in which it represents workers have economic problems which union and

---

5. See *AFL-CIO Conference on Shorter Hours of Work* (Washington, D.C.: AFL-CIO, 1956). Some shorter hours have been the result of an effort to obtain more hours at premium pay. This seems to be an element in the 25-hour week negotiated in 1961 by Local 3 of the International Brotherhood of Electrical Workers in New York City.

management should try to solve together. Here is the statement on shorter hours, in part:

Since 1953, the number of production workers in our industries in the United States and Canada has declined by 391,000—165,000 in auto and supplier plants, 198,000 in aircraft, and 28,000 in agricultural implements. . . .

Many partial solutions are available. Jobs can be created through reduction in work time, through lowering the retirement age, and through limitations on overtime in times of unemployment. . . . We are flexible as to the choice of methods. . . .

More jobs can be created by agreement on a shorter workweek or a shorter workday with no loss in pay.

Such a reduction in the workweek can be accomplished by negotiating it directly on a graduated basis downward. Another way of meeting this objective is to tie automatic downward adjustment of the workweek . . . to levels of unemployment in the industry, without reducing pay. When unemployment in the industry rises above a specified percentage for a specified period of time, the standard workweek would be automatically reduced; and if it rose still higher, the hours would be still further reduced. The reverse process would be applied as unemployment declined. This method would not be vulnerable to a charge that national needs in time of a world crisis are being slighted. The cost could be met by a fund, negotiated company by company or industry-wide, on the basis of a specified percentage of payroll. Reduction in the workweek has already been effected in some industries. . . .

Other means of creating jobs are to increase the number of paid holidays or to extend vacation time with pay, or both. . . . More paid holidays and longer paid vacations would both cut unemployment and lay the basis for a more creative approach to the increasing problems of meaningful leisure in a technological age.

Another approach would be that of sabbatical leaves of absence with pay, a standard practice in the teaching profession. . . . Australia . . . provides sabbaticals—called "long service leaves"—for workers. . . .

Still another approach to the creation of job opportunity is through a lowering of the retirement age. Early retirement can be made possible and more attractive by increasing company pension benefits and making up, in addition, for the unavailability of social security benefits to those who retire early.

Another possibility is that of a program of phased retirement—a planned transition in which work time would gradually be reduced and the worker would gradually adjust himself to the new conditions of retirement. . . .

We are prepared to explore the following approaches in seeking a solution:

Reduction of the workweek without loss in pay;
Reduction of the workday without loss in pay;
Reduction of the workyear without loss in pay;
Longer vacations;
Additional paid holidays;
Industrial sabbaticals;
Early retirement;
Control of overtime.[6]

Shorter hours without reduction in pay clearly mean higher labor costs unless productivity rises sufficiently so that weekly output per worker is maintained at a level at least as high as before the hours reduction. Since productivity cannot increase that suddenly, the UAW proposals were bound to meet resistance from automobile, aircraft, and farm implement employers. Others have also raised objections. The President of the United States, supported by his Secretary of Labor, declared that in the present stage of the Cold War we cannot as a nation afford a general reduction in the length of the workweek. This view was supported by the impartial members of the Armour Automation Fund Committee who opposed

the permanently shorter workweek as a matter of national policy because they believe it is a solution which reduces the nation's productive capacity at the very time when it ought to be expanded. They recognize, however, that unless full employment can be achieved through a rapidly growing economy the demand for the reduced workweek will become increasingly insistent.[7]

6. United Automobile Workers, *Workers' Problems Are Democracy's Problems* (Detroit, Mich.: UAW, April, 1961), pp. 26–29.

7. Armour Automation Fund Committee, *Progress Report* (Chicago, Ill.: June, 1961), p. 12. The impartial members were Clark Kerr, President, University of California, and Robben W. Fleming, Professor of Law, University of Illinois.

The union members of the committee filed a supplementary statement, noting that total employment in the meatpacking industry had declined by about 30,000 jobs since 1956. The union representatives stated:

the shortened workweek [is] not merely desirable but an economic imperative. . . . The immediate goal to be achieved through a shortening of the workweek is not more leisure but substantially less enforced and unpaid leisure for those who now seek work.[8]

The company members of the committee argued that a shorter workweek would not achieve its goal, at least in meatpacking, because in this low-profit industry the higher costs would only accelerate efforts to automate.

The United Automobile Workers have tried to meet both the arguments of higher labor costs and the arguments of maintaining national output by proposing a flexible workweek under federal law. The UAW agrees that the position of the President is sound but becomes meaningless when there is widespread unemployment.

We therefore propose that the Fair Labor Standards Act be amended to provide for automatic adjustment of the standard workweek based upon the level of unemployment. When unemployment is less than a specified percentage of the labor force, the standard workweek would remain at 40 hours. If unemployment should rise above that percentage for a specified period of time, the standard workweek would automatically be reduced; if unemployment rose to still higher levels, the standard workweek would be further reduced accordingly. The reverse process would be applied as unemployment declined.

The specific figures to be written into the law would have to be developed on the basis of studies to determine how many unemployed workers are likely to be re-employed as a result of each successive hour of reduction in the standard workweek. . . .

When unemployment is high, the individual employer—particularly the small employer—is least able to afford the compensating pay required to maintain take-home pay in the face of reduced workweeks. We therefore propose that such compensation be financed . . . through a National Workweek Adjustment Fund to be accumulated out of revenues from a small payroll tax on all employers. This method of financing would have a stabilizing influence on the economy, since in

8. *Ibid.,* p. 25.

good times when demand is high, money would be drawn into the Fund, and in bad times when demand needs to be stimulated it would be withdrawn from the Fund and used to increase purchasing power. When a reduction in the standard workweek comes into effect, . . . any employer who reduced hours worked accordingly would be reimbursed from the Fund for the added cost of continuing to pay his workers for 40 hours a week at their normal wage rates. An employer who did not reduce hours . . . would not be so reimbursed. He would pay out of his own pocket full wages for the hours in excess of [the reduced] standard plus premium overtime rates for those hours. This would provide a stimulus to reduce scheduled hours and to hire additional workers.

The cost of this proposal, when spread over the entire business cycle, would require only a small tax on payrolls—quite likely less than one per cent. The small cost involved would be offset to a significant degree by reductions in unemployment compensation contributions and SUB payments now borne by employers as a result of high unemployment. Whatever net cost remained would be far less than the cost of unemployment.[9]

Other unions have adopted proposals similar to those of the UAW, both for collective bargaining and for national legislation. The United Packinghouse Workers in its 1961 negotiations sought, but did not achieve, leaves with pay of 13 weeks after each five years of service with a company. As for national legislation, both the UPW and the United Steelworkers of America have proposed a permanent reduction in the standard workweek through an amendment to the Fair Labor Standards Act, with no mention of a flexible standard. The Communications Workers of America, however, in its Twenty-third Annual Convention in 1961, proposed a "national security fund" to cover both retraining costs and the cost of maintaining a 40-hour pay level when hours are reduced below 40 hours per week "as a result of automation."

REDUCTION OF WORK FORCES THROUGH ATTRITION

Frequently, firms can introduce labor-saving equipment with few or no layoffs. The solution is to introduce the new equipment

---

9. United Automobile Workers, *op. cit.,* pp. 79–80.

slowly enough so that normal attrition (deaths, retirement, quits) will bring about the required shrinkage of the work force.

Most instances of work-forces reduction through attrition have resulted from unilateral decisions by management, but devices to delay and slow up automation have increasingly become a subject of collective bargaining. The attrition approach, however, is most feasible where the quit rate is high—in offices and similar establishments, with a large proportion of women workers and relatively little unionism.[10] When male production workers are involved, attrition is apt to be a slow process and would often seriously impede the introduction of new technology. Interplant transfer, discussed later in this chapter, increases the possibilities of reduction in force through attrition.

Since American unions are generally proud of the fact that they do not stand in the way of progress and rising standards of living accomplished by technological change, it is not surprising that there are relatively few examples of unions pressing for or achieving no-layoff policies. The nature of the industry, and particularly its degree of competition, will influence the ability of companies to adopt a no-layoff policy. In the New York transit industry with no direct competition, the New York City Transit Authority, as the result of a verbal agreement with the Transport Workers Union, reduced its work force by more than 7,500 in five years, or about 4 per cent a year, without any layoffs.[11] Any widespread use of reduction of force through attrition is unlikely because it would result in the slower introduction of technological change. Further, the process saves the jobs of some but makes little contribution to the general reduction of unemployment.

---

10. The U.S. Bureau of Labor Statistics has studied the introduction of electronic data processing in offices and found that a number of employers use the attrition process. To adjust their labor demands to such a policy, employers hire only temporary employees as needed or schedule overtime rather than hire people into regular jobs who later would have to be displaced. U.S. Bureau of Labor Statistics, *Adjustments to the Introduction of Office Automation* (Washington, D.C.: The Bureau, Bulletin No. 1276, 1960).

11. International Association of Machinists, *Meeting the Problems of Automation through Collective Bargaining* (Washington, D.C.: IAM Research Department, December, 1960), p. 8.

GUARANTEED EMPLOYMENT

Because of uncertainties about future labor requirements, few companies are willing to agree in advance to a no-layoff policy. Such a policy is really one of guaranteed employment for regular employees, and guaranteed employment has only rarely been successful in American industry. Guaranteed employment or guaranteed annual wage plans have been tried on a number of occasions, but most of the plans have not lasted very long.

While management can take many actions that will have an effect on preserving jobs—including producing for inventory during slack seasons, adjusting sales techniques, careful timing of new models, diversification that helps regularize production through the year, and many others—not many companies are in a position to agree in advance to guarantee employment for a specified period of time.

One plan that has received a great deal of publicity is the Agreement on Mechanization and Modernization between the Pacific Maritime Association and the International Longshoremen's and Warehousemen's Union, in effect since early 1961. In return for the freedom to change working rules, particularly those involving the size of loads, multiple handling, and the use of mechanized equipment, the employers (the PMA) established a fund for which the Association and the Union act as joint trustees and to which the employers are contributing $5 million a year for five and one-half years.[12] The fund is used for payments to "fully registered longshoremen" (that is, the year-round workers who are full members of the union) upon retirement, including early retirement, and to guarantee payment of wages for a specified number of straight-time hours per week. The guaranteed weekly payment applies only when the opportunities for work have been reduced because of the contract provisions and not when there is a lessening of "economic activity."

A significant aspect of this plan is that it reduces unemployment by permitting shorter hours without a reduction in worker income. Whether a similar approach would be feasible in many other in-

---

12. See Max D. Kossoris, "Working Rules in West Coast Longshoring," *Monthly Labor Review,* January, 1961, pp. 1–10.

dustries is open to question, but the possibilities are being explored by many unions. It would appear to be most likely to occur where labor costs are relatively low in relation to total costs.

In the 1961 negotiations with the major meatpacking firms, the United Packinghouse Workers proposed that the companies agree not to close any plants during the life of the contract and that, if a plant is to be closed upon the termination of a contract period, "substantial notice of intention" would be required. In the three-year agreement reached by the Packinghouse Workers and Meat-cutters with Armour in September, 1961, the parties settled for a 90-day notice to workers and the unions of plant or department shutdowns. The same provision was included in the agreement with Swift.

These are only some of the examples of collective bargaining efforts to preserve jobs. Further innovations are quite probable. What might become a pioneering agreement was signed in June, 1961, between the American Cable and Radio Corporation and the Communications Workers of America. The parties agreed that employees who have completed their probation cannot be laid off if their jobs are rendered obsolete by automation. Adjustments in the work force must come through attrition and/or reassignment. Workers assigned to lower classifications retain their pay and their regular classification. Layoffs can still occur if business declines. In a number of other cases, however, although mostly in smaller companies, there have been collective agreements providing for guaranteed employment on a yearly basis without specific reference to automation.[13]

Finding Jobs for Displaced Workers

How much unemployment is actually prevented by management efforts and collective bargaining agreements designed to avoid or delay layoffs cannot possibly be measured; yet there is little doubt that unemployment would be noticeably worse if all business decisions were based solely on the criterion of paying only for hours of work needed. Similarly, when layoffs do take place, much can be done to reduce the length of unemployment by helping the dis-

13. For examples, see Bureau of National Affairs, *op. cit.,* 53:901–904.

placed workers locate new jobs but, again, no measurements are available of the effectiveness of such job-finding assistance.

Unfortunately, as all labor market studies (including those in this book) have shown, displaced production workers are largely on their own when it comes to finding jobs. Although many companies and unions endeavor to assist permanently laid-off workers in their search for work, companies and unions typically do not have the facilities and experience to act as employment agencies. Exceptions are those unions with hiring halls.

THE PUBLIC EMPLOYMENT SERVICE SYSTEM

The most logical source of job-seeking advice for displaced workers is the public employment service system. This system, which first became nationwide when the Wagner-Peyser Act of July, 1933, created the United States Employment Service, is today a federal-state system with local offices within reach of virtually every worker and employer in the United States.[14] The system, however, has never been as widely accepted or used by employers and workers as have comparable systems in some other industrialized countries. The relative inability of the public employment service to help the displaced Armour and ABC workers was described in Chapter 5. The experiences of these workers are fairly typical of manual workers in the labor market.

The fact that the public employment service has not been able to realize its full potential in services to employers and workers is recognized by the state services and by the U.S. Department of Labor. Arthur Goldberg, in an address to employment service officials, said that the employment service needs to become a

far more active and aggressive force than it has been in the last ten years. . . .

The picture of the Employment Service offices is too often colored by their unemployment insurance functions. Therefore, to change this impression, we must begin now to subordinate the claims processing

---

14. For an official history of the growth of the employment service, see "The Public Employment Service System, 1933–1953," *Employment Security Review,* June, 1953 and "The Employment Service in an Expanding Economy, 1953–1958," *Employment Security Review,* October, 1958, entire issues.

functions in the local offices to their job market services. The Employment Service office should be primarily a placement office to match workers and jobs. . . .

Primary emphasis on the placement functions means, in some instances, reorganization of offices, modernization of facilities, greatly expanded employer relations, increased job listings, and increased efforts to place qualified applicants in jobs quickly and promptly to meet local hiring needs first while at the same time keeping abreast of needs on the national scene.[15]

In order to strengthen the public employment service system, local office staffs were increased, starting in 1961, with the objective of changing the average ratio of employment office staff members to wage and salary workers from 1 to 4,900 to 1 to 4,000. Plans were also adopted to modernize and intensify interstate and interarea recruitment and placement, particularly for occupations in short supply. Finally, reorganization of the employment service in a number of metropolitan areas was undertaken in order to provide more effective counseling and placement services.

In order to finance the strengthening of services, President Kennedy requested and obtained a $21 million increase in the 1962 Department of Labor budget and a $25 million advance from the employment security trust fund to be used to hire additional workers in the Bureau of Employment Security and in the state systems. The advance is being repaid from unemployment compensation tax receipts.[16]

The Area Redevelopment Act of 1961 and the Manpower Development and Training Act of 1962 have also given the employment services system new responsibilities. Under the former Act, the employment service develops the data to determine which areas are eligible under the law; selects, registers, counsels, tests, and refers workers who are to receive retraining; surveys manpower and training needs in each area; and makes retraining sub-

15. Arthur J. Goldberg, address before national conference of state employment security administrators and employment service directors; reported in Bureau of National Affairs, *Daily Labor Report,* April 20, 1961, pp. A 6–7.

16. *Ibid.,* March 15, 1961, pp. A 17–19. Regulations were also amended to facilitate the construction of new employment security local offices. *Ibid.,* March 30, 1961, p. A 10.

sistence payments through the unemployment insurance machinery. The Manpower Act provides for similar responsibilities.

Because of insufficient data about fast-moving occupational changes and the occupational experience of the long-term unemployed, the Department of Labor has taken other steps to improve the flow of information and to analyze the nation's labor requirements. The Department assigned to the new Office of Manpower, Automation and Training the task of conducting studies of the impact of automation and the changing needs in training and placement. Also being deliberated in 1962 were ways of measuring the extent and specifics of job openings in labor markets across the nation.

In addition, the Bureau of Employment Security in the Department of Labor set up a Bureau-State Agency-University Task Force on Automation and Technological Change to consider what the employment service might do, in cooperation with management and labor, to provide greater help for technologically displaced workers. One of the first efforts in 1961–62 was the conducting of ten "demonstration projects" in which the employment service worked with employers who were planning or making technological changes that would displace workers. The purpose of the projects was to determine how employment service techniques and facilities, community training resources, and advance planning by management, labor, and the employment service could smooth and speed the transition of the displaced to other jobs.

The Bureau of Employment Security also decided to experiment with an "early warning system" on worker displacement, conduct more area skill surveys on current and future job opportunities, study the characteristics of the long-term unemployed, and establish a system for exchanging information between the Bureau and the state agencies, as well as among the states, on facts, plans, and suggested action programs.

In addition to these activities, a number of the state agencies have been stressing the theme that referral and placement of workers should be on the basis of ability and job qualifications. In most of the industrialized states of the north and west, fair employment practices laws give the employment service the authority to bar job orders that discriminate on the basis of race, religion, or national origin.[17] In some of the states, the employment services have also been making special efforts to help older workers secure new jobs. As time goes on, the employment services are likely to have an increasing role, both direct and indirect, in reducing discrimination in the hiring of workers by private industry.

PUBLIC-PRIVATE COOPERATION

The major burden of finding new jobs is likely to remain with the unemployed workers. Rapid occupational changes and industrial relocation, however, indicate the importance of a greater role for employment agencies and particularly for the publicly supported employment service agencies. The work of the public employment service can be greatly strengthened if it receives full cooperation from employers and unions. Such cooperation is particularly important when large numbers of workers are laid off at one time.

In each of the five shutdown situations that we studied, more cooperation between company, union, and employment service could have been beneficial to the displaced workers. The greatest efforts were made in Oklahoma City as a result of the work of the Armour Automation Fund Committee. Even there, more could have been done, particularly in advance planning of ways in which the laid-off workers might be helped. As Robben W. Fleming, who was Executive Director of the Committee, commented:

One of my conclusions from the Oklahoma City experience is that it casts real doubts on the efficacy of "crash" programs which must be inaugurated after the crisis is at hand. The kind of program which is likely to be much more successful is the carefully thought out, carefully administered, continuing program which can be administered during "normal" times.[18]

17. As of January, 1962, according to the U.S. Bureau of Labor Statistics, 23 states had adopted fair employment practice laws, with seven of these including age.

18. R. W. Fleming, "Collective Bargaining Approaches to Job Security," Seventh Annual Industrial Relations Conference, University of Michigan, March 29, 1961.

The Relocation of Experienced Workers

Thus far in this chapter we have discussed the possibilities of reducing unemployment by shortening the hours of work and speeding the process of finding new jobs when workers are displaced. This discussion has largely ignored several problems: (1) Even with shorter hours, work sharing, and reliance on attrition, there may not be enough jobs in a particular establishment, making layoffs inevitable. (2) There may not be enough jobs in the community for those who are displaced. (3) Workers whose jobs have become obsolete or have otherwise disappeared may not have the qualifications for existing jobs within the plant or place of business or within the community.

The first two of these problems have, as possible solutions, transfer to jobs elsewhere in the company or relocation in jobs with other companies in other labor market areas. First, we shall consider existing and proposed practices in transfer and relocation. Then, we shall analyze the problems and potential of retraining as a means of avoiding or ending unemployment.

INTERPLANT TRANSFER RIGHTS AND SENIORITY

The most fundamental question concerning interplant transfer, or relocation of a worker in a different establishment of the same company is whether the worker has the *right* to such transfer. Traditionally, transfer has been viewed by management as one of its prerogatives and as part of its right to assign employees to jobs. When seniority systems put limitations on management's right to assign workers, they are generally applicable to single establishments only.

As a result, the right of transfer has for the most part remained in the hands of management. Very few collective bargaining agreements have contained formal provisions for interplant transfer. Union concern about worker displacement, however, has resulted in increased pressure on management for transfer arrangements, and many companies have become convinced that their responsibilities to their long-service workers include attempting to do something about transfer.

Four kinds of transfer arrangements illustrate varying degrees of rights to transfer.[19] The first is preferential hiring, which gives the laid-off workers first consideration when they apply for a job at another plant of the same company. In other words, they apply as new employees and are put at the head of the application list but behind any employees on layoff status at that plant. The ABC workers, for example, were given preferential hiring consideration at other appliances plants of the parent company.

When preferential hiring is used, limits are sometimes imposed on the workers' transfer rights. These limits include the requirement of a given number of years of service as well as applications at a specified number of other plants or within a particular geographic area. For example, when Lever Brothers closed its Cambridge, Mass., plant, it allowed each of the laid-off workers interested in transfer to apply at only one of the five remaining plants. Ford and Chrysler each have "Detroit Availability Lists" for preferential hiring within the Detroit metropolitan area. General Motors has some 25 geographic-area preferential hiring pools. The 1962 Steel Agreement has a similar provision: preferential hiring at other plants of the same company within designated geographic areas.

Weber comments that the geographically-limited preferential arrangements tend to be "more authoritative" than those not so limited, because the company assumes a greater obligation in trying to use the displaced workers and the worker more of an obligation in seeking transfer. In the automobile industry, the labor market area approach is also tied in with supplemental unemployment benefits (SUB); that is, if the worker refuses another job in the area, he may lose his SUB benefits. A similar arrangement was negotiated by the two major meatpacking unions with Armour in 1961. Permanently displaced workers with five or more years of seniority are eligible for Technological Adjustment Pay (TAP). To be eligible for TAP, however, employees must request transfer

19. This is the classification used by Arnold R. Weber in his paper, "The Inter-plant Transfer of Displaced Employees," which was prepared for the Armour Automation Fund Committee and is included in Gerald Somers, ed., *Adjustments to Technological Change,* scheduled for publication by Harper & Row, New York, in 1963. We have drawn on this paper in the preparation of our discussion of interplant transfers.

to another Armour plant covered by the collective bargaining agreements. Transfers are made as openings in other plants occur. If a worker who applied for transfer refuses a proffered job, TAP payments and other company-paid benefits are deducted from his severance pay.

Another feature in preferential hiring is that the worker has to have an "employee status," usually meaning that he has retained seniority rights of recall. Generally, workers who have accepted separation allowances or early-retirement benefits have severed their employment relationship and, therefore, are not eligible for preferential hiring. The offer of preferential hiring in Kansas City to former Armour workers in Oklahoma City was a special case and an exception to this rule. Any Oklahoma City worker who had received separation pay and then accepted transfer would either start as a new employee with respect to severance pay and pension rights or would reinstate these rights by repaying his severance money.

Intercompany preferential hiring is rare. One such arrangement was set up in 1962 in the glass container industry in a contract between the Glass Bottle Blowers Association (AFL-CIO) and The Glass Container Manufacturers Institute. Preferential hiring rights for laid-off workers, with transfer of job classifications and pay scales but not pension rights, apply to some 6,500 machine operators in 24 firms.[20]

The second type of transfer right, a variation on preferential hiring, was instituted by Chrysler and the United Automobile Workers. Under this plan, displaced employees with high seniority are given preferential hiring rights at other plants before all employees on layoff at those plants are recalled. Weber labels this "attrition rights" because the high-seniority workers are placed on an "attrition list" which gives them recall rights at any of the Detroit area plants. If a given plant loses a worker through attrition (death, retirement, quit), it rotates its recalls on a one-and-one basis between its own recall list and the attrition list. A man called in from the attrition list carries his accumulated seniority with him.

A third approach applies to situations in which operations are

20. *Wall Street Journal,* February 13, 1962, p. 2. See also footnote 24.

transferred from one plant to another and management agrees to transfer the workers with the operations. Under this type of arrangement, workers who want to transfer have the right to do so if there are enough jobs. Since transfers of operations often mean the introduction of automated equipment, there may be fewer jobs in the new installation. In such cases, seniority usually determines priority. In any event, full seniority rights go with the transfer.[21]

Most examples of transfer rights when operations are transferred come about through collective bargaining. Companies, in some cases, do not want to transfer their workers. A plant relocation may result, in part, from a desire to escape collective bargaining or to obtain a new and lower-paid work force. A plant which is relocated for the purpose of breaking an existing collectively bargained contract might be charged with being a "runaway shop." The courts have generally agreed that "runaway shops" constitute an unfair labor practice under the Taft-Hartley Act. Until 1961, however, there was nothing to stop a company from relocating its operations and hiring a new work force when a collective agreement expired.

This freedom may be restricted in the future as the result of recent court cases. The Glidden Company in 1957 transferred operations from a plant in Elmhurst, New York, to Bethlehem, Pennsylvania, after an agreement expired between the company and the Brotherhood of Teamsters. Five employees who were offered transfer, as new employees, sued for damages for violation of contract; they charged that the company was depriving them of benefits under the company's pension and group life insurance plans and under the negotiated welfare plan. The Federal District Court in New York ruled for the company but the Second Court of Appeals held (March 28, 1961), in a two-to-one decision, that "the more rational, not to say humane" construction of the contract required the company to honor the seniority rights in question. In language which has proven somewhat controversial, the court also spoke of seniority as a "vested right," equivalent to "valuable unemployment insurance," and not terminable by unilateral action. The case has been appealed, but the Supreme Court has agreed to hear only a technical aspect of the case. If the Court finds error

---

21. A number of cases are cited in International Association of Machinists, *op. cit.*, pp. 10–15.

the case will be returned to the Court of Appeals; otherwise the decision in its present form will stand.[22]

The Gemmer Manufacturing Company, a Detroit division of Ross Gear and Tool Company of Indiana, was planning to move its operations to Lebanon, Tenn., which had provided it with a new plant financed by a bond issue and with a 20-year lease, on the condition that the company would recruit workers among local residents. In July, 1961, the U.S. District Court in Michigan, on the basis of the Glidden decision, ruled in favor of the United Automobile Workers' contention that the Detroit workers had a "vested right" to jobs in the new plant. In July, 1962, however, the Sixth Court of Appeals overruled the District Court on the basis that the Glidden ruling did not apply.[23]

If and when the Supreme Court has an opportunity to rule on lower court decisions upholding seniority as a "vested right," the decision can have a great impact on collective bargaining and worker rights of transfer. Even if the rulings are upheld, however, many collective bargaining problems will remain. For example, will the principle apply to a multiplant company that is displacing workers but not transferring any operations? In unionized companies, the chances are that transfer to existing plants will continue to depend, in most instances, upon collective bargaining arrangements.

A complication that sometimes arises with plant relocation is change of ownership. Courts have generally held, however, that a collective bargaining agreement continues even when a plant comes under new ownership. The Glidden-Ross Gear "doctrine," if upheld, may have to be further tested when a plant closes simultaneously with or after a collective agreement expires and operations are transferred or consolidated elsewhere under new ownership.

Under collective bargaining, the fourth type of transfer right is interplant bumping. Under such a plan, a senior laid-off worker could displace a more junior employee at another plant, whether or not operations are being transferred. According to Weber's

---

22. *Wall Street Journal,* July 21, 1961, p. 1.

23. Bureau of National Affairs, *Daily Labor Report,* July 7, 1961, p. A-5, and July 20, 1962, p. A-1. In 1962, another U.S. District Court ruled, in a case involving the Mack Truck Company and the UAW, that a company and a union may change any rights to transfer, by agreement, without the consent of all the individual employees.

survey, unrestricted interplant bumping is rare because of the many problems posed for company and union. One plan, which was under consideration by the UAW, would establish under the master agreement company-wide seniority for displacement purposes to begin as of a specified date. On that date, all employees would begin to accumulate company-wide seniority. After that date, new employees would have company-wide seniority beginning with the date of hire. The theory is that new employees would accept an existing arrangement and established employees would be put on an equal footing, thus avoiding intra-union problems resulting from transfer. If company-wide seniority is to be adopted, a gradual plan such as this would seem to have the greatest possibility of success. The Armour Company and the meatpacking unions did adopt this plan in their 1961 agreement; it went into effect for employees hired after August 7, 1961.

Some further experimentation with the device of permitting high-seniority workers to bump low-seniority workers in other plants may be undertaken, but the intra-union political problems inherent in such experimentation will probably limit this development. Pressures for transfer with some degree of seniority, however, are likely to be greatest where entire plants close or where displacement is the result of technological change rather than lack of business.[24]

SPECIFIC PROBLEMS IN INTERPLANT TRANSFERS

Transfer and seniority rights in transfer situations still leave many knotty problems, some of which are worth discussing briefly. One problem is how to integrate transferred employees into the seniority lists of the plant to which they move. When full seniority is retained, integration is largely a question of dovetailing the transferees into the plant seniority roster on the basis of length of service with the company. The mechanics are simple, although the

---

24. Even preferential hiring is frequently limited to displaced workers whose jobs were eliminated by technological change. An industry-wide agreement in the cement industry, affecting 27,000 workers represented by the United Cement, Lime and Gypsum Workers International Union, calls for plant-wide bumping and preferential hiring at other plants for those displaced only when technological changes are introduced. Bureau of National Affairs, *Labor Relations Reporter,* Vol. 48 (1961), p. 461.

rearrangement may cause political problems for the local union. When those transferred have date-of-entry seniority in the new plant, another type of problem may arise. The transferred employees may leave the old plant in reverse order of seniority and, as a result, the seniority order of the transferred employees may be inverted in the new plant. The solution found for this problem in a number of cases has been "pegged seniority" under which the displaced workers all receive the same pegged seniority date regardless of when a transfer actually occurs and/or retain their former seniority order after transfer.

Other problems occur when the plant from which transfers are made is not closed. Unions generally claim or seek bargaining recognition of the principle that transferred employees retain their seniority and recall rights at their original location. In transfers of operations, where employees keep their full seniority in the new plant, they generally lose their seniority rights in the old plant. With preferential hiring, however, seniority in the original plant is usually retained. In the automobile industry, with the area transfer arrangements, for example, the workers have their original seniority in their first plant and plant-service seniority in the second plant. If recalled by the first plant, the workers must either accept recall or lose their seniority in that plant. If they do accept, they lose seniority in the second plant. Multiple seniority rights are probably carried furthest in contracts between various railroads and the Brotherhood of Railway Clerks. A typical agreement permits a transferred employee to retain seniority in his original "district" and to bump back or apply for open jobs in that district.

Although in most cases of transfer, the worker is, in effect, a new employee with respect to job rights (layoff, promotion, and recall), he almost always will retain his seniority rights with respect to fringe benefits. In other words, his company length of service continues to apply with respect to pensions, severance pay, vacation pay, holiday pay, life insurance, and health insurance.

In cases where transfer involves a move to another labor market area, the displaced worker may face some complex calculations of the relative advantage of moving his family and being at the bottom of the seniority ladder or remaining in the local area and seeking another job. Separation pay, early-retirement benefits, and in some cases accumulated profit sharing or savings through company plans may increase an employee's reluctance to transfer. A number of unions are seeking early retirement with augmented rather than reduced benefits in cases of technologically induced displacement, as a way of reducing the work force and preserving jobs at other plants (see Chapter 8).

As we have shown in Chapter 5, however, interest in transfer will be greatly influenced by the workers' perceptions of the local job market. One of the problems that occurs is that displaced workers may have to decide between transfer and separation pay (including termination of their employment status) before they are fully aware of local employment opportunities. For this reason, unions such as the UAW have sought or agreed to waiting periods before separation pay can be claimed.

RELOCATION ALLOWANCES

An unusual feature in the transfer agreement for the Armour Oklahoma City workers was the provision for moving allowances. The funds were to come from the Armour Automation Fund and would cover the following expenses:

(a) The worker's actual moving expenses (supported by a bill) up to a maximum of $325 (the amount being related to the distance between the two cities, and to the amount of goods an average family might be expected to have).

(b) If he chose to leave his family in Oklahoma City temporarily, he could receive a $5 per day living allowance for the first three months of his employment in Kansas City, or until he decided to move his family, whichever occurred first.

(c) Actual moving expenses back to Oklahoma City up to a maximum of $325 if, any time during the first year of employment in Kansas City, the individual was put on layoff judged by the Automation Committee to be permanent. From this $325 would be deducted any amount received under the $5 per day living allowance previously mentioned.[25]

Moving allowances for transferred production and maintenance workers have been relatively rare, except on the railroads, but are likely to increase in instances where transfer involves a change of

---

25. Armour Automation Fund Committee, *op. cit.,* p. 9. The provision for moving expenses back to the home city in the event of layoff during the first year is probably unique.

residence.[26] One of the more comprehensive plans is contained in an agreement between the Brotherhood of Railway Clerks and the Norfolk and Western Railway Company. Included are at least two days off with pay and free transportation for house-hunting; guarantee by the company against loss in the sale of a home or the cancellation of a lease; household moving costs; traveling and living costs for the worker and his family during the move; and coverage of wage loss on the day of transfer and up to five days thereafter.[27] These provisions are quite similar to those many companies have adopted when executive and professional personnel are transferred.[28]

Some of the 1961 contracts negotiated in the meatpacking industry by the United Packinghouse Workers and the Amalgamated Meatcutters include a provision for paying part of the moving costs. The Swift agreement, for example, establishes a maximum payment of $500. Moving allowances were also negotiated by the United Automobile Workers with the major automobile manufacturers in 1961.

The major limitation of moving allowances is that they apply only to transfers between plants of the same company. Thus, their usefulness is contingent upon the existence of job opportunities in other plants of the same employer.

GOVERNMENT SUPPORT OF WORKER RELOCATION

Proposals have been made in Congress for government measures to accelerate the relocation of some of the long-term unemployed,

---

26. In the nineteenth century, railroad companies, farmers, and others paid passage for immigrants who agreed to work for them. In World War II, also because of labor shortages, there were instances of transportation and moving allowances made to workers hired by defense plants.

27. Bureau of National Affairs, *What's New in Collective Bargaining*, No. 416, Part 1, May 12, 1961. Transfers have a long history in railroading, dating back at least to the Washington Job Protection Agreement of 1936.

28. See American Management Association, *Company Practices in Employee Transfers and Relocation* (New York: The Association, Research Report No. 33, 1954). United Airlines moved three hundred mechanics from the East Coast to the West with benefits very similar to those provided executives. The move resulted from reorganization of United's maintenance operations.

particularly in labor surplus areas. One way of doing this would be government-financed relocation allowances. In the original versions of the Manpower Development and Training Act (in 1961), provision was included for government payment of one-half of "the expenses incurred in transportation of persons and household effects" for relocation of workers who had been unemployed for six months or more, who could not reasonably be expected to find local employment, and who had received bona fide offers of employment of extended duration. Although the objective was only to supplement other measures to help the unemployed, a number of Congressmen, particularly those from states with depressed areas, objected to a program which might result in the movement of better-qualified workers out of such areas. Another objection was that it would be difficult to administer. As a result, the provision was dropped by both Senate and House Labor Committees and was not included in the bill that passed in 1962. Experience under collectively bargained plans may lead to reconsideration of government subsidies for worker relocation.

A bill was introduced in the same session of Congress to amend the Internal Revenue Code to allow income tax deductions for expenses incurred in relocation for the purpose of "obtaining or accepting employment." The bill would also have allowed deduction for capital loss in the sale of a home as a result of a job move.[29] Other recommendations have been to permit deduction from income of a worker's expenses in retraining and to change the tax definition of place of residence so that workers temporarily working away from home can deduct per diem expenses.[30]

The Retraining of Experienced Workers

Almost everyone seems to be in favor of retraining for displaced workers with obsolescent or negligible skills, but there is a great deal of disagreement over where the primary responsibility lies and how retraining should be financed. Some argue that the primary responsibility falls on industry, or on industry in cooperation with

29. Bureau of National Affairs, *Daily Labor Report,* March 28, 1961, pp. A 10–11.
30. Report of Subcommittee on Special Projects, House Republican Policy Committee, August 14, 1961.

the decentralized public school system, to provide the upgrading in work skills needed in the economy. Others contend that, while industry and established community facilities should do all they can, the retraining needs have become so great it is necessary to institute a much enlarged federal program that will underwrite a great increase in retraining, especially for the long-term unemployed.

In discussing the problem on the basis of available data, it is possible to make a broad distinction between retraining for employed workers, either for upgrading or to provide new skills when their jobs are to disappear, and retraining for the unemployed who are having difficulty finding suitable work. This distinction helps in allocating responsibility. Industry has always had primary responsibility for retraining of employed workers, but in our view government (federal, state, and local) has primary responsibility for retraining of the unemployed. One of the questions, of course, is how much coordination and cooperation there should be between government and industry and between the two broad aspects of retraining. For example, how should responsibility be shared for the retraining of employed workers whose jobs are becoming obsolete and whose services companies will not need in the future?

RETRAINING OF THOSE WITH JOBS

Although there are few data on the extent and characteristics of retraining within industry, there seems to be little doubt that formal job instruction of employed persons far exceeds even the most visionary plans for publicly financed retraining of the unemployed. A study by the U.S. Bureau of Apprenticeship and Training of training programs in private nonfarm industry in New Jersey shows that, in 1959, 16 per cent of 38,000 establishments with four or more workers were conducting training programs. The range was from 11 per cent of the firms with 4–19 employees to 82 per cent of the firms with 500 or more workers. Of an estimated 729,000 employees in establishments with training programs, one in nine participated in training during the year.[31]

31. U.S. Bureau of Apprenticeship and Training, "Employee Training in New Jersey Industry," reprinted in *Manpower Utilization and Training* (Washington, D.C.: Subcommittee on Unemployment and the Impact of Automation, House of Representatives, U.S. Government Printing Office,

These data for New Jersey cannot be projected for the economy as a whole to measure the over-all extent of training, but the patterns by industry and size of firm and the techniques used are probably representative of current practices in industry.

In manufacturing industries, larger firms were much more likely to have training programs than smaller firms, but among firms with programs the proportions of employees in the programs did not vary greatly with the size of the firm. Before going further, it should be noted that these statistics include management, safety, and sales training programs; in fact, these types of programs covered more than half of the employees receiving training. Nevertheless, large numbers were also involved in "short-term job-skill," apprenticeship, and technical training courses for production and maintenance workers.

Another major aspect of industry training revealed in the New Jersey survey is the extent to which facilities outside the plant are used.[32] More than half the establishments with programs used facilities outside the plant to supplement training conducted in the plant. Larger companies used outside facilities more frequently than smaller, and manufacturing firms used public vocational-technical high schools more than any other industry group.

Although only a minority of the firms with training had training departments (from 4 per cent of the smallest to 41 per cent of the establishments with 500 or more employees), two out of three used special techniques to encourage participation in the programs. Of the firms with programs, 34 per cent paid tuition and other costs, 28 per cent paid employees for their time, 31 per cent considered completed training in promotions, and 19 per cent guaranteed promotions and raises when training was completed.

1961), pp. 29–76. A subsequent sample survey by the Bureau of Apprenticeship and Training indicates that approximately one-fifth of industrial establishments have some form of apprenticeship or other training programs. See Bureau of National Affairs, *Daily Labor Report,* July 17, 1962, p. A-9.

32. These facilities for manufacturing included vocational schools, mostly public (24 per cent), colleges (16.5 per cent), technical institutes (12.5 per cent), correspondence courses (9 per cent), trade associations (6 per cent), and labor union or joint labor-management facilities (20 per cent). Some used more than one type, but 51.4 per cent of the manufacturing firms used outside facilities.

These proportions are similar for manufacturing and for all industries. Promotion and pay raises on completion of training were used about equally in large and small establishments.

In the New Jersey study, no differentiation was made between training designed for general upgrading of the work force and promotion from within, on the one hand, and training designed to retrain workers whose jobs were being replaced by machines or were otherwise disappearing, on the other. Various reports in the business press and trade journals indicate that many firms are expanding programs to retrain workers for new jobs, but there seems to be no way of estimating how widespread this may be. Many businessmen undoubtedly agree with the point of view expressed by Frank H. Cassell, Director of Personnel Administration of the Inland Steel Company, who said: ". . . retraining makes maximum use of manpower and contributes to the long-range security of the individual. . . . We think this is smart because it minimizes resistance to change, enables us to get production up faster than when people fear they won't keep their jobs, and gives us a quicker return on our investment."[33]

Retraining to prevent layoffs is illustrated by the experience of the U.S. Steel Company when it replaced its old structural mills at its South Chicago works with modern facilities. As a result of retraining, 953 of 1,346 workers whose jobs were cancelled between 1956 and 1960 were transferred to the new mill. Among the more obvious advantages to workers who are retrained and retain their seniority is the protection given to older workers who would have difficulty finding other jobs if laid off. Some of the retraining programs have fairly high age limits. At the Whiting Refinery of the American Oil Company, for example, where 1,800 jobs have been eliminated since 1956, men up to age 58 have been retrained.[34]

Although there is much room for disagreement between management and labor on retraining of workers displaced by automation or other technological change, a sharp increase in collective bar-

33. Quoted in *Wall Street Journal,* August 23, 1961, p. 6.

34. *Ibid.,* p. 6. In large companies, retraining covers an impressive number of workers. General Motors, for example, is reported as retraining more than 7,000 workers in a year. "The Hard Realities of Retraining," *Fortune,* July, 1961, p. 242.

gaining clauses on the subject gives evidence that the principle is becoming more widely accepted. One of the problems is the relative weight to give to seniority and to management's estimate of individual worker capacity for retraining. Some representative examples of contract clauses indicate both the extent of agreement on the principle of retraining and the problems left for management-union interpretation in individual cases:

In case of automation, employees with greater seniority shall be given first opportunity for training on the new machine tools insofar as possible, recognizing capabilities of such candidates for training in the new work. (Griscom-Russell Company and International Association of Machinists.)

In the event such mechanical or electronic office equipment is installed, management shall provide reasonable training arrangements for the employees who were displaced from their positions by such installation in order that such employees may have an opportunity to become qualified as required for newly established jobs on such installations. The balance of the employees whose jobs are discontinued will be given reasonable training in order that they may become qualified to take other jobs in the unit to which their seniority entitles them. (Memorandum of Agreement between the American Can Company and the United Steel Workers of America, December, 1959.)

. . . employees entitled to and making application for positions advertised to work in the Computer Center will be schooled or trained for the positions at the carrier's expense and without loss in compensation to them; also that employees securing positions in the Computer Center desiring to take promotion to other positions for which they have not been trained will be accorded similar treatment and consideration. (Brotherhood of Railway Clerks and the Chesapeake and Ohio Railway Company, 1956.)[35]

The impact and potential of automation have led to some experiments in collective bargaining which provide benefits to others than the members of the contracting local. U.S. Industries, manufacturer of automated machinery, in an agreement with the IAM, late in 1961 set up a company-financed foundation, to be privately administered by the union and the company, that will study retraining and perhaps make grants. Contributions are, in effect,

---

35. The three examples are from the International Association of Machinists, *op. cit.,* pp. 19–20.

royalties on the automated machines that are sold.[36] A similar agreement between the International Brotherhood of Electrical Workers and International Good Music, Inc., sets up a fund based on company contributions of 5 per cent from sales of automated radio station equipment and program services. The fund is being used to pay tuition and fees at established schools for those radio station personnel who are displaced by the new equipment. The U.S. Employment Service conducts the aptitude tests for the displaced workers.[37]

Many companies and unions have also expanded their apprenticeship programs to train employees for new jobs. In some cases, long-standing age limitations have been eased. The Ford Motor Company, which enrolls about 2,000 employees a year in apprenticeship programs, abolished the age limit in 1957 in agreement with the UAW. A seniority employee who can pass the necessary mental and aptitude tests is eligible for apprenticeship training, regardless of age. Points based on length of service are awarded to the seniority employees, improving their standing on the waiting lists.[38]

RETRAINING OF THE UNEMPLOYED

One of the issues in retraining is the determination of the limits of responsibility of management, labor, and the labor-management relationship. Industry could take the position that its responsibility for retraining is limited to providing retraining for employees only when it is unable to find the necessary new skills in the labor market. Many companies, with or without the push of unions, have gone far beyond this, however, and are retraining employees even when it might be less costly to displace workers and hire others with the necessary skills.

Beyond this, when workers are permanently laid off or are about

36. *Wall Street Journal,* Feb. 7, 1962, p. 6.
37. *AFL-CIO News,* June 3, 1961.
38. Ken Bannon and Nelson Samp, "The Impact of Automation on Wages and Working Conditions in Ford-UAW Relationship," in *Automation and Major Technological Change,* Industrial Union Department, AFL-CIO, April 22, 1958.

to be, does a company have any direct responsibility for retraining them for new jobs with other companies? Also, to what extent should a company hire from the ranks of the unemployed those who will need retraining if they are to meet the company's requirements? Generally, companies have not entered either of these areas, although the position with respect to retraining of new hires will depend upon the availability of the necessary skills in the labor market. Apprenticeship programs, for example, are a traditional method of providing training for skilled jobs when the necessary number of journeymen are not available in the market. Also, companies have been training new employees in various technical operations (e.g., computer operators), when workers with such training are not available. Finally, companies may contribute in various ways to community training programs but perhaps cannot be expected to underwrite such programs, except through taxes.

The most publicized case of company-paid training of former employees for jobs in other industries has been the experiment of the Armour Automation Fund Committee in Oklahoma City. Perhaps because of the uniqueness of the sponsorship by a special management-labor committee and the possibility that this might be a trail-blazing experiment in finding a solution for a major social problem, much was expected of the efforts of the committee. The experiment, as it turned out, was a relatively minor effort, rather hastily developed some months after the plant shutdown.[39]

The retraining experience of the Armour Automation Committee proves neither a lack of interest on the part of the unemployed nor an inability to develop successful retraining programs. The committee estimated that three out of five of those without jobs reported for testing and counseling. No information was obtained on how many may have been discouraged from reporting for counseling when they heard that many of the workers were not being recommended for retraining. Even if this were not a factor, the proportion of unemployed who came in for testing is impressive.

As for the 65 per cent rate of "rejection," that is, those who were tested and not offered retraining, there are several explanations. The maximum training allowance authorized by the Automation

---

39. See the discussion of the results of the program in Chapter 3.

Committee was only $150. Many of the unemployed were those with very low levels of education whose only industrial experience had been in nontransferable meatpacking occupations. The occupations for which training was considered most feasible in the area (welding, basic electronics, air conditioning, and auto repair, among others) were beyond the capabilities of many, if not most, of the former Armour workers. Also there was some indication that the State Employment Service, which made the determination of who could benefit from training, was exceedingly careful about those it recommended. The subsequent poor employment record of those who did receive retraining offers apparent justification for this caution. On the other hand, it should not be implied that retraining of workers with little education and obsolete work experience is hopeless. It is quite possible that greater experience with retraining programs will show that these personal limitations are not necessarily a bar to successful retraining.[40]

The Armour Automation Committee recognized the limitations of its approach and commented as follows:

Retraining on a "crash" basis is likely to benefit only a minority of employees in a situation involving middle-aged individuals who have limited formal education to start with.

A carefully planned, continuing education program, promoted and supported by both company and the union, would help employees develop abilities and skills which would improve their positions in the labor market in a time of crisis. . . .

It may be that the displaced employee's best prospect of a new job is to be found upon completing some kind of retraining.[41]

An immediate lesson of the Armour experience seems to be that the costs and complexities of retraining are such that industry is not likely to go much beyond improving the training programs for established employees. Retraining of the unemployed is being left primarily to government, ranging all the way from local school districts to the federal government. At the local community level,

---

40. Functional illiterates can be taught basic reading, writing, and shop arithmetic in a relatively short time.

41. Armour Automation Committee, *op. cit.,* pp. 7, 8, 13. In addition to the Oklahoma City experiment, the Committee has done some work in providing retraining for Armour employees not yet laid off but subject to layoff.

where retraining has its ultimate test, the basic problem is financing. As is often the case in matters of public policy, the communities with the greatest need for retraining for their unemployed are likely to be the ones with the least ability to pay. For this reason, most of those who have studied retraining have advocated state and/or federal assistance in retraining programs for the unemployed.

The precedent for a federal-state system of retraining has long been in existence. Federal aid for vocational education dates back to the Smith-Hughes Act of 1917, with the major amendment being the Vocational Education Act of 1946 (the George-Barden Act). Under the terms of this legislation, funds have been made available to the states for financing instruction in four broad fields —trade and industrial occupations, agriculture, home economics, and distributive occupations. In 1960, there were 3,769,000 individuals enrolled in publicly sponsored vocational education. The cost in 1960 was $239 million; 46.5 per cent of the funds were local, 34.5 per cent were state, and only 19 per cent federal.[42]

Several state governments, including California, Michigan, Ohio, Pennsylvania, and West Virginia, did not wait for further federal legislation to expand retraining for the unemployed. Pennsylvania permanently amended its School Law in 1957 to provide for the vocational training of recipients of public assistance and unemployment compensation. No retraining allowances are made to the individual trainees, however. In 1958, out of 28,000 persons receiving training in state-sponsored programs, about 1,700 were in programs designed for the unemployed. Courses included welding, power sewing, and skills required by the opening of a shoe factory. The state covers the cost of the programs, which are administered by the State Board for Vocational Education. Funds for the program have been severely limited. The 1,700 unemployed receiving retraining in 1958 were only a tiny fraction of the average of 475,000 unemployed in the state during that year.[43]

---

42. House Subcommittee on Unemployment and the Impact of Automation, *op. cit.,* p. 112.

43. Jacob J. Kaufman and Helmut J. Golatz, *Chronic Unemployment in Pennsylvania* (University Park, Pa.: Bureau of Business Research, The Pennsylvania State University, 1960), pp. 15, 97–98.

The State of Ohio in 1961 appropriated $200,000 for a program to retrain unemployed workers. Those who are approved for retraining by the ten-member Worker Training Committee are eligible for unemployment insurance but are required to seek or accept suitable work that will not interfere with the retraining course.[44]

The major test of publicly financed retraining, however, began in 1962 when programs under the Area Redevelopment Act of 1961 began to go into effect and when the Manpower Development and Training Act of 1962 was passed. The former applies only to industrial areas certified as having chronic unemployment and rural areas with very low average income. The Manpower Act is more general and has a potential impact in all states and labor market areas. Its "statement of findings and purpose" includes the following:

The Congress finds that there is critical need for more and better trained personnel in many vital occupational categories, including professional, scientific, technical, and apprenticeable categories; that even in periods of high unemployment, many employment opportunities remain unfilled because of the shortage of qualified personnel; and that it is in the national interest that current and prospective manpower shortages be identified and that persons who can be qualified for these positions through education and training be sought out and trained, in order that the Nation may meet the staffing requirements of the struggle for freedom. . . . It is therefore the purpose of this Act to require the Federal Government to appraise the manpower requirements and resources of the Nation, and to develop and apply the information and methods needed to deal with the problems of automation and technological changes and other types of persistent unemployment.

The Act established a three-year retraining program (July, 1962, through June, 1965), with $419 million allocated for the selection and training of the workers and $16 million for such purposes as planning programs and making manpower surveys. Estimates were that 110,000 would be trained during the first year, 160,000 in the second and 300,000 in the third.

---

44. Bureau of National Affairs, *Daily Labor Report,* August 15, 1961, p. A 13.

256 Unwanted Workers

The U.S. Department of Labor, through the federal-state employment service system, is responsible for testing, counseling, and selecting workers for occupational training. Priority is given to the unemployed and underemployed, including workers in low-income farm families, "who cannot reasonably be expected to secure appropriate full-time employment without training." Employed workers who need job improvement are also eligible, however. Priority in referral for training goes first to those who can be trained for local labor market area jobs and, second, for jobs within the State of residence. Training periods vary from two weeks to 52 weeks. Training allowances go to the unemployed heads of households with at least three years of employment experience.[45]

Two general types of training are permitted. Training in public and private schools is arranged by state vocational education agencies under agreements with the U.S. Department of Health, Education, and Welfare. Priority goes to public schools. Secondly, the Department of Labor develops or arranges for on-the-job training programs, in cooperation with the states, private and public agencies, employers, trade associations, labor organizations, and other qualified industrial and community groups. The Labor Department is responsible for all aspects of on-the-job training programs, although related classroom instruction has to be arranged by agreement with the Department of HEW.

Both federal departments share responsibility in establishing and administering standards for an equitable apportionment of federal funds among the states. Factors considered are the size of the labor force, the amount of total and insured unemployment, and the average weekly unemployment benefits in each of the states.

At the time the Act was passed, there was very little knowledge of the extent of retraining actually needed for re-employment; it is, therefore, fortunate that the Act stipulated a program of

45. The retraining allowances under this Act are discussed in Chapter 8. Training for less than two weeks is permissible when there are immediate employment opportunities, but no allowance can be paid if the training period is less than six days. Youths over 19 but under 22 can receive $20 a week while in training regardless of family responsibility or labor force experience.

research and evaluation both of the impact of retraining and of employer and union practices that influence the mobility and re-employment of workers. These special studies should make it possible not only to evaluate the effectiveness of the present law but also to develop criteria for any extension of the law. Also, since the total job of retraining involves a very large degree of private as well as governmental action, the most significant new contribution that government can make may be the collection and analysis of data that will help introduce more order and sense into the complex world of vocational education. A "clearing house" of information can provide guidance for the employer, the trade union, the vocational school, and the individual worker.

This discussion of retraining has been focused on the experienced worker; consequently we have said little about the very serious problems of more adequate and up-to-date vocational training, as well as more thorough general education, for the youth who are entering the labor market. The predicted 7.5 million who will enter the labor force in the 1960's without completing a high school education, with 2.5 million of these not completing even a grade school education, is a problem of great importance which we do not have the space to discuss. We have also omitted any consideration of various tax proposals to encourage employers to expand their training activities, although we have mentioned tax incentives for individuals.

Area and Regional Redevelopment

Since a significant proportion of long-term unemployment is concentrated in areas of chronic labor surplus, it has been contended that one of the ways in which long-term unemployment can be reduced is to undertake redevelopment programs in these areas. Redevelopment is usually understood to mean improvement of public and private facilities and the attraction of new industry that will employ some of the labor surplus. One of the problems in area redevelopment is the extent to which any gains in employment provide a net reduction of unemployment in the economy. To our knowledge, no one has been able to demonstrate the over-all employment effects of area redevelopment, one way or the other.[46]

In our view, area and regional redevelopment should be supported, but not because it is a major or necessarily an effective
means of solving the national unemployment problem. When the
nation's unemployment rate is running well above a minimum frictional level, shifting industry into depressed areas may have as one
of its main consequences the redistribution rather than the reduction of unemployment. The situation would be quite different when
the economy as a whole is at or near a full employment level;
under such conditions, shifts of industry into areas of labor surplus could then reduce this surplus and be more likely to reduce
over-all unemployment. In some European countries, as noted
later, area redevelopment first became effective in a full-employment economy.

Area redevelopment, however, can be supported on other
grounds. Whenever an area has the potential for redevelopment and
retention of a reasonably balanced population in terms of labor
force skills, it would seem wise as social policy to preserve the
huge investments of capital in homes, stores, public facilities, and
all of the institutions that go to make up a community. Further,
as labor market studies have uniformly shown, the great majority of
people prefer to remain in their "home towns" with all their familiar ties and associations.

It is questionable, however, whether it is possible to "save"
every area that has had a declining industry and many years of
inadequate opportunities for its labor force. It is also questionable
social policy to encourage communities to lure or "pirate" jobs
away from other communities by offering buildings, tax conces-
sions, lower wage rates, and other inducements. Finally, it is questionable economic policy to limit retraining in depressed areas to
locally available jobs. Workers willing to migrate should be eligible

---

46. For general analyses of depressed areas, see Kaufman and Golatz,
op. cit.; National Planning Association, *The Rise of Chronic Unemploy-
ment* (Washington, D.C.: The Association, Planning Pamphlet No. 113,
April, 1961), 44 pp.; Committee for Economic Development, *Distressed
Areas in a Growing Economy* (New York: The Committee, June, 1961),
74 pp.; and William H. Miernyk, *Depressed Industrial Areas—A National
Problem* (Washington, D.C.: National Planning Association, Planning
Pamphlet No. 98, January, 1957).

for retraining and relocation allowances that would enable them to secure jobs in other areas.

Areas (or regions) that have lost industry but have natural locational advantages and can attract new or expanding industries should, in our opinion, be developed, and it is appropriate for government to assist in such development. This, however, is a long-range type of program and must be viewed as peripheral to our immediate question of how to reduce long-term unemployment.

Long-term unemployment is a national phenomenon and exists in areas of expansion as well as in depressed areas. An illustration of this is given by Kaufman and Golatz who present data for 1956, a year in which there was presumably very little cyclical unemployment. They estimate that in Pennsylvania, which has had a large number of chronic labor surplus areas, chronic unemployment (which they define as neither frictional nor cyclical) was 60,000 in 12 depressed areas. The remainder of the state had 42,000 chronically unemployed. Unemployment rates in the 12 areas were double the average rate for the state, and almost 80 per cent of the unemployed in these areas were chronically unemployed compared with about 25 per cent of the unemployed elsewhere in the state.[47]

Chronic unemployment, therefore, is higher in depressed areas but also is substantial outside these areas. Further, when looking at the national picture, the depressed areas probably contain less than one-tenth of the nation's population and labor force, although the exact size depends upon the definition. In a definition that included 21 major labor market areas (out of 150) and 70 smaller areas, the Bureau of Labor Statistics reached this conclusion:

Unemployment in chronically depressed areas accounted for at least one-fifth of total unemployment in the full-employment period of 1956–57. Not all the unemployment in chronically depressed areas was "structural," i.e., the result of long-term changes in the economy. . . . If the rate of unemployment in these areas could have been reduced to the national average, the jobless total would have been roughly a quarter of a million lower at that time.[48]

47. Kaufman and Golatz, *op. cit.,* pp. 13–15.

48. U.S. Bureau of Labor Statistics, *The Structure of Unemployment in Areas of Substantial Labor Surplus* (Washington, D.C.: Joint Economic Committee, Eighty-sixth Congress, Second Session, Study Paper No. 23, January 30, 1960), p. 3.

Thus, if above-average unemployment had been eliminated in these areas, it would have reduced the national level of unemployment by about 9 per cent. Unfortunately, however, there is no assurance that area redevelopment, however desirable for other reasons, would in fact reduce unemployment in depressed areas to the national average.

The above conclusions do not mean that unemployment in depressed areas should be ignored; rather they reflect our conviction that programs designed to reduce long-term unemployment should be available to all unemployed workers, wherever they may be. Lengthy unemployment is just as serious for the individual in an area of high-level employment as in a depressed area. The long-range economic development of depressed areas, however, appears to be desirable if it is based upon careful and intensive analysis of the economic potential of these areas.

The Area Redevelopment Act of 1961 authorized the federal government to spend $4.5 million a year to help finance state and local programs for retraining of the unemployed and underemployed in areas of substantial and persistent unemployment. In addition, $10 million a year was authorized to enable the states to make subsistence payments up to 16 weeks to those undergoing retraining.[49] Compared with the Manpower Act of 1962, this is a relatively modest bill. In our judgment, it is wise public policy because it permits time to evaluate the success of a number of projects and to determine the feasibility of larger-scale area redevelopment.

Brief Review of Policies in Other Countries

In considering national approaches to unemployment reduction, the most useful comparisons are between the United States and the highly industrialized countries of Western Europe with which it shares many political and social traditions. The differences are

---

49. The Act also provided for assistance to designated "redevelopment areas" in the form of (a) grants for the purchase or development of land and facilities for industrial or commercial use, (b) loans and grants to assist in financing the land for and construction of public facilities, and (c) technical assistance in evaluating the needs of a community.

sufficiently great, however, that few would advocate any direct borrowing of European policies and practices without adaptation to American traditions and experience.

Not only are there long-run differences in labor mobility, institutional practices, and degree of government involvement, but also the unemployment situation has differed in recent years: the United Kingdom and most of the countries of Western Europe have had substantially less unemployment than the United States. For this reason alone, policies with respect to reducing unemployment through improved functioning of the labor market and retraining can be expected to differ.

One factor that may contribute to lower unemployment rates in Western Europe is a generally lower level of turnover (intercompany mobility) and, therefore, a lower level of frictional unemployment. This is the opinion of Gladys L. Palmer, who attributes the lower turnover largely to a different tradition with respect to layoffs. As she points out:

While no one in northern Europe challenges the right of an employer to lay off workers, except when legally forbidden as in the nationalized industries in some countries, permanent layoffs seldom occur in practice, and temporary layoffs in nonseasonal industries occur less frequently than in the United States. . . .

. . . it is fair to say that the risk of layoff is a greater threat in the United States, partly because of general acceptance of the idea and partly because of more rapid changes in the structure and location of employment. . . .

. . . In Europe, permanent layoffs reflect an emergency in the history of a business enterprise; temporary layoffs (in nonseasonal industries) are made with reluctance and only after consultation with workers.[50]

Because of different traditions, the parties to collective bargaining in the United States have been much more concerned with questions of layoff and recall procedure, subcontracting, work sharing, and similar issues than have their European counterparts. European employers are accustomed to making decisions designed

---

50. Gladys L. Palmer, "Contrasts in Labor Market Behavior in Northern Europe and the United States," *Industrial and Labor Relations Review*, Vol. 13, No. 4 (July, 1960), pp. 522–524.

to regularize employment and share the work during slack periods.

In spite of these differences, however, workers are displaced in Europe as a result of technological and market changes. The typical European approach is to establish government or government-sponsored programs to retrain, relocate, and place such workers. The whole process is usually called "readaptation." We shall briefly examine some of the major features of government programs in Great Britain, France, and Sweden, and also the program of the European Coal and Steel Community.

GREAT BRITAIN

Great Britain has been attempting to reduce unemployment in areas of labor surplus ever since the Special Areas Development and Improvement Act was passed in 1934.[51] This and subsequent legislation in the 1930's was not notably successful, presumably because of the generally high level of unemployment at the time. Before the end of World War II, the British government had outlined a postwar unemployment policy which essentially called for maintaining a high level of total demand in the economy and for a concerted attack on unemployment in local areas. The latter policy was to have three facets: governmental influence on the location of new enterprises, removal of obstacles to the transfer of workers between areas and occupations, and the provision of training facilities to retrain workers moving from declining to expanding industries.

The basic postwar policy that was adopted, beginning with the Distribution of Industry Act in 1945 and culminating with the Local Employment Act of 1960, has been to persuade and assist industries in the establishment of new plants in regional "development" areas and thus to put the emphasis on moving industry to

---

51. British efforts to reduce unemployment are discussed by William H. Miernyk in "Foreign Experience with Structural Unemployment and Its Remedies," in *Studies in Unemployment* (Washington, D.C.: U.S. Senate Special Committee on Unemployment Problems, 1960), pp. 412–422, and "British and American Approaches to Structural Unemployment," *Industrial and Labor Relations Review*, Vol. 12, No. 1 (October, 1958), pp. 3–19. See also Jean A. Flexner and Ann S. Ritter, "Experience in the Development Areas in Great Britain," *Monthly Labor Review*, May, 1957.

the available workers rather than on relocating workers. As Miernyk comments:

. . . the British Government has done more to influence the location of industrial plants—at least since the end of World War II—than other governments in the free world. . . .

Much has been done to direct work to places of above-average unemployment rather than allowing market criteria to determine the location of industry, which would have necessitated far more vigorous efforts to increase the mobility of labor. It must also be pointed out that if there had been no development area program the problem of congestion in the South of England would be far more serious than it is today.[52]

In spite of the efforts of the Board of Trade, which is roughly equivalent to the U.S. Department of Commerce and which administers the distribution-of-industry laws, the economics of industrial location, as well as noneconomic factors such as personal preference, have meant that unemployment in some areas has remained well above the national average. All of the development areas, however, have shown some improvement.[53]

A major weakness in the British program is the lack of adequate retraining assistance. Government assistance for retraining is still largely limited to ex-servicemen and handicapped workers. Miernyk concludes that retraining of workers for branch plants in development areas could mean that firms would be more likely to relocate in these areas. The United Kingdom, however, does put pressure on unemployed workers by disqualifying for unemployment benefits those who refuse retraining. This policy also exists in France, West Germany, Belgium, the Netherlands, and Switzerland.[54]

---

52. Miernyk, "Foreign Experience with Structural Unemployment and Its Remedies," *loc. cit.*, p. 422.

53. Under the Local Employment Act of 1960, according to the Board of Trade's first annual report required by the law, some 57,000 new jobs were created, with a large proportion in durable goods industries.

54. Phyllis P. Groom, "Retraining the Unemployed: I. European Government Programs," *Monthly Labor Review*, August, 1961, p. 824. The data on retraining in France and Sweden in the following paragraphs are largely from this article.

FRANCE

French workers resist change in either residence or place of work perhaps more than other European workers and certainly far more than American workers.[55] Because of this resistance, the French government puts as much emphasis on moving jobs to the worker as does the British government. The French have gone further, however, with respect to government assistance in retraining.

The French government program, which was adopted in 1954, calls for assistance to areas of relatively high unemployment and underemployment, but requires first that extended regional economic studies be made. When an area is approved by an interministerial committee, government can make loans for land, plant and equipment, and working capital and can also grant up to 20 per cent of the total investment costs of an enterprise. Further, the national government will assist regional development corporations with a 50 per cent tax exemption on investment income and provide government aid to local governments or other organizations, in the form of loans and interest subsidies, for the purpose of acquiring and improving industrial sites and constructing plants for tenant occupancy.[56]

The basic French legislation on vocational training and retraining was passed in November, 1946, and provides for occupational training centers of two types—some 130 community centers run by associations, trade unions, employers, or public corporations and open to all candidates presented by the public employment service and, secondly, special centers to meet the needs of a particular industrial establishment. The Ministry of Labor and Social Security finances the community centers; individual firms finance

---

55. Gladys L. Palmer, *op. cit.*, pp. 526–528.

56. Joint Economic Committee, *Economic Programs for Labor Surplus Areas in Selected Countries of Western Europe* (Washington, D.C.: The Committee, Eighty-sixth Congress, Second Session, U.S. Government Printing Office, December, 1960), table following p. 11. The provisions of French law are similar in many respects to the Area Redevelopment Act of 1961 (U.S. Public Law 87–27). See "Major Provisions of the Area Redevelopment Act," *Employment Security Review,* June, 1961, pp. 3–4.

the special centers. The Ministry contributes part of the cost of instruction in both types of centers and provides subsistence allowances to, and pays for the social insurance of, those undergoing retraining. Some 200 thousand workers received training between 1946 and 1960.

Under the regional development law of August, 1954, financial aid is available to firms in development areas for retraining of their workers, including those who are scheduled for displacement but have been promised employment by other firms.

The Government pays the wages, totally or partially, including the social insurance charges, of trainees and instructors during the training period, as well as the costs of material and training equipment. . . . Between January 1, 1955 . . . and the end of 1959, nearly 200 enterprises received aid from the Government. About 13,000 workers underwent retraining at an average cost per worker of 600 francs. Workers were most commonly retrained in mechanical skills and for occupations in the electrical, textile, chemical, and paper and cardboard box industries.[57]

A weakness of the French program is that it has been, with some exceptions, limited to workers under 35.

SWEDEN

Of all the European countries, Sweden has the most comprehensive program for reducing unemployment and matching workers and jobs. Further, Sweden, more than the other countries, has emphasized encouraging workers to move to jobs. These programs function in the context of over-all national economic planning.

As a small nation with a population of less than eight million, Sweden has been able to place its public employment service, its policies of furthering geographical and occupational mobility, and its policies of stimulating employment under the centralized direction of the Royal Labor Market Board. This Board and its provincial subsidiaries have the following responsibilities: (1) approval of investment in plant and equipment by companies that

---

57. Phyllis P. Groom, *op. cit.,* p. 828. The 600 francs roughly equals $200.

have placed part of their earnings in blocked, tax-free investment
accounts which were established for the purpose of countering
cyclical unemployment; (2) approval of loans to provincial industrial associations for stimulating industrial diversification in
areas dominated by one industry, in rural areas undergoing de-
population, and in areas with restricted employment opportunities;
(3) recommendations to parliament to expand loans and grants to
local governments for short-run public works projects; (4) advising
investors on suitable locations for new industrial plants; (5) operating the public employment service; (6) planning emergency public
works programs to alleviate regional unemployment; (7) management of vocational guidance and rehabilitation services; (8) payment of transportation, subsistence, family, and resettlement allowances to workers who are relocating; (9) selection of unemployed
workers for retraining, a program run by a central board of training, which also has provincial offices; and (10) research and data
collection related to the above responsibilities.[58]

The Royal Labor Market Board, therefore, has been placed in a
powerful position as an overseer of Sweden's full-employment
policy, and it seems to have been successful in using its variety of
powers to keep unemployment close to minimum levels. A number
of factors help account for this success. The most important, perhaps, is the program's comprehensiveness and flexibility, enabling
the Board, on the basis of continuing studies, to stress those
measures needed most at any given time. Secondly, the Board
operates the public employment service, and Swedish workers and
employers use this service as the major means of finding jobs and
hiring workers. Swedish employers report most of their job openings to the Board's local offices and are required to report impending layoffs to the Board usually at least two months before the
layoffs. In the third place, more emphasis is given to worker relocation than to area assistance, thus enabling the Board to avoid the

---

58. The functions of the Swedish Royal Labor Market Board are discussed by Miernyk, "Foreign Experience with Structural Unemployment
and Its Remedies," *loc. cit.,* pp. 426–429; Joint Economic Committee,
Economic Programs for Labor Surplus Areas, loc. cit., Groom, *op. cit.,*
pp. 825–826; and Carl G. Uhr, "Employment Security in Sweden," *Employment Security Review,* October, 1959, pp. 11–14.

high costs and administrative problems of attempting to create "artificially high levels of economic activity at national expense."[59] Workers who relocate are given travel grants and a family allowance for as long as six months if suitable housing is not available.

By providing facilities for retraining both the employed and the unemployed, by permitting retraining for older as well as younger workers, and by making it financially feasible for workers and their families to relocate, the Board is able to facilitate geographic and occupational mobility in directions that strengthen the total economy. In these programs, there is no compulsion for workers to accept retraining or relocation. Unlike the situation in a number of countries, the worker does not lose his unemployment benefits if he does not accept retraining, but if he does participate in retraining he is eligible to receive unemployment benefits for a maximum of 52 weeks. If assigned a job by the employment service during the retraining, the trainee is required to interrupt the course, but such interruptions rarely take place.

Retraining in Sweden, as elsewhere, has the dual purpose of reducing unemployment and meeting shortages in specific skills. While the Central Board of Vocational Training develops and operates the retraining program, the Labor Market Board makes the assessments of employer manpower needs and worker training needs. The retraining can be either in regular vocational schools or on-the-job training in private firms, subject to union approval of schedules and pay rates. The individual courses are administered and certificates are issued by local vocational training committees consisting of manpower experts, named by the county labor board, and representatives of the appropriate unions and employers. In the fiscal year 1960–61, 14,000 workers received training allowances, and it was expected that more than 20,000 would be retrained in 1961–62. In March, 1961, 9,200 persons were being trained at a time when 20,700 persons were registered for unemployment insurance.

59. Joint Economic Committee, *Economic Programs for Labor Surplus Areas, loc. cit.,* p. 15. Area assistance is given in the form of loans, but no national grants are made except for forest conservation. Further, tax incentives are limited to the tax exemptions for the blocked investment funds, whose purpose is the control of cyclical rather than regional unemployment.

THE EUROPEAN COAL AND STEEL COMMUNITY

Article 56 of the 1951 Treaty establishing the European Coal and Steel Community, with Italy, France, West Germany, Belgium, Luxemburg, and the Netherlands as members, took into account the possible displacement of workers through technological change. This article, as implemented, has provided displaced coal miners and steelworkers with separation allowances for up to a year, with a gradual reduction from 90 per cent to 70 per cent of regular earnings; an allowance of 90 per cent of regular earnings during retraining, plus allowances for special expenses; family moving allowances if relocated elsewhere, and a resettlement allowance equal to two months' wages. Workers who retire voluntarily on pension so that other workers can be kept on receive a substantial lump sum in addition to the pension. The Treaty also contains provisions, more difficult to carry out, that are intended to encourage new job opportunities in other industries or in "new and economically sound activities capable of insuring productive employment to the workers thus released."[60]

Because coal mines cannot be moved and steel mills have special locational requirements, the ECSC has concentrated on moving workers to jobs when there are labor shortages. Also, displaced workers have been encouraged to relocate by means of moving allowances. Because much of the migration is across national boundaries, many social problems have developed—language difficulties, poor housing, assimilation into the local community—and, in addition, there have been problems of adjustment at the work place.

The Community, however, has been increasingly successful in facilitating the adjustment of those workers who resettle permanently. The major lessons have been that adequate housing is very important, as is the provision of equivalent wages and working conditions for both foreign and local workers. Experience under the

---

60. Article 56 of the Treaty. For accounts of "readaptation" under the ECSC, see "Obstacles to Labour Mobility and Social Problems of Resettlement," *International Labour Review,* Vol. 76, No. 1 (July, 1957), pp. 72–83, and Miernyk, "Foreign Experience with Structural Unemployment and Its Remedies," *loc. cit.,* pp. 423–426.

ECSC has been useful to other industries as the development of the Common Market in the same countries has led to additional international worker migration.

The problems of relocation and retraining are not easily solved, however. When large numbers of workers are displaced at one time, many have become long-term unemployed. In one area of Belgium, for example, some 7,000 coal miners were displaced between 1958 and 1961. Many had lengthy unemployment because they could not be relocated or were unwilling to move. Further, only a small proportion received retraining because of the limited number of new jobs in the area and because many did not have the educational background for training in the occupations with job openings.[61] The experience of these workers is reminiscent of the experience of the former Armour workers in Oklahoma City. Most of the coal miners, like most of the meatpacking workers, had skills and work experience that were not transferable, many had low levels of education, and many were older workers.

Summary

The problems of reducing long-term unemployment are difficult, although not insoluble. Although any basic solution requires steps that will accelerate economic growth, economic growth will probably not, by itself, place in jobs those long-term unemployed who are in depressed areas or are handicapped in the search for work by age, low levels of education, obsolete skills, or by virtue of being in minority groups. In this chapter we have discussed some of the specific measures open to employers, to joint labor-management action, and to government at all levels to match workers with jobs more quickly and efficiently.

WORK SHARING AND SHORTER HOURS

We have found that work sharing within industry is a temporary and spottily used measure that can have only a minor effect in reducing unemployment. Because of the conflicts it creates between

61. "Retraining Works—for the Fortunate Few," *Business Week,* June 17, 1961, pp. 73–74.

labor and management and between different groups of workers, it is not likely to become a universal practice.

Permanent reductions in hours have been tried in several unionized industries, but there is no sign that a widespread adoption of a shorter workweek will be achieved in the near future through collective bargaining. Unions will press for the shorter workweek only if it can be obtained without loss in take-home pay, and few employers are in a position to accede to such a demand. Further, few American workers seem to have reached the point of wanting to accept the gains of greater productivity in substantially greater amounts of leisure rather than in earnings. Instead of a permanently shorter workweek, the reduction of hours during a workyear through increases in vacations, holidays, and other kinds of paid time off appears to us to be more probable.

Neither the reduction of the standard workday or workweek under the Fair Labor Standards Act nor the adoption of a federally legislated flexible workweek, geared to the level of unemployment, appears to be very likely in the next few years. The former will not gain much support because of general concern about the nation's output during the Cold War. The latter would be cumbersome to administer and would require substantial federal interference in private enterprise. If other measures fail to have much effect on long-term unemployment, however, the demand for shorter hours will become more insistent.

Unions and managements can be expected to increase their efforts and their experiments to provide as much job security as possible without jeopardizing the economic health of the enterprise. There will probably be wider experimentation with such steps as gradual introduction of automated equipment so that work force reduction is accomplished through attrition, guarantees for specified periods against layoff resulting from automation, and establishment of funds to make possible early retirement or guaranteed workweeks when new methods are adopted or equipment installed.

FINDING JOBS FOR DISPLACED WORKERS

For workers who are displaced, both public and private assistance in finding new jobs can be improved. Employers and unions might make special efforts to assist the laid-off workers with early notice, counseling, job information, and personal recommendations. Both can cooperate with an expanded public employment service.

The public employment service is being strengthened and can play a much greater role if given the directives, the funds, and the cooperation of employers and unions. Much more can be done to make information on job openings available over wide areas rather than confining much of it to local communities. Electronic data processing of job information may help bring about enormous improvements in this respect.

THE RELOCATION OF EXPERIENCED WORKERS

Many thousands of American workers migrate to jobs, often at considerable financial sacrifice, but many thousands of others do not because of lack of information and inability to cover the costs. One type of inter-area move is the transfer of workers from one plant to another in a multiplant corporation. Management has not, in general, ceded the right of transfer to bargaining unit employees, but transfer clauses in collective contracts are increasing in number. The most common arrangement is to give workers displaced from one plant preferential hiring consideration as new employees at other plants of the same firm. When operations are moved, however, some unions have obtained the right to have the employees transferred with jobs—with full seniority.

Recent court cases indicate that a worker's seniority may come to be construed as a vested right, existing independently of the life of a collective contract, and applicable even if a plant is relocated. If the Supreme Court has the opportunity to uphold the lower court rulings, more workers will be able to preserve their jobs through transfer, when plants move.

Still relatively rare, other than in transfers of operations, is inter-plant bumping on the basis of company-wide seniority. Because of intra-union problems, company-wide seniority can most easily be introduced by applying it only to those hired after a specified date.

Moving allowances for transferring production workers are still quite uncommon but may be adopted more frequently as companies agree to transfer privileges. As yet, no governmental financial assistance is made available to workers who relocate.

THE RETRAINING OF EXPERIENCED WORKERS

The primary responsibility for retraining of the employed whose skills are obsolescent falls upon private enterprise, but public facilities and financing have been utilized extensively by industry. A study of training in New Jersey industry showed that more than half of the firms with programs used outside facilities, many of them public. In the body of this chapter a number of illustrations have been given of collective bargaining clauses on retraining and of company training programs.

Retraining of the unemployed has been, for the most part, beyond the capacity of private firms and trade unions. The experiment of the Armour Automation Fund Committee in Oklahoma City illustrates the difficulties of privately sponsored retraining for the unemployed. The costs and complexities of retraining for the unemployed suggest that the major burden will fall upon various levels of government—from local school districts to the federal government.

A federal-state system of vocational education has long existed, and is being expanded for the retraining of the unemployed. The Manpower Development and Training Act of 1962 was designed to accomplish this. While some states had established retraining programs for unemployed workers, the federal law has established them in all states.

The Manpower Act is designed primarily for the retraining of experienced unemployed workers who are heads of households, but it is open also to employed workers who need it. Retraining takes place in vocational schools, or the equivalent, and on the job. The Area Redevelopment Act of 1961 provides funds for retraining of the unemployed and underemployed in areas of substantial and persistent labor surplus.

AREA AND REGIONAL REDEVELOPMENT

Area redevelopment, if defined as attracting industry to surplus-labor areas, can only be a partial and probably minor factor in reducing long-term unemployment. As long as national unemployment levels are relatively high and the long-term unemployed are located in labor market areas throughout the country, the relocation of industry is likely to create more of a redistribution than a reduction in unemployment. European experience suggests that area redevelopment will be much more effective after the over-all labor demand in the economy has been greatly strengthened and "full employment" is being approached. Although the economic and social problems of these areas should not be ignored, it would clearly be unwise economic policy to concentrate too much of the national effort on these areas as long as there is widespread long-term unemployment.

GOVERNMENT POLICIES IN OTHER COUNTRIES

Economic and social programs of other countries cannot usually be imported "as is" because of differences in political and economic organization; however, experience under such programs is worth examining for the possible lessons they may teach. The programs in Great Britain, France, Sweden, and the European Coal and Steel Community, which we have briefly reviewed, suggest that government programs for readaptation of workers can have some positive effects. Britain and France have emphasized moving jobs to workers and have had some success in doing so, partly because their governments are more centralized than ours and greater pressure can be exerted on private industry. Sweden and the ECSC have emphasized the movement of workers to jobs; Sweden, particularly, has demonstrated that a flexible, comprehensive, but noncompulsory program of information gathering, retraining, and moving allowances can increase mobility and decrease unemployment.

10

The Problem
in Perspective

IN OUR INTRODUCTION we described the upward trend in long-term unemployment that has occurred since the early 1950's; we discussed the characteristics of the long-term unemployed; and we raised some questions about both the causes of extended jobless-ness and the possible cures. Our case studies have provided detailed evidence for five groups of workers on the relationship between lengthy unemployment and the permanent displacement from jobs, the economic and personal factors that contribute to long-term unemployment and underemployment, and the impact of unemployment on the individual and the family. In the two chapters preceding this one, we went beyond the case studies and analyzed both public and private efforts to reduce long-term unemployment and relieve its burdens.

We have two final tasks. The first is to analyze the causes of the rising totals of long-term unemployment. A correct analysis of these causes, we believe, is an exceedingly important factor in determining the scope and nature of remedial measures. The second task is to propose remedies for the problem of long-term unemployment that are consistent with our analysis of the causes.

274

The Causes of Long-Term Unemployment

In a "perfect" market long-term unemployment would not exist. Unemployment of more than a few weeks would represent either a failure of the economy to provide jobs for those able and willing to work or inefficiencies in the labor market that prevent the matching of qualified workers and available jobs in a reasonable length of time. In a complex, dynamic, and free labor market such as exists in the United States, a certain amount of long-term unemployment is unavoidable.

An appropriate goal of public policy is to reduce long-term unemployment to the lowest level that is consistent with a dynamic and free labor market. Further, in the interest of maximum utilization of manpower and the reduction of personal hardships, socially responsible company, union, and collective bargaining policies would attempt to support the national goal.

The specifics of both public and private policies, however, will be considerably influenced both by what is considered a practicable national goal for the level of long-term unemployment and by the conclusions drawn from an analysis of the causes of such unemployment. The appropriate national goal, in other words, must take into account the causes of long-term unemployment and what would be required to attack these causes.

If, as some allege, much of the lengthy unemployment is "structural"—meaning that the long-term unemployed don't know about, can't get to, are not qualified for, or will not accept available jobs—the chances of substantial reductions in such employment without massive governmental interference in the private economy are poor. The structural hypothesis means that, if long-term unemployment is to be reduced, either the workers' qualifications will have to be raised on a truly grand scale or employment for these workers will have to be subsidized either by payments to employers or direct hiring by the government in a vastly expanded public works program.

If, on the other hand, much of the excess in long-term unemployment is basically not structural but instead the result of a serious lag in aggregate demand—as we shall argue in the following pages—public policy can more realistically and with less violence to the private sector aim for low levels of prolonged joblessness. Interim goals of no more than 0.5 per cent of the labor force with 15 or more weeks of unemployment and no more than 0.2 per cent with 27 or more weeks of unemployment seem reasonable to us on the basis of our analysis in the following pages. In fact, these suggested levels of long-term unemployment are higher than those achieved in 1952 and 1953.

We call them interim goals for the same reason that the Kennedy Administration has labeled a 4.0 per cent level of total unemployment as an interim goal. The assumption is that a lower level of total unemployment *may be* inflationary unless special measures are taken to improve the functioning of the labor market. Our interim goals for long-term unemployment, however, are based not only on our argument that higher levels of aggregate demand can greatly reduce long-term unemployment but also on our assumption that a number of policies, including government support of retraining, strengthening of the public employment service, and various collective bargaining provisions, can have some effect on the level of unemployment if they are accompanied by a rising rate of aggregate labor demand. In other words, we would expect specialized public and private labor market measures to push the potential level of long-term unemployment *below* what would otherwise be possible without creating a serious inflationary situation.

In order to support our viewpoint, however, we need to show that much of the long-term unemployment is *not* predominantly a structural problem.

IS LONG-TERM UNEMPLOYMENT STRUCTURAL?[1]

The "structural transformation theory" attributes the higher unemployment in good years to an accelerated rate of technological

1. In this section we have drawn upon James W. Knowles and Edward D. Kalacheck, "Higher Unemployment Rates, 1957–60: Structural Transformation or Inadequate Demand," study paper prepared for Joint Economic Committee, Eighty-seventh Congress, First Session (Washington, D.C.: U.S. Government Printing Office, December, 1961), 79 pp.; Richard C. Wilcock and Walter H. Franke, "Will Economic Growth Solve the Problem of Long-term Unemployment?" *Proceedings of the Fourteenth Annual Meeting* (Madison, Wis.: Industrial Relations Research Association, 1962), pp. 37–49; and Wilcock and Franke, "The Unemployment Boom: Is Growth the Answer?" *New Leader*, April 29, 1962, pp. 13–15.

and market changes in the economy. The process of transformation in the economy has brought a large-scale shift from blue-collar occupations and goods-producing industries to white-collar occupations and service industries. It has also meant higher rates of worker displacement from jobs in declining industries and occupations and growing numbers of workers with obsolete work experience who are not qualified for the occupations that are expanding. More workers have to change jobs involuntarily, and the process of adjustment is slower; thus, in effect, the level of frictional unemployment is higher, at least temporarily.

A variation of this theory has been advanced by Clarence Long, who argues that the "upward creep of prosperity unemployment" is primarily the result of the "social minimum wage" exceeding the personal productivity of a growing number of workers.[2] He contends that the social minimum wage, which he defines as "the wage below which custom, employer ethics, or law forbids workers to be employed," maintains at least a constant relation to the average wage. As the average wage and the level of productivity increase, those with little education and low skill are likely to fall below the rising level of the social minimum.

What is the evidence that structural factors are the basic cause of the higher rates of unemployment? For one thing, the rate of worker displacement has apparently increased in recent years. This is illustrated by a trend toward higher layoff rates in manufacturing during prosperity periods—1.0 per one hundred employees in 1947, 1.3 in 1953, and 1.6 in 1959. In broad one-digit industry groups which had an absolute decline in employment between 1947 and 1953 (agriculture and mining), the loss of jobs was 2.8 per cent of 1947 total employment. The comparable loss between 1953 and 1959—for agriculture, mining, manufacturing, and transportation and communication—was 4.7 per cent of 1953 total employment. In 27 two- and three-digit industry groups with absolute employment declines—such as bituminous coal, meat products, canning and preserving, bakery products, apparel, rubber products, and interstate railroads—the loss of jobs was 4.0 per

---

2. Clarence D. Long, "A Theory of Creeping Unemployment and Labor Force Replacement," paper delivered before Catholic Economic Association, St. Louis, Mo., December 27, 1960.

cent between 1947 and 1953 and 5.1 per cent between 1953 and
1959. Establishment data would almost certainly show higher rates
of displacement. Displacement from declining occupations also
appears to have accelerated since 1955.

A crucial question, of course, is what has caused the acceleration
in the rates of displacement. Is it a faster pace of technological
change and thus of accelerated manhour productivity? Knowles
summarizes the evidence:

Output per man-hour has increased during the postwar period as a
whole at a rate faster than the average for the past 50 years. The
postwar rates, however, are not particularly high when compared
with other periods of expanding employment and mild recessions such
as the 1920's. In manufacturing, the rate of advance has been slower
during the postwar period than in the 1920's, while some nonmanufacturing industries have shown faster rates of advance than in the
1920's. The evidence for 1957–60 is ambiguous, but, on balance,
indicates no acceleration compared to the 1948–57 period.[3]

Furthermore, even if productivity had accelerated, there is no
clear evidence that this would have been responsible for higher
unemployment rates. Historically, at least over long periods of
time, employment has increased most rapidly when productivity
has increased rapidly.

Technological change does not necessarily cause widespread or
prolonged unemployment. While the introduction of new machines,
new products, and new methods of transportation invariably means
the elimination of firms, occupations, and jobs, it also creates new
firms, industries, occupations, and jobs. Further, the increased
productivity that results can also mean expanded demand and output and shorter hours for the work force.

Another facet of the structural-transformation argument is that
the shifting of job opportunities to white-collar, service, and professional occupations has contributed to the higher unemployment
rates. The evidence does not support this relationship. If the structural argument were correct, there would have been unusually
heavy concentrations of unemployment among blue-collar workers
and in goods-producing industries and, at the same time, above-

---

3. Knowles and Kalacheck, *op. cit.,* p. 77.

average levels of job vacancies and unusually long workweeks in the expanding occupations and industries. Instead, unemployment in recent years has risen among all groups of workers. Further, the composition of unemployment in the prosperity years has been very similar to its composition in recession years.

Those who advance the structural argument also speak of increased immobility of labor, but there is little evidence to demonstrate that mobility rates have been declining. Various studies, including our own, show that interindustry and interoccupational mobility continue to take place on a considerable scale, even for workers with relatively low levels of education. While it is argued that institutional factors such as the job security measures obtained through collective bargaining and the expansion of private pension plans, health and welfare plans, and the like tie workers to their employers, it has not been demonstrated that voluntary mobility has lessened in periods of comparable labor demand. On the contrary, it may be argued that a decline in voluntary mobility has resulted primarily from the lag in aggregate demand which has reduced alternative job opportunities.

Geographic immobility might seem to be more of a problem because of the depressed areas, yet there has been no evidence that workers are any less willing to make geographic moves than in earlier years.[4] For example, in each of the prosperous years of 1953, 1957, and 1960, (using data for the month of May) unemployment rates in labor surplus areas exceeded the national rate by about the same proportion.[5] Also, our case studies show a very substantial degree of willingness to move under the spur of economic necessity and in spite of attachment to the "home town." Reluctance to break local ties, the financial burdens and risks of moving, and lack of information about out-of-area jobs do limit geographic mobility and mean higher unemployment than might otherwise exist. Nevertheless, geographic immobility has not been a major contributing factor in the *rising* rates of total or long-term unemployment.

4. *Ibid.*, pp. 40, 77.
5. Council of Economic Advisers, "The American Economy in 1961: Problems and Policies," Statement before the Joint Economic Committee, U.S. Congress, March 6, 1961, pp. B 4, B 15.

IS DEMAND DEFICIENCY THE CAUSE?[6]

The proponents of the structural-transformation theory implicitly assume that, in prosperity periods, we have had adequate rates of aggregate spending and economic growth. The rival theory, or "aggregate-demand theory," holds that economic growth has not been adequate. Instead, the basic problem is a "chronic slack" in the economy, a "growing gap between what we can produce and what we do produce."[7] The aggregate-demand theorists contend that dislocations in the labor market are not significantly different than they were earlier in the postwar period when unemployment was at a 4 per cent level or lower.

We can test the aggregate-demand theory by measuring the consistency of the relationship between increases in demand, on the one hand, and changes in employment and unemployment, on the other. First, we shall examine the relationship between increases in real gross national product (GNP) as a measure of higher labor demand and associated rates of decline in total and long-term unemployment during postwar economic recovery periods.

In examining data for the recoveries after the 1948–49, 1953–54, and 1957–58 recessions, we find that in the first year of each recovery increases in GNP were of about the same magnitude. Further, declines in total unemployment were closely related to the increases in output. In the first year of each recovery, total unemployment declined between 3.3 and 3.7 per cent for each percentage increase in real GNP.

Second, we find that while long-term unemployment closely followed total unemployment, there was a delayed reaction between GNP and long-term unemployment in each economic upturn. In each of the second years, long-term and very long-term unemployment declined much faster in relation to economic recovery than in the first years. For the two-year periods, we find a fairly consistent relationship. For each percentage increase in GNP, long-term unemployment fell 7.0 per cent in 1949–51, 6.6 per cent in 1954–56, and 6.7 per cent in 1958–60.

---

6. This section summarizes data in our articles listed in footnote 1.
7. Council of Economic Advisers, *op. cit.*, p. 9.

In the third place, we find that when total unemployment expanded, long-term joblessness increased at a more rapid rate, but when total unemployment declined, long-term also fell at a more rapid rate (see Figure 1, p. 10).

The relationships between long-term unemployment and total unemployment seem to refute Long's argument that the social minimum wage prevents re-employment of the long-term unemployed. His argument is valid only if one assumes that labor demand in the prosperity periods was adequate and that unemployment at such times was entirely frictional. The consistent nature of the declines in long-term unemployment in the three recoveries suggests the possibility that if the total rate of unemployment can be reduced to, say, 4 per cent, long-term unemployment will approximate the levels previously achieved. This historical relationship does not suggest any decline in employer willingness to hire the long-term unemployed when labor demand rises over a period of time.

The only major evidence of a change in the relationship is that long-term unemployment reacted more slowly to economic recovery in the early stages of the 1958–59 and 1961–62 upturns than it did in earlier recoveries. At this writing, it is too early to say whether this change in the relationships was temporary or symptomatic of a permanent change. The slow decline in long-term unemployment between 1961 and 1962 may reflect the relatively slow pace of the economic recovery.

The analysis of the GNP-unemployment relationship discussed thus far ignores changes that occur over time in such variables as the civilian labor force, size of the armed forces, and average hours of work. We therefore inquire next into the relationship between short-term economic growth and the utilization of the total labor force.

The relationship between the increase in GNP and net employment change, shown in Table 17, is very similar in the first two recovery periods even though the growth rate was quite different. In each case, approximately 80,000 new full-time equivalent jobs were created by each billion-dollar increase in GNP. In both cases, the unemployment rate was about 4 per cent at the end of one

Table 17
Relation of Changes in Real GNP to Changes in Employment,
Four Postwar Recoveries

Changes in Employment and GNP	Recovery Periods			
	IV '49–IV '50	III '54–III '55	II '58–II'59	I '61–I '62
1. Change in employment and size of armed forces (seasonally adjusted)	2,620,000	2,510,000	2,020,000	1,210,000
2. Equivalent employment change attributable to change in hours of work[a]	470,000	380,000	570,000	(no change)
3. Net employment change (line 1 + line 2)	3,090,000	2,890,000	2,590,000	1,210,000
4. Change in GNP (billions of 1954 dollars)	38.6	35.4	39.4	35.0
5. Per cent per quarter	3.2%	2.4%	2.4%	2.0%
6. Increase in GNP per increase in job (line 4 ÷ line 3) in dollars	12,500	12,200	15,200	28,800
7. New jobs per $1 billion increase in GNP ($1 billion ÷ line 6)	80,000	82,000	66,000	35,000

Source: U.S. Department of Labor, *Monthly Report on the Labor Force,* and U.S. Department of Commerce, *Survey of Current Business,* various dates.

[a] Equivalent employment change is obtained by multiplying the average increase in hours by the number employed and dividing by the average hours of work per week.

year. In the 1958–59 recovery, however, only about 66,000 and in the 1961–62 recovery only about 35,000 new full-time equivalent jobs resulted from each billion-dollar increase in real GNP. The smaller effect of changes in GNP on employment in the first year of the 1961–62 recovery seems to reflect more rapid advances in productivity. Under these circumstances, the modest pace of the recovery (only 2.0 per cent per quarter) was clearly inadequate. The 1961–62 recovery was the weakest of the postwar recoveries in its first year, and the unemployment consequences of this weakness emphasize the importance of an accelerated rate of increase in national output in order to create jobs and reduce long-term unemployment.

Other evidence gives additional support to the contention that the basic problem is the level of aggregate demand. As summarized by Knowles:

Real gross national product increased at a considerably slower rate in 1957–60 than in 1948–57, though the growth of productive capacity did not slow, and in fact probably accelerated. . . . The rise in unemployment was particularly sharp among inexperienced workers, the group subject to the fewest wage and mobility constraints. The absence of any unusual concentration of unemployment in 1957–60, studies of interindustry mobility, and the high level of geographic mobility . . . all of these factors indicate that if an adequate number of jobs had been available, workers would have sought them out, regardless of their geographic or industrial concentration.[8]

None of the above is meant to deny the existence of structural problems in the form of workers who have obsolete skills, inadequate job qualifications, or are located in the wrong place. We do take the position, however, that these problems can be met more successfully in the context of a rising aggregate demand for labor.

THE PROBLEM IN THE SIXTIES

The foregoing analysis shows that most of the *increase* in the level of long-term unemployment during the fifties can be attributed to a lag in demand. The prospects for reducing the level of long-term unemployment thus depend in the first instance upon maintaining a generally high level of economic activity.

Long-term unemployment, however, is not the result of any one cause. Even if the rate of economic growth were to accelerate somewhat in the years ahead, a number of general economic and population trends indicate the problem of keeping long-term unemployment at tolerable levels is likely to persist or even become more difficult.

One factor likely to increase the difficulty of keeping unemployment at minimum levels during the sixties is the expected rapid increase in the size of the labor force. Although labor force projections are at best imprecise, the estimates of both the Bureau of the Census and the Bureau of Labor Statistics indicate that the labor force will increase at a more rapid rate during the current decade than it did during the 1950's: whereas the increase was only about 12 per cent during the fifties, a 20 per cent increase is

---

8. Knowles and Kalacheck, *op. cit.*, p. 79.

predicted during the sixties. Further, while the total population increased faster than the labor force during the fifties, the reverse is expected during the sixties.

In addition to a more rapid growth in the labor force, there may be a faster pace of automation and technological change during the 1960's, necessitating complex labor market adjustments. As we have shown previously, involuntary displacement from jobs has been increasing, and the chances are that a rising displacement rate would accompany a more rapid rate of technological change. Whether the result would be higher levels of long-term unemployment would depend upon both the ability of the economy to create jobs and the ability and willingness of workers to make drastic shifts in occupation, industry, and location.[9]

Finally, in assessing the prospects for minimizing long-term unemployment in the 1960's, it is necessary to take account of the anticipated relationship between economic growth and employment. The major problem during the last half of the 1950's was that of sustaining economic recoveries for periods long enough to reduce total and long-term unemployment to tolerable levels.

What are the prospects for the sixties in maintaining economic expansion at rates high enough and for periods long enough to absorb increases in the labor force and in productivity? The data in Table 17 suggest that output will have to expand more rapidly than in the fifties in order to create the same number of new jobs. Clearly, an *accelerating* rate of economic growth will be required to keep long-term unemployment at low levels. Even an accelerating growth rate, however, should be accompanied by an expansion of special efforts to help those workers who are most disadvantaged in the labor market.

A Coordinated Approach to the Problem

The only satisfactory solution to the problem of unemployment is putting the jobless back to work. But unemployment has proved

---

9. For a more extensive discussion of the effects of labor force and technological changes on the prospects for employment and unemployment in the 1960's, see Ewan Clague, "A Profile of Unemployment in the Early 1960's," paper presented at Forty-fifth Economic Conference, National Industrial Conference Board, May 18, 1961, 14 pp. (mimeographed).

to be a persistent problem, and whatever steps are taken, short of a highly planned and managed economy, they will fall short of maintaining high levels of employment at all times. Fluctuations in economic activity and structural changes in the economy will continue, as they have in the past, to produce unemployed, and sometimes "unwanted," workers.

REDUCING LONG-TERM UNEMPLOYMENT

In any program to reduce long-term unemployment, we would argue that it is neither necessary nor desirable for government to "make work" on any large scale or to pay subsidies to private employers to hire the long-term unemployed. Government-subsidized employment for the sole purpose of creating jobs, we believe, would not only be grossly inefficient in allocating labor but would also seriously endanger the freedom of choice in the labor market. It is our contention that the basic governmental policy to bring about a reduction in lengthy unemployment should be to stimulate an accelerated rate of economic expansion through appropriate fiscal and monetary measures.

The failure of such expansion to occur would seriously weaken the effectiveness of the public and private labor market programs which we discussed in Chapter 9 and evaluate briefly below. If a faster pace of expansion does occur, however, this will not only create jobs but will also mean that programs to improve the functioning of the labor market will have greater impact. Our reasoning, which is based on our case studies and our analysis of national trends, is that economic expansion creates the new jobs but special programs help prepare workers for the new jobs and assist in the matching of workers and jobs.

Perhaps the most frequently mentioned remedy is a general shortening of the hours of work, in the form of shorter days, weeks, or years. The difficulty with the shorter-hour solution to long-term unemployment, however, is that there is no guarantee that shorter hours *per se* will create more jobs. Shorter hours in the form of work sharing (that is, shorter hours with less total pay) can mean more jobs, but it is not a very satisfactory solution and is not likely to be accepted by very many workers for very long.

Shorter hours can be widely accepted only if they mean fewer hours without reduction in pay. To have a favorable impact on unemployment, shorter hours with the same pay require increased productivity so that total output will be as high in the shorter hours as it was previously. Shorter hours based on productivity increases may create more jobs to the extent that the higher productivity stimulates demand for either capital or consumer goods.

In our view, therefore, shorter hours for the most part must come about in a piecemeal fashion whenever and wherever productivity changes make it possible. Employers and unions can contribute to potential employment expansion by adopting shorter hours whenever warranted by productivity changes. Such shorter hours can be taken in shorter workweeks or in longer vacations, more holidays, or "sabbaticals" that would reduce the length of the work year.

In general, we advocate leaving shorter hours to the decisions of labor and management. A careful study of possible changes in the Fair Labor Standards Act is warranted, however, to see whether it is practicable to vary the standard workweek as a countercyclical device. The United Automobile Workers have proposed an automatic reduction in the standard workweek, under the Fair Labor Standards Act, whenever unemployment exceeds a given rate. The cost of maintaining weekly wages would be covered by a federal fund built up through a payroll tax. A simpler solution, however, might be to raise the required overtime premium during high unemployment. The premium could be increased and decreased by small amounts in the multiplier (1.5 times the regular wage, 1.6, 1.7, and so forth). This by itself might reduce the average workweek substantially, particularly in the early stages of recovery when lengthening of the workweek reduces the number of new jobs available to the unemployed. A longer workweek during 1961 was one of the factors that kept unemployment rates on a high plateau close to 7 per cent until late in the year.

Much can be done, through both public and private efforts, to assist displaced workers in finding jobs. Our case studies show the extent to which laid-off workers are on their own, and they make a clear case for much more extensive assistance. Assuming enough jobs exist, the process of matching unemployed workers and available jobs can be speeded when workers have early notice of layoff, job information on both area and out-of-area jobs, and letters of recommendation. Employers and unions can work out procedures, and sometimes financial assistance, that will smooth the shift of displaced workers into other occupations and industries. Cooperation of private committees and the public employment service has been tried and could become an established practice, particularly when whole plants or large departments of establishments are closed.

The recent expansion of the federal-state employment service system may have a positive effect on the more efficient relocation of workers in the labor market. If it can obtain significantly greater cooperation from employers and unions, the public employment service should be able to increase its effectiveness in referring workers both in and between labor market areas on the basis of job qualifications, capacity, and equal opportunity. We advocate an interarea and interstate clearance of job-opportunities information at *all* occupational levels.

The public employment service has also begun to play a larger role in the labor market as a result of the Manpower Development and Training Act of 1962. This Act should significantly improve and accelerate the process of labor market adjustment. In our view, publicly supported retraining has as much justification as publicly supported education. Retraining will not create jobs, but it will assist in the process of needed upgrading of the labor force.

The original version of the Manpower Act included a provision for financial assistance in the relocation of workers; we think it unfortunate that this provision was dropped by both the Senate and House Labor Committees. One of the major lessons of the 1950's is that geographic mobility needs to be facilitated in order to obtain an efficient allocation and full utilization of manpower. Both Sweden and Great Britain have found that relocation allowances are of substantial assistance to both workers and employers, particularly in an expanding economy.

Proponents of area redevelopment programs object to encouraging workers to leave labor surplus areas. However, it is not necessarily inconsistent to advocate worker relocation and also to support area redevelopment. Our case studies convince us that the great majority of workers will seek local jobs for a reasonable period of time, and many who do leave will return to the home town when job opportunities improve. It would appear to be short-sighted not to encourage unemployed workers to migrate to areas of better job opportunities. The provision of relocation allowances, with suitable safeguards, would appeal primarily to the long-term unemployed, who deserve every opportunity to secure satisfactory employment.

Relocation of workers need not be limited to government assistance or to movement of workers out of depressed areas. Interplant transfers and company-wide seniority are two means that might be more widely used in maintaining jobs for many workers who might otherwise be permanently laid off. Collectively bargained plans to expand worker training and education for those who are still employed may also improve the job chances of many workers if and when they are displaced. The Armour and ABC workers who had skills and training applicable to a number of industries were significantly more successful in their job search.

Other programs would help the long-term unemployed in a more indirect fashion. For example, comprehensive federal legislation on fair employment practices, which would cover discrimination based on race, creed, color, and age, would help reduce the labor market disadvantages of minority groups who are, as we have shown, overrepresented among the long-term unemployed. We recognize, however, that fair employment practices legislation is only part of the story. Any substantial reduction in discrimination requires not only "equal opportunity" policies on the part of employers and unions but also effective administration of such policies.

Also of indirect assistance would be greater coordination of government manpower policies. Miernyk, for example, has suggested a Cabinet Committee on Employment and Unemployment which could develop a unified labor market policy and provide some coordination among the various agencies whose actions and investigations influence job placement, job training, and employment practices.[10]

---

10. William H. Miernyk, "Labor Market Lessons from Abroad," paper for Fourth Annual Social Security Conference, the University of Michigan, January 23, 1962.

RELIEVING THE BURDENS OF LONG-TERM
UNEMPLOYMENT

Even a faster rate of economic expansion combined with a comprehensive program of retraining, relocation, and other assistance
to the long-term unemployed would not eliminate all long-term unemployment. Further, there are no guarantees that expansion will
be adequate or that special programs could cover all contingencies.
For these reasons it is important to strengthen both public and
private programs designed to provide income to those who suffer
from prolonged joblessness.

The basic mechanism through which the unemployed receive
support is the federal-state system of unemployment insurance.
The system falls short in a number of respects in adequately meeting the needs of the long-term unemployed.

Tests of the adequacy of unemployment insurance benefits indicate that benefits generally replace less than half the net wage
loss and fail to cover nondeferrable expenditures fully, particularly
for primary breadwinners. While low benefits are of concern to
all of the unemployed, they result in particularly difficult situations
for the long-term jobless because of the difficulty of postponing
"deferrable expenditures" over long periods of time. Adoption of
federal benefit standards seems to be the only hope of bringing
about desirable improvements. A federal standard that would result in benefits of at least 50 per cent of earnings for the large
majority of beneficiaries does not appear to be excessive. This
might be accomplished gradually by adopting the federal standards
for maximum benefits proposed in the Employment Security
Amendments Bill of 1961. States should also consider changes in
their benefit provisions that would favor primary earners, such as
providing dependency allowances or varying maximum benefits
with the number of dependents. In fact, in the absence of federal
standards, either of these two provisions would relieve some of the
most serious burdens arising from inadequate benefits.

A more serious problem for the long-term jobless is the limited
duration of benefits. Substantial numbers of the unemployed are
jobless for periods far beyond their eligibility for benefits, during
both recession and prosperity. Of the estimated 2.2 million unem-

ployed who were not receiving benefits in January, 1961, for example, about half a million were persons who had exhausted their benefit rights.[11] Also, large proportions of the displaced workers in our case studies were still without jobs long after they had received their last unemployment insurance checks.

The temporary extension of unemployment insurance benefits during recessions is only a partially satisfactory approach to income maintenance for the long-term unemployed. Long-term unemployment is not limited to recessionary periods. Further, emergency extension of benefits tends to undermine the insurance principle of making benefits available as a right. When extended benefits are not a permanent part of the system, contributions in anticipation of needs do not build up the necessary funds.

The problem, therefore, is how to provide greater protection, as a matter of right, to the long-term unemployed without sacrificing the insurance character of unemployment compensation. Further, if benefits are made available to the long-term unemployed in both recession and prosperity, how can the risk be minimized of workers' taking compensation when they could find jobs? Our proposals for meeting these problems are as follows:

1. Establishment of a *permanent* federal program of extended benefits to certain workers who exhaust their regular state benefits. At least some federal responsibility can be justified on the grounds that the states can do little to control the extent of long-term unemployment and should, therefore, not be burdened with the entire cost. Further, competition among the states to keep costs low is likely to result in slow progress in improving duration provisions if changes are left solely to state action.

The federal government could meet the entire cost of the extended benefits or it might match state-provided extended benefits on a fifty-fifty basis.[12] The benefits might be financed by increasing the payroll tax on employers and increasing the taxable wage base. Although it runs counter to social insurance principles,

---

11. Richard A. Lester, *The Economics of Unemployment Compensation* (Princeton, N. J.: Princeton University Press, 1962), pp. 125–126.

12. Lester suggests a program of federal matching with the states. See *ibid.,* p. 127.

financing part of the federal share out of general revenues could be justified as a social cost to the country as a whole.

The federal government, we believe, should participate in the financing of extended benefits from the twenty-seventh through the fifty-second week. Analysis of exhaustions under the TEC program in the 1961 recession shows that a 39-week limit on benefits is far from sufficient in periods of relatively high unemployment. Our case studies indicate that in nonrecession periods most of the unemployed who find new jobs obtain them within a year. The job prospects of those who have not found jobs in that length of time are very low, and for them unemployment insurance cannot be viewed as a between-jobs source of income. Their services are so little in demand that they are members of the labor force only in a marginal sense, and sources of support other than unemployment insurance would appear to be more appropriate.

Eligibility for extended benefits should be more strict than for regular state benefits. The Kennedy proposal for limiting federal benefits to workers who have employment in half of the weeks in the three years prior to unemployment would limit benefits to workers with a substantial and sustained attachment to the labor force. Benefits would then tend to go to primary breadwinners who are generally in greatest need when unemployed for extended periods. States could still, of course, extend benefits during recessions beyond the twenty-sixth week on the basis of their own eligibility requirements without federal participation.

Extended benefits should be made contingent upon the unemployed worker's participation in an occupational training course, if one is offered and available to him. Voluntary migration of the worker to an area with more promising employment opportunities might also qualify him for extended benefits. These tests of availability and suitability for employment would help to safeguard the program from malingerers.

2. The federal government should contribute financially to the state general assistance programs on a matching basis similar to the special assistance programs. There does not appear to be a good case for distinguishing between the two types of programs in the financial arrangements. Since even with extended benefits some of the unemployed will exhaust their benefits, an adequate general

assistance program is required to meet such needs and underpin the unemployment insurance system. The matching grants should be contingent, of course, upon the states' making payments available to the needy unemployed.

3. We also propose study and consideration of some other possible changes in the federal-state unemployment insurance system. States might reexamine their eligibility requirements with a view to tightening them to exclude from the benefit rolls workers with only "casual" attachment to the job market. Also, after more experience with the program of allowances for retraining the unemployed under the Manpower Development and Training Act of 1962, consideration can be given to the feasibility of making retraining allowances a permanent part of the unemployment insurance system.[13]

As a final governmental measure appropriate to relieving the individual burdens of long-term unemployment, we would suggest more experimentation than has occurred thus far with countercyclical public works programs to try to provide jobs when unemployment is high or rising. Although many economists are dubious about the propriety of public works programs as a countercyclical device, we think the 1962 Kennedy proposal for standby authority to trigger public works programs to stem recessions should be given a try.

Most of the above suggestions have already been proposed in some form and considered in bills introduced in the Congress. Controversial as many of them may be, we believe the findings of our case studies demonstrate the urgency of adopting these provisions. Further, their adoption would provide a base of minimum protection for the long-term jobless that would make supplementary efforts in the private sector of the economy more feasible and meaningful.

Supplemental unemployment benefits, for example, could become a more important device for meeting the economic needs of some of the long-term jobless. Experimentation would be worthwhile in making severance pay more of an instrument than it has been for developing a new career. Perhaps more easily and effec-

---

13. See *ibid.*, pp. 126–129 for detailed recommendations on other issues in unemployment insurance.

tively than those of government, private resources can be used for such matters as extension of fringe benefits to the unemployed and the provision of early retirement pensions to older workers who have difficulty finding appropriate employment. Further, provisions for advance notice of permanent layoffs could be negotiated with some hope that a period of time before separation could be used constructively in preparing for the adjustments that would be required.

Programs of these types have inherent limitations, as we noted in Chapter 8; nonetheless they can offer important supplementary protection if a solid base of minimum income protection is available to the unemployed.

Conclusion

In conclusion, it is our view that a program of economic recovery should include, as an essential and coordinate part, a program of governmental assistance to workers and employers in the process of labor market adjustment. Programs of retraining, relocation, and improved nondiscriminatory placement services will make a contribution of their own in reducing total and long-term unemployment. Finally, since these programs can improve the efficiency of the labor market, they make it possible for public policy to have a more ambitious goal with respect to noninflationary levels of total and long-term unemployment.

The Kennedy administration has spoken of an "interim goal" of 4.0 per cent, based on the conclusion of the Council of Economic Advisors that the high levels of unemployment have been primarily the result of inadequate demand. If sustained economic growth should be achieved, we believe that noninflationary levels of unemployment *below* 4.0 per cent and long-term unemployment of 0.5 per cent or lower are attainable through carefully tailored programs of retraining, relocation, and job placement, buttressed by effective fair employment practices legislation and by labor-management programs that supplement and strengthen the government programs.

Government expenditures required to make these programs successful cannot possibly be measured because of the unknown variables involved in the pace and scope of economic growth. It seems highly likely, however, that the savings in unemployment insurance benefits and in public assistance and the additional revenues resulting from the income created by new jobs would be far greater than the government expenditures on retraining programs, employment service expansion, and the like. Increases in tax revenues resulting from the new jobs might alone offset the additional expenditures. A careful study of the expenditures and revenues associated with the programs we have discussed is certainly warranted.

Finally, we believe that retraining, relocation, and job placement services will, if accompanied by job-creating economic expansion, make it much more feasible both to reduce long-term unemployment to minimal levels and to strengthen programs of income maintenance for those who under any set of circumstances may become long-term unemployed. Even without the assistance of accelerating economic expansion, however, the American economy surely has the wealth and resources to provide an acceptable level of income for those workers whose services the economy at any given time is not able to utilize.

▶ APPENDIXES

Some Notes
on
Methodology

The purpose of these notes on methodology is to provide details on both the procedures and the reliability of results of the displaced-worker surveys in each of the five communities. These notes will supplement the brief description of the study design presented in Chapter 2.

Survey Procedures

For the Armour plants, we defined the survey populations as all of the bargaining-unit production and maintenance workers who at the time of the plant shutdowns were eligible for severance pay. They were "seniority" employees who had worked for Armour for at least a year. For the ABC plant in Peoria, the survey population consisted of all the hourly-paid production and maintenance employees, the foremen, and the salaried office workers up through first-line supervisors who were on the payroll during the week prior to the in-plant survey. Names and addresses for all workers in the survey populations were obtained from company payroll data.

In addition, the companies provided, for each individual, data on personal characteristics and wage rates.

In Peoria, only about 2 per cent of the workers quit before the shutdown occurred and no workers were on layoff as of the date the list of employees was compiled. In the four Armour plants, virtually all who were working when the closings were announced remained on the job until final layoff. Two hundred of the 460 Oklahoma City workers, however, had been on layoff for some months before the shutdown was announced. These 200 were designated the "early-layoff group" and were not included in the in-plant or personal-interview surveys. Because they were still employees when the announcement was made, we did obtain data from them in the mail-questionnaire survey. These data, however, were analyzed separately from those received from the "final-layoff group" of 260 persons. In the other three Armour plants, only about 20 per cent of the workers eligible for the survey had been on layoff at the time of the shutdowns, and they were not treated separately either in data collection or in analysis.

THE IN-PLANT SURVEYS

The in-plant surveys conducted in Peoria and Oklahoma City prior to the shutdowns provided few procedural problems. In both cities, a company official was assigned the task of scheduling the "interviews" and given the responsibility for seeing that appointments were kept. Groups of about 15 workers each met with us during working hours and on the company premises. The purposes of the survey and the procedures to be followed in filling out the form were explained, and each person then filled out the entire form at his own pace. With our graduate assistants we supervised the "interviews," answered questions, and assisted those who had difficulties in reading or writing. Between 30 and 45 minutes were required to complete the form.

The schedules were completed by all of the eligible workers with the exception of those absent during the survey period and a few who refused to participate. Workers on jobs that were difficult to leave were interviewed at their work place or just before or after their shift. Two and one-half days were required to complete the survey in Oklahoma City and four and one-half days in Peoria. The in-plant survey was completed about three weeks before the plant closed in Oklahoma City and about a month before the closing of the Peoria plant.

MAIL-QUESTIONNAIRE SURVEYS

The mail-questionnaire forms with prepaid return envelopes were sent to the entire roster of names provided us by the companies. Except in Oklahoma City, the initial mailing was made approximately one year after the plant shutdowns. In Oklahoma City, because of a deadline for submitting a report to the Armour Automation Committee, the mail survey began about four and one-half months after the plant closed. In each city two follow-up mailings at about ten-day intervals were made to those who had failed to return the form. The response rate on these three mailings was as follows in each city: Peoria, 76.8; East St. Louis, 79.5; Columbus, 64.3; Fargo, 74.8; and Oklahoma City (final-layoff group), 78.1 per cent. Returns were received from 67 per cent of the early-layoff group in Oklahoma City.

A personal follow-up of nonrespondents to the mail questionnaire was conducted in connection with the interview survey in each city. The interview samples included a random sampling of nonrespondents who were asked to complete the mail questionnaire form at the time they were interviewed. When their completed forms are added to the mail returns, the total response for each city becomes: Peoria, 85.0; East St. Louis, 82.1; Columbus, 70.9; Fargo, 78.5; and Oklahoma City, 96.3 per cent. Thus, in each city, data on post-shutdown experiences are available from a very large majority of the displaced workers.

The age, sex, and race distributions of the survey populations, the mail respondents, the nonrespondents who were interviewed, and the total interview samples are shown in Table 18. In all five cities, the workers who completed the mail questionnaire conform closely to the total group of displaced workers in age, sex, and race distribution. On these important determinants of post-shutdown experience, therefore, the mail returns are representative of the total group of displaced workers.

Table 18

Distribution of Laid-Off Workers by Age, Sex, and Race—Total Work Forces, Mail Questionnaire, and Personal Interview Samples, Five Cities

	TOTAL PLANT WORK FORCE		RETURNS BY MAIL		NON-RESPONDENTS CONTACTED		TOTAL RESPONDENTS		INTERVIEWS COMPLETED	
	No.	Per Cent	No.[a]	Per Cent	No.	Per Cent	No.	Per Cent	No.	Per Cent
AGE										
East St. Louis										
Under 45	754	46.5	598	46.8	21	50.0	619	46.9	48	48.5
45 and over	867	53.5	679	53.2	21	50.0	700	53.1	51	51.5
Columbus										
Under 45	212	51.8	142	55.0	12	44.4	154	54.0	37	50.0
45 and over	197	48.2	116	45.0	15	55.6	131	46.0	37	50.0
Fargo										
Under 45	165	43.3	126	44.4	7	50.0	133	44.6	35	50.0
45 and over	216	56.7	158	55.6	7	50.0	165	55.4	35	50.0
Peoria[b]										
Under 45	325	58.5	244	57.3	32	69.6	276	58.5	118	60.2
45 and over	230	41.5	182	42.7	14	30.4	196	41.5	78	39.8
Oklahoma City[c]										
Under 45	76	31.0	59	31.4	14	28.6	73	30.8	34	31.0
45 and over	170	69.0	129	68.6	35	71.4	164	69.2	77	69.0
SEX										
East St. Louis										
Men	1,286	79.3	1,012	78.5	29	69.0	1,041	78.2	68	68.7
Women	335	20.7	277	21.5	13	31.0	290	21.8	31	31.3

Columbus										
Men	353	88.5	224	85.2	26	96.3	250	86.2	64	86.5
Women	56	11.5	39	14.8	1	3.7	40	13.8	10	13.5
Fargo										
Men	318	83.5	236	82.8	12	85.7	248	82.9	60	85.7
Women	63	16.5	49	17.2	2	14.3	51	17.1	10	14.3
Peoria[b]										
Men	435	78.5	328	77.2	36	78.3	364	77.3	135	68.9
Women	119	21.5	97	22.8	10	21.7	107	22.7	61	31.1
Oklahoma City[c]										
Men	197	80.0	150	79.8	39	79.6	189	79.7	89	80.0
Women	49	20.0	38	20.2	10	20.4	48	20.3	22	20.0
RACE										
East St. Louis										
White	688	42.4	521	40.4	25	59.5	546	41.0	54	54.5
Negro	933	57.6	768	59.6	17	40.5	785	59.0	45	45.5
Columbus										
White	374	91.4	240	91.3	26	96.3	266	91.7	68	91.9
Negro	35	8.6	23	8.5	1	3.7	24	8.3	6	8.1
Peoria[b]										
White	509	91.7	396	93.0	38	82.6	434	91.9	168	85.7
Negro	46	8.3	30	7.0	8	17.4	38	8.1	28	14.3
Oklahoma City[c]										
White	156	63.0	122	64.9	30	61.2	152	64.1	71	64.0
Negro	90	37.0	66	35.1	19	38.8	85	35.9	40	36.0

[a] Eighteen unknown by age; one unknown by sex.
[b] Excludes 115 short service and office salaried employees from the figures for TOTAL PLANT WORK FORCE. Figure includes 13 persons who did not complete the in-plant questionnaire and were, therefore, not included in the mail survey.
[c] Excludes 14 persons from the figure for TOTAL PLANT WORK FORCE who were still working for Armour at the time of the survey.

Respondents to the mail questionnaire in East St. Louis, Columbus, and Fargo who at the time of the survey lived more than 100
miles from these three cities were sent an additional questionnaire.
Only one mailing was made and returns were received from 41 of
the 64 in the sample, or 64 per cent. It cannot be assumed that
those who responded are representative of all migrants. The data
received from them should be viewed as only a rough approxima-
tion of the post-shutdown experiences of workers who migrated.

THE INTERVIEW SURVEY

The interview surveys had two major purposes. One was to obtain from a representative group of workers in each city information that could not be obtained through a mail questionnaire. The
other was to check the reliability of the mail-questionnaire results. In addition, we wanted the samples to contain a sufficient
number of individuals with certain characteristics so that reliable
comparisons could be made between such groups as men and
women, old and young, and white and Negro.

Because budget limitations precluded the full attainment of
each goal, compromises were necessary. For example, reliability
of the mail-questionnaire returns could best be checked by interviewing only nonrespondents. Doing so, however, would bias the
interview results on items not included in the mail survey. Also,
comparisons by major variables could be maximized by selecting
equal numbers of persons in each subsample or stratum, but again
the representativeness of the interview sample would be reduced.

The interview design used in each city varied with the populations to be sampled. In Oklahoma City, interviews were conducted
only with a sample of the final-layoff group. Since the population of
that group was relatively small, all nonrespondents who could be
located were included (49 persons). The remainder of the 111
interviews were with respondents and were stratified by sex, race,
and age. The numbers in the strata were calculated in such a way
as to make the total interview sample identical to the total work
force on sex, race, and age characteristics. Within each stratum,
those to be interviewed were selected randomly.

The interview design in Oklahoma City maximized the reliability of the mail-questionnaire data because, except for the nine non-respondents who could not be located, data on the mail-questionnaire items were obtained from everyone. The interview sample, however, overrepresents nonrespondents. Since the nonrespondents, on the average, had less unemployment than respondents, the interview results probably understate the difficulties occasioned by the shutdown.

Because of report deadlines, the sample design for the interview surveys in the other three Armour cities had to be chosen before the mail surveys were complete. It was not known, therefore, how many nonrespondents there would be or who they would be. On the basis of partial mail returns in East St. Louis and Columbus, we attempted to select a sample that would consist half of respondents and half of nonrespondents. For Fargo, the sample had to be selected before any response to the mail survey had been received. Because of this timing problem and the high response rate in each of the cities, only a little over a third of the 243 interviews in the three-city study were with nonrespondents. Nevertheless, sufficient nonrespondent interviews were obtained to allow comparisons with the mail-questionnaire data.

In addition to the stratification by response status, the East St. Louis sample was stratified by sex, race, and age and the samples for Columbus and Fargo by sex and age. The Columbus work force contained only a few Negroes and Fargo none, and for this reason race was not used as a stratification factor in those cities.

Two factors influenced the size of each subsample or stratum. The first was the known distribution of the work forces by sex, race, and age. The other was the anticipation that these characteristics would be important determinants of post-shutdown experience; since the budget limited the total number of interviews, we wanted to make sure that the subgroups were large enough to allow reliable comparisons.

Since the proportions above and below age 45 were relatively equal in all three cities and since the numbers of white and Negro in East St. Louis were also relatively equal, it was decided to seek equal subsample sizes for these groups. Too few women had been employed in any of the plants to justify equal subsamples of men and women. In order to have sufficient interviews with women for purposes of analysis, however, the decision was to set up proportionate samples of men and women in Columbus and Fargo and a more-than-proportionate sample of women in East St. Louis.

A result of these decisions is that the distribution of interview respondents by age, sex, and race differs slightly from the distribution of both total workers in the plants and the mail-questionnaire respondents. Only a few of the differences are at all substantial, however, and these occur primarily in the East St. Louis sample (see Table 18). Compared with the original population and the questionnaire respondents, men are underrepresented and women overrepresented in the East St. Louis interview sample; in the same sample, white workers are more heavily represented than Negroes. The only other sizable difference occurs in the Fargo sample, where workers 45 years of age and over are underrepresented.

These differences, it should be noted, refer only to the proportions found in the several age, sex, and race subgroups and have no bearing on the degree to which each subsample represents the population of its group. For example, the fact that the East St. Louis interview sample has a smaller proportion of men than the East St. Louis work force does not mean that the interview subsample is in any way inadequately representative of East St. Louis men. In other words, since the subsamples were chosen randomly from the relevant population, they are subject only to the usual random sampling errors.[1]

For the three cities combined, the most serious bias in the interview sample results from an underrepresentation of Negroes. As in Oklahoma City, the result is that the interview data probably understate post-shutdown problems.

Because the Peoria shutdown differed from those of the Armour plants in a number of respects, the interview design also differed.

---

1. See the section on sampling errors below. Another source of error is the use of alternates in some subsamples. Although this error cannot be precisely assessed, it is assumed that it is of small consequence, both because the alternates were chosen randomly and because their use had virtually no effect on the age-sex-race distribution of the samples. The reduction in the proportion of Negroes between the original and completed interview samples in East St. Louis is the result of the lack of alternates in one of the subsamples of Negroes and the greater difficulty of locating Negroes for interviewing.

First, the shutdown was announced further in advance than in the other cities. It was anticipated that the advance notice would make it possible for a number of workers to line up new jobs before the plant closed, and we wanted an adequate number of them in the sample. Twenty-six persons indicated in the in-plant survey that they had already lined up new jobs. Since the number was small, we decided that all should be interviewed. We succeeded in obtaining interviews with 21 of them.

Peoria also differed from the Armour cities in that salaried office workers were included in the interview portion of the study. Interviews were obtained from 22 of them, three of whom were also in the job-lined-up group.

The other special sampling problem in Peoria was that of Negroes. The plant employed only 46 Negroes, 43 of whom were less than 45 years old. A random sampling of the entire work force would probably have yielded only a few Negroes. We therefore set a goal of interviews with 28 Negroes under 45 and obtained that number through random sampling of the 43 possibilities.

Sixty-eight of the 196 interviews, therefore, were held with the salaried persons, Negroes, and those who had lined up jobs. The other 128 interviews were obtained after stratifying the remaining population by age, response status, and length of unemployment. The categories used were (1) under age 45 and age 45 and over, (2) respondents and nonrespondents to the mail questionnaire, and (3) those with less than six months of unemployment and those unemployed six months or more at the time of the mail survey.

Each stratum was sampled randomly. The number in each group was selected to produce a total interview sample with approximately the distribution of the total work force in age, mail-questionnaire response status, and length of unemployment. Also, in determining the size of each subsample, account was taken of the proportions with these characteristics in the separate subsample of salaried, Negroes, and those with jobs lined up.

The result of the interview design is that the sample overrepresents persons with jobs lined up before the shutdown, salaried persons, and Negroes. The sample is large enough, however, so that the bias has a minimal effect on the interview data.

The characteristics of persons in the interview samples in each of the five cities are summarized in Table 18. In the important variables of sex, age, and race, the interview samples conform closely to the total population, with the exceptions noted in the above discussion.

THE 1962 RESURVEY

Because of the great amount of very long-term unemployment found in the original surveys, we decided to resurvey the displaced workers in the spring of 1962 to determine what changes had occurred in labor force status, jobs, and sources of income since the original surveys.

Questionnaires were mailed to the 2,629 workers in the five cities for whom we had responses on the original surveys. After two follow-up mailings, returns had been received from almost 75 per cent. A limited follow-up of nonrespondents by phone and home visits was conducted in each city. An attempt was made to contact each nonrespondent who was still in the local area, but rather severe budget limitations made it impossible to search out the hard-to-find among the nonrespondents. Nevertheless, the mail and personal follow-up returns resulted in completed forms from over 85 per cent of those eligible for the study, a rather phenomenal return for a study conducted so long after the shutdowns. The high response rate on this as well as the original surveys probably is a function of the serious personal consequences of the shutdowns for the majority of the workers and their resulting willingness to cooperate in anything that might even remotely be related to assistance to them.

PROCESSING OF DATA

Both the in-plant surveys and the interview program in Peoria were under the direct supervision of the authors. In each of the four Armour cities, the interview program, although under our general supervision, was directed by a member of the economics faculty at a university in the local area. Interviewers in all five cities were graduate students or faculty members at the same schools. We gave the interviewers a short but intensive training session, and additional training and supervision was provided by the faculty supervisors.

The in-plant, mail-questionnaire, interview, and resurvey data were coded at the University of Illinois by graduate students under our direction. Randomly selected 10 per cent samples of each set of data were recoded by someone other than the original coders to ensure that there had been no systematic errors introduced into the coding. The coded data were then punched on IBM cards for machine recording and tabulation. Every precaution possible was taken, within the limits of the time and resources available, to ensure accuracy in the collection and processing of the data.

Reliability of the Results

Two of the major problems of data reliability arise from the degree of nonresponse in mail-questionnaire data and disproportionate representation of some groups in interview samples. Comparisons of mail-questionnaire and interview data and weighting of the data by response status and various personal characteristics demonstrate the effects of nonresponse and disproportionate representation on the reliability of our data.

COMPARABILITY OF MAIL-QUESTIONNAIRE
AND INTERVIEW DATA

The mail-questionnaire and interview data on length of unemployment for East St. Louis, Columbus, and Fargo are shown in Table 19. Column 1 under each city shows the results obtained when the interview data are not adjusted for disproportionate representation of sex, race, and age groups in the sample. Column 2 shows the results when the data in each sex, race, and age stratum in the sample are weighted in accordance with the occurrence of these groups in the original work forces. The effects of the weighting are very small. In most cases the result is not changed by more than one percentage point and the largest change is three percentage points.[2] Column 3 presents the data on length of un-

---

2. It should be noted that when the interview data for each of the three cities are combined for a total, the result is affected by whether or not the data are weighted to take account of the differences in the sizes of the three plants. Since most of the interview data used in the book are qualitative, the data were presented without weighting by plant size.

Table 19
Percentage Distribution of Laid-off Workers by Number of Months of Unemployment, East St. Louis, Columbus, and Fargo

Months of Unemployment	East St. Louis				Columbus				Fargo			
	INTERVIEW		MAIL QUESTIONNAIRE		INTERVIEW		MAIL QUESTIONNAIRE		INTERVIEW		MAIL QUESTIONNAIRE	
	Un-weighted (N = 99)	Weight-ed[a] (N = 99)	Un-weighted (N = 1331)	Weight-ed[b] (N = 1331)	Un-weighted (N = 74)	Weight-ed[c] (N = 74)	Un-weighted (N = 290)	Weight-ed[b] (N = 290)	Un-weighted (N = 70)	Weight-ed[c] (N = 70)	Un-weighted (N = 299)	Weight-ed[b] (N = 299)
	(1)	(2)	(3)	(4)	(1)	(2)	(3)	(4)	(1)	(2)	(3)	(4)
Less than 3 months	17	17	14	15	42	42	38	38	36	33	29	31
3–6 months	10	10	10	10	20	20	22	23	24	24	26	25
7–12 months	50	52	58	56	35	35	39	37	34	37	40	39
Over 12 months	23	21	17	18	3	3	1	2	6	6	4	4
Unknown	—	—	1	1	—	—	—	—	—	—	1	1

Source: Mail questionnaire and interview data.
[a] Weighted by sex, age, and race.
[b] Weighted by respondent and nonrespondent status.
[c] Weighted by sex and age.

employment obtained from the mail-questionnaire respondents, and column 4 shows the effect of weighting-in the data from non-respondents obtained during the interview. Again, weighting changes the results only slightly; in most cases, the change is only about one percentage point. Although nonrespondents had sub-stantially less unemployment than respondents, the high response rate on the mail survey greatly mitigates the effect on the mail-questionnaire data. Consequently, the bias in the mail-question-naire data due to nonresponse is quite small.

Finally, by comparing column 1 with column 4, the differences between the unweighted interview and mail-questionnaire data can be noted. Here the differences are larger, and the mail-ques-tionnaire data indicate more unemployment than the interview data. This is due to the overrepresentation of nonrespondents in the interview samples.

Because the mail-questionnaire data (which include data from nonrespondents who were interviewed) appear to have less bias than the interview data, the mail data have been used in the book whenever available. Also, the mail data are not weighted because the effects of weighting are so small. As noted earlier, the inter-view data probably understate to a small degree the magnitude of post-shutdown problems.

The Oklahoma City interview data are biased in the same direc-tion as the three-city data. The mail-questionnaire data have little or no bias for the final-layoff group because responses were ob-tained from nearly everyone in that group.

Finally, the Peoria interview data, because nonrespondents are not overrepresented, appear to be an accurate representation of the entire work force.[3] A comparison of interview and mail data on length of time required to obtain the first post-shutdown job (the item most directly comparable in the two surveys) shows the re-sults in Table 20. The largest difference between the two sets of data is less than two percentage points—the interviews, therefore, confirm the mail-questionnaire results. Comparisons of other items included in both the mail-questionnaire and interview surveys show no greater differences.

---

3. The interviews include data from a very small group of office salaried workers not included in the mail questionnaire data.

Table 20
Peoria Interview and Mail Data Compared on Time Required
to Obtain First Post-shutdown Job

Months to First Job	Interviews	Mail Questionnaire
	Per Cent	
Less than 3 months	56.0	54.6
3–5 months	14.5	16.1
6–8 months	14.5	13.9
9–11 months	3.5	3.4
12 or more months	11.5	12.0
	100.0	100.0

Although the compromises necessary in the design of the interview samples resulted in some undesirable bias in the interview data, the study results are not seriously affected. Since the bias, where it occurs, is in the direction of understating post-shutdown problems, and since the data show widespread and serious problems, the findings based on interview data can be viewed as conservative. The mail-questionnaire data appear to be free of serious bias.

SAMPLING ERROR

The probable sampling error in any of the findings reported in the community studies varies among the cities and with the particular percentages or proportions reported. The sizes of the interview samples in each city, however, were selected so that the maximum sampling error, as measured by the standard error, associated with any computed percentage (such as the per cent unemployed) would be no greater than 5 percentage points. The Peoria and Oklahoma City samples were designed to give smaller sampling errors.

Although it is not strictly appropriate to apply probability sampling theory to the mail-questionnaire data, since the mail respondents are self-selected rather than randomly selected, the high response rate in all of the cities greatly reduces the danger of doing so. We have, therefore, computed standard errors for the mail-questionnaire samples, fully realizing that they deviate by

some unknown (but probably small) amount from the true
sample variation. Table 21 shows the maximum standard error
for both the mail-questionnaire and interview data in each city.

Table 21
Maximum Standard Error for Data, Five Cities

City	Mail Questionnaire Samples	Interview Samples
	Per Cent	
East St. Louis	0.6	4.8
Columbus	1.6	5.2
Fargo	1.3	5.4
Oklahoma City	0.6	3.5
Peoria	1.0	2.9

The calculations of standard error are based on the least favorable percentage distribution, namely, a fifty-fifty split in a dichot-
omy. When the actual figures deviate from equal proportions, the
sampling error decreases. Also, no allowance is made in the computations for the possible effect of sample stratification in reducing
the sample error. In most instances, therefore, the actual sampling
error is likely to be well below the figures shown above.

Other tests of data reliability were made. For the three cities,
for example, we made a person-by-person check of the data obtained by mail questionnaires and personal interviews where we had
obtained similar data in both schedules. The comparison shows
highly consistent results from the two data sources, suggesting that
the methods of data collection as such did not bias the results.

Finally, in our interpretations of the survey data, we have attempted to limit major conclusions to findings that are clearly significant statistically.

Survey
Schedules

Five different schedules, with some variations, were used in the community studies. The questions used in these schedules are presented in the following pages, but with the layout simplified in order to conserve space. The schedules are:

1. In-plant questionnaire (used in Peoria and Oklahoma City for interviews with workers prior to layoff).
2. Mail-survey questionnaire (used in all five cities; the ABC mail questionnaire was revised for the Armour studies).
3. Personal interview schedule (used in all five cities for post-shutdown interviews; the ABC schedule was revised for the Armour studies).
4. Special mail questionnaire for migrants (used in East St. Louis, Columbus, and Fargo).
5. Mail questionnaire for resurvey (used in all five cities).

Variations in questions between the ABC and Armour studies and between the three-city and Oklahoma City Armour studies are shown by indicating which questions apply only to specific studies. When no designation is given, the questions were used in all cities listed in the heading.

A. *Employment Experience*

1. What is your present job with Armour (ABC) [job title or classification]?
2. How long have you been on this job?
3. What job have you held longest at Armour? (at ABC?)
4. How long were you on that job?
5. (Oklahoma City) How many years have you been employed by Armour altogether?
6. (Peoria) How did you find your first job with ABC? (check *one*)

   Applied at the gate, told about it by State Employment Service, heard about it through newspaper ad, heard about it through a friend or relative, other (please specify).

B. *Plans After Leaving*

7. When you leave which of the following will apply to you? I already have a job lined up (check this only if *sure* you have another job); I am looking for a job now or will be very soon; I plan to take some time off and then look for work (if you check this one, about how long will you wait before looking for work? _____ months); I plan to retire and not look for work; I plan to do housework at home and not look for another job in the next year or so.

C. *Job Ratings*

1. On the following characteristics of jobs, how do you rate the job you have now?

   Pay (wage or salary), interesting work, impression of people you work with, immediate supervision, working conditions, use of your training and education, impression of company as a place to work, retirement plan.

   (Peoria only) Variety in the work, and other fringe benefits.
   The answer categories are: Good, Fair, Poor, and Very good.

2. A lot of things are involved in any job. For each of the following, please check whether it is *very important, fairly important,* or *not important* TO YOU in ANY job you might have. What the job pays (wage or salary); how steady the employment is (few or no layoffs); whether it is interesting work (type of work you like); whether job makes use of your training and education; working conditions (light, heat, ventilation, safety, etc.); your chances of promotion (to a job requiring a higher level of skill); what the retirement or pension plan is like. (Peoria only) Whether job has variety (not monotonous); what your fellow workers are like; what your immediate supervision is like (that is, supervisors you report to directly); the reputation of the company as a place to work; what other fringe benefits are like (health and hospitalization, vacation plan, holidays).

D. *If you have a job lined up, complete the following:*

1. What is the job? (title or description)
2. Where will the job be? (city and state) (company)
3. How did you hear about this job? (check one)
   Through friends or relatives, through State Employment Service, just went out and applied, saw an ad in the paper, other (specify).
4. Are you satisfied with this job change? Yes, No, Don't know.
5. Compared to your present job—
   Is skill and training required:
   Higher, Lower, About same, Don't know;
   Will your pay be:
   Better, Worse, About same, Don't know;
   Will the working conditions be:
   Better, Worse, About same, Don't know;
   Will you like the type of work:
   Better, Worse, About same, Don't know.
6. In deciding to accept this job you've lined up, you had to consider a number of things. Please check whether each of the following was *very important, fairly important,* or *not important to you* before you decided to *accept* it. For any of these you don't know about, check "don't know."
   [The job factors used here are the same as in question C(2) above.]

E. *If you are looking or will look for another job, complete the following:*

1. How are you going about looking for a job? (Check *all* answers that apply)

Using the State Employment Service, applying directly to a company (or companies), reading the want ads, I expect help from friends or relatives, I expect some help from Armour (ABC), I expect some help from the union.

(Questions 2–5 for Oklahoma City):

2. Who do you expect to be of the greatest help in finding a new job? Please number in order of where you expect the greatest help—1 for greatest help, 2 for next greatest help, and so on.

The company, the union, the Oklahoma State Employment Service, friends or relatives, other (what?).

3. Do you think you could find a job that will make use of your skill and experience at Armour? (check *one*)

No; Yes, in the Oklahoma City area; Yes, but I will have to go to another area.

4. You may have had some jobs outside of meatpacking which lasted for some time (in other industries or in the armed forces). If so, list below the two jobs where you had the *most experience.*

Job title; what the company made or did; how many years were you on that job?; what was the last year you worked on that job?

5. Do you think you could find a job that will make use of any skills or experience you have had on jobs other than at Armour? (check *one*)

No; Yes, in the Oklahoma City area; Yes, but I will have to go to another area.

6. Where are you looking for work? (or where *will* you look?) (check *all* that apply)

Oklahoma City (Peoria) and vicinity; elsewhere in Oklahoma (Illinois); outside of Oklahoma (Illinois); particular cities, other than Oklahoma City (Peoria), where I will look—.

(Questions 7–11 for Oklahoma City):

7. Do you plan to move away from the Oklahoma City area after this plant closes? Yes, No. If "Yes," where do you plan to move? (City or town, state) Do you expect to be able to find a job in that area? Yes, No.

8. If you had this choice, which would you do: (check *one*)
   Move to another city (200 or more miles away) for a meat-packing job at the same pay you now get; or take a meat-packing job in Oklahoma City at 40 cents an hour less than you now get?

9. If you had this choice, which would you do: (check *one*)
   Take a job outside of meatpacking in Oklahoma City at 40 cents less an hour than you now get; or move to another city (200 or more miles away) for a job outside of meat-packing at the same pay you now get?

10. Would you take a job in another area (200 miles away) at about the same pay if the moving costs for you and your family were paid? Yes, No.

11. If moving costs were *not* paid, would you take a job in another area (200 miles or more away) if it pays 40 cents an hour more than your present job? Yes, No.

12. Where will you *prefer* working?
    Oklahoma City (Peoria) and vicinity; elsewhere (where?).

13. Please list up to three types of work (occupations) you are looking for *and* you think you have a chance of finding. (Example: roustabout in oil field, truck driver.)

14. (a) For your first choice, what are your chances of a job in this occupation? Fair, Good, Poor, Very good.
    (b) Where are your chances better? Oklahoma City (Peoria) and vicinity; elsewhere (where?).

15. We are interested in your *best guess* about your next job. Do you think your pay will be: better, worse, about same? *Other than pay,* do you think your next job will be: a better job, a worse job, about same? Do you think your working conditions will be: better, worse, about same?

16. What type of work or occupation do you consider your *regular* or *usual* line of work?

17. What are the best places to work in or near Oklahoma City (Peoria)? (list in order) Best, next best, next best.

18. Do you plan to apply for work at any of these places: Yes, No.

19. Are there any places in or near Oklahoma City (Peoria) you would *not* want to work? Yes; No; if "Yes," where?

20. Have you applied or do you plan to apply for a job with Armour (the parent company of ABC) in another area? Yes,

No. If "Yes," do you see any possibility of such employment?
Yes, No.
21. Have you put in applications for work with *any* companies?
Yes, No. If "Yes," please list them *in order:* (asked to list
three choices)
22. What is your best guess on how long you will be unemployed?
Less than 1 month, 1 or 2 months, 3 to 6 months, 6 months
or more.
23. (Peoria) In looking for a job now or very soon, you will
consider a number of things about any job you might be offered. Please check how important each of the following will
be *to you* before you *take* or *accept* a job.
[The job factors and response categories used here are the
same as in question C(2) above.]

F. *If you plan to retire and don't plan to look for work, answer
the following:*

1. Why do you plan to retire now? (check any of these that apply
to you)
Because I have reached retirement age; because I don't think
I can find a suitable job; other (please explain).
2. If this job were not ending, when *would* you have retired?
(month, year)

G. *If you plan to do housework at home and not look for work
for a year or more, answer the following:*

3. Why are you not going to look for work? (check any of these
that apply to you)
Personal reasons (for example, needed at home); because
I don't think I can find a suitable job; other (please explain).

H. *Personal Data (everyone answer)*

1. (Oklahoma City) How many years of school have you completed?
2. Have you served an apprenticeship? Yes, No. If "Yes," what
was the trade? How long was the apprenticeship? (months)
3. Have you had vocational training, other than apprenticeship?
Yes, No. If "Yes," what was the subject matter? How long

did the training last? (months) (if more than one type of training, enter the most important)

4. How many years have you lived in or near Oklahoma City (Peoria)? (that is, within daily commuting distance of city)

5. (Oklahoma City) If you have lived around here less than 10 years: Where did you live before you came here? (city or town, state) Why did you move to this area?

6. (Peoria) When did you first come to Peoria? I was born here. I came (month, year).

7. I own my home (or paying off mortgage); I rent my home.

8. If you have relatives (husband, wife, son, daughter, etc.) *who live in the same household with you* and have worked during the past year, please answer the following for each one:
   Relationship to you, number of months worked in past 12, is he or she now working?

9. If you have children, how many are 18 years or older; how many are under 18 years of age; how many of your children live at home?

10. Other than your job at Armour (at ABC), do you NOW do any other work for pay or income? Yes, No. If "Yes," job title; usual number of hours worked each week; usual weekly income from this job; who do you work for?

11. (Peoria) Are you a member of a labor union? Yes, No.

12. How far is your home from this plant? (miles)

The value of this study will depend upon our knowing what your job is three months to one year from now. For this purpose, we need your name and address. Name, address.

Since it is possible that you might move, would you give us the address of someone who would always know where you are. C/o, address.

MAIL-SURVEY QUESTIONNAIRE (FIVE CITIES)

Note. The mail-questionnaire form developed for the ABC study was redesigned for the Armour studies. Because of the differences, both lists of questions are shown, omitting the spaces for answers.

ABC QUESTIONNAIRE (PEORIA)

I. *On what day did you leave ABC? Month, day, year.*

   Date you fill this out (today's date): Month, day, year.

II. *Employment and unemployment since leaving ABC:*

1. How long did it take to find your *first* job after leaving ABC? (months)

   Date started this job: Month, day, year. Date left this job (if not still on it): Month, day, year. Check here if you have not worked at all since leaving ABC.

2. Since leaving ABC: Please fill in blanks (1) to (4).

   I have actually worked for pay a total of (months); I was out of work because I did not want to work or was not able to work a total of (months); I was able to work and looking for work but could not find a job a total of (months); total months since leaving ABC (months).

   Note: (1), (2), and (3) should add up to the total time since you left ABC (4).

3. Since leaving ABC, have you applied for State unemployment compensation at any time? Yes, No. If "Yes," how many weeks of benefits did you receive? (weeks)

III. *Have you worked for any one employer for a month or more since you left ABC? Yes, No. If your answer is "No," go immediately to question IV. If your answer is "Yes," please answer the following questions for the* longest *job you have had since leaving ABC.*

1. When did you first start on this job after leaving ABC? Date started: Month, day, year.

2. Name of employer or company. City, state, kind of business.

3. Your usual number of hours worked each week for this employer. (hours)

4. Your usual rate of pay (answer one, not all three):
   Per hour, per week, per month.

5. Your usual kind of work for this employer (occupation or job title).

6. How did you first hear about this job? (check one)
   From ABC; Unemployment Office (Illinois State Employment Service); a union; friends or relatives; a newspaper, radio or TV advertisement; none of the above; I applied directly for work at the company; other (please explain).

7. How would you rate this job on each of the following items?
   Pay, interesting work, variety in the work, people you work with, immediate supervision, working conditions, use of

your skills, company as a place to work, retirement plan, other fringe benefits; steady work, chances for promotion. The categories are: Good, Fair, Poor, Very good.

8. In general, compared to your job at ABC, would you rate this job.

A better job, a worse job, about the same.

9. Are you working for the same employer now? Yes, No. If "No": When did you leave this job? (month) Are you working now? Yes, No. If "Yes," date started present job: month, year, name of employer, city and state. If "No," are you *now* able to work and *looking* for work? Yes, No.

IV. *Answer this question if you have not worked for any one employer for a month or more since you left ABC (that is, if your answer to question III was "No").*

1. Are you working now? Yes, No. If "Yes," date started present job (month, year), name of employer, city and state. If "No," are you now able to work and looking for work? Yes, No.

Your correct address: Would you please give us your correct address? Number, street or road, town or city, state.

Comments: Have you had any special problems in finding work? If so, what?

Please check to make certain you have answered all of the questions. Then mail in the enclosed self-addressed envelope which needs no stamp.

ARMOUR QUESTIONNAIRE
(EAST ST. LOUIS, COLUMBUS, FARGO, OKLAHOMA CITY)

I. *Personal data.*

1. Sex: Male, Female.
2. Are you married? Yes; other (single, widowed, separated, divorced).
3. What is the highest grade of school you completed? (grade)
4. When you worked at Armour, did you own (or were you buying) your own home? Yes, No.
5. Do you now own (or are you buying) your own home? Yes, No.
6. How many children do you have who are under 18 years of age and living at home?

7. In your last year working at Armour, what was your usual occupation (or job title)? (Examples: Shrouder, Ham Boner, Pork Shoulder Boner, etc.)

II. *On what date did you last work at Armour? Month, day, year.*

1. Please fill in today's date—month, day, year.
2. Then, it has been _____ months since you last worked at Armour.
3. For the total time since you last worked at Armour:
   I have worked for pay a total of (months); I was able to work and wanted to work, but could not find a job a total of (months); I was out of work because I was not able to work, or did not desire work a total of (months). Total months since I last worked at Armour (months).

III. *After you last worked at Armour—*

1. How long did it take you to get your next job? (months) Date started that job? (month and year) Date left that job (if not still on it)? (month and year) I am still on this job.
2. How many different companies have you worked for, since leaving Armour?
3. Since you last worked at Armour, have you applied for State unemployment compensation? Yes, No. If "Yes": Since July 1959 have you at any time used up (exhausted) your benefits? Yes, No. Since July 1959 how many weeks of benefits have you received? (weeks) (If you drew benefits more than once, put *total* number of weeks.)

IV. *Are you now working for pay? No, Yes, I am temporarily laid off.*

1. If "No," check the answer that applies to you. (check one) I am actively looking for work; I am doing housework in my own home; I am not able to work; I have retired; other reason (please explain); check here if you have not worked at all since you left Armour.
2. If "Yes" or if you are on temporary layoff:
   Who is your employer; where do you work (city, state); date you started this job (month, year); what does this company make or do; what type of work do you do (please give job title and describe duties)—(Example: Loader—I put loads on freight cars or trucks); what is your usual rate of

pay (answer *one,* not all three)—per hour, per week, per month; your usual number of hours worked each week.

In general, compared to your job at Armour, would you rate this job:

A better job, a worse job, about the same.

How did you first hear about your present job? (check one) The Unemployment Office (The State Employment Service); newspaper, radio, or TV ad; through friends or relatives; through Armour; through the union; none of the above —I applied directly for work at the company; other (please explain).

Your correct address: Would you please give us your correct address? Number, street or road, town or city, state.

Comments: What special problems has the Armour shutdown created for you and your family (finding work, financial, or other)?

Have you answered all the questions?

PERSONAL INTERVIEW SCHEDULE (FIVE CITIES)

A. *The Armour (ABC) Shutdown*

1. (Peoria) Looking back, what was your reaction when you first heard that the plant would close?

2. (Armour studies) Looking back, what did you do when you first received official notice that the Armour plant was going to close down? (Probe and record as fully as possible.) (action or inaction) (attitude)

3. (Three cities) When the plant closed: what did the union do to help its members; what did the company do to help its employees; did any other groups provide assistance in finding jobs or giving other kinds of help; on the basis of your experience, what additional help, if any, did you need?

4. (Oklahoma City) We are interested in what specific help *you* have received during the time since you have left Armour. Have you had any help from the Union? What? Have you had any help from the Company? What? Have you had any help from the Automation Fund Committee (the joint union-management group)? What? Have you had any help from the Oklahoma State Employment Service? What? From any other agency? What? On the basis of your experience, what additional help (if any) (1) could you have used? (2) could you use

now? Have you been taking any specific training or schooling? (If "Yes") What? (length of program) (If "No") Did you ask for any training? (If "Yes") Why didn't you get it?

5. (Peoria) Who do you think should try to do something to help in this kind of problem? Which organizations? What should they do? What about the government—what should it do? What level(s) of government should do this? Do you feel that the union did all it could to help its members when the plant closed? Why do you say that? Not a union member and doesn't know. How about management—do you feel that they did all they could to help the workers? What else could they have done that might have helped?

6. (Armour studies) At the time your job at Armour was terminated and you had to find another job, what possibilities were open to you? (Probe: find out what the respondent considered to be the main job possibility and whether he or she saw any alternatives.) (possibilities, in order) (if necessary to ask) Which of these seemed to be the best possibility? Why do you say that _____ was your best possibility?

7. (Oklahoma City) Have you had an offer of the possibility of a job with Armour in another plant? (If "Yes") If you are offered a job, will you take it? (If "Yes") Why would you take it? (If "No") Why would you turn it down?

8. (Three cities) If you had been offered a job at another Armour meatpacking plant in another city, would you have taken it if: Armour had offered you a job at about the same rate of pay as you were making here? (If "No") Why do you say no? The above *and* you could have kept your seniority rights? (If "No") Why do you say no? Both of the above *and* the Company had paid part of your moving costs to a new location? (If "No") Why do you say no?

9. (Peoria) Did you give any thought to trying to get a job at the parent company's plant in Grand Rapids, Michigan? (a) If yes, why did you decide against it? If no, why didn't you give it some consideration? (b) Do you think you would have taken a job at the Grand Rapids plant if [ask (1); then, if necessary, (1) and (2) together; then, if necessary, (1), (2), and (3)]: (1) The company had offered you the same work there that you were doing at ABC? and (2) The company had given you your full seniority rights? and (3) The company had paid the cost of moving up there?

B. *Work History*

On what date did you last work at Armour (ABC)? Month, day, year.

What was your first job after you left Armour (ABC)?

1. Jobs since leaving Armour (ABC). First and last job for each employer. A form was used to record the following data for each post-shutdown job:

    Starting and ending dates (to nearest month), employer and location, kind of business, occupation and duties, usual pay or earnings, usual weekly hours, how heard about job, why left job, and residence.

    Before leaving question on work history, ask: Other than the jobs you've told me about, did you do any other work for pay since you left Armour (ABC)? If so, record on form.

2. Periods not working. (Ask following questions for each such period lasting two or more weeks. Also, ask about first period of unemployment after leaving Armour [ABC] regardless of length.) From (month, year) to (month, year).

    (a) Were you looking for a job during this entire period? Yes, No. If "No," why not? How many months not looking? If "Yes," or if looking for work *part of time:*

    (b) During the time you were looking for work, what kind of job did you look for? Full time, part time? Kind of work? In this area only, outside this area? Where?

    (c) (Armour studies) (If has not found type of work mentioned in [b] What are the reasons you were not able to find that type of work?

    (d) At what companies did you apply for work? (name and industry) (If more than 4, list 4 and then put number of additional places applied.)

    (e) (Armour studies) During this period were you offered any jobs which you did not accept? Yes, No. (If "Yes," obtain reason for not taking.)

    (f) Did you apply for State unemployment compensation? Yes, No. Number of weeks received, weekly amount received. If not, why didn't you apply?

3. (Armour studies) Ask after all periods of unemployment are covered. (Ask only of those with two months or more without regular employment since the closing of Armour [three cities: July 1959] [Oklahoma City: since July 1960].) You were

without a regular job for quite a long period of time. What are the main reasons why you were not able to find a regular job sooner?

4. (Peoria) Ask of those with short period of unemployment (three months or less): You were quite successful in finding work after a relatively short period of unemployment. What do you think is the main reason you were able to find a job so quickly? Ask of those with long period of unemployment (more than three months): You were without a job for quite a long period of time. What do you think are the main reasons you were not able to find a job sooner?

5. (Peoria) Effect of unemployment compensation. Ask after covering all periods of unemployment: applicable only if collected 10 weeks or more of U.C. Did the fact that you got U.C. in any way affect how you went about looking for work? (If "No," or "I don't think so") Why? (If "Yes") In what ways? (If not answered) Did it affect where you looked? Any effect on kind of jobs looked for? Did you turn down any jobs you didn't think suitable because you were receiving U.C.?

C. *Skills and Experience*

1. (Armour studies) At Armour ([a]–[d], three cities): (a) How long did you work at Armour? (b) Did you have any job training while at Armour? What? (c) What was your highest-rated job at Armour? How long were you on this job? (If less than a year, obtain highest-rated job held for a year or more, if any.) (d) What were your duties on this job? (Obtain job title and description.) (e) In what ways is your present job like the job at Armour? (f) In what ways is your present job different?

2. (Three cities) Other companies or industries: Since you first went to work, have you had any jobs as good or better than what you did at Armour? (Good or better on basis of skill, pay, or both.) If so, what jobs? (List each such job, approximately when held and how long, the industry, and description of type of work.)

3. (Armour studies) Present job interests:
(a) In what ways has your job (have your jobs) since leaving Armour used any skills, training, or experience you have had in the past?

(b) Of jobs you have ever had, which one do you think you are best qualified for?

(c) (If [b] is different from present job) Do you plan to try and get a job as _____? (If "No") Why not? (Is it because he believes he cannot get such a job? If so, probe on reasons.) (If "Yes") Why haven't you made the change yet? (Probe on reasons.) Do you expect to make the change soon? (If "Yes") When? (If "No") Why not?

(d) Of jobs you have ever had, which one have you liked the best?

(e) (If [d] is different from [b] or present job) Do you plan to try and get a job as _____? (If "No") Why not? (Is is because he believes he cannot get such a job? If so, probe on reasons.) (If "Yes") Why haven't you made the change yet? (Probe on reasons.) Do you expect to make the change soon? (If "Yes") When? (If "No") Why not?

D. *Evaluation of Jobs Since Termination*

1. (Armour studies) Your first (regular) job after the closing of Armour was _____. What was *most* important to you in deciding to accept that job? (unstructured response) What else was important?

   First job (first job is first regular job; that is, do not count any job that is clearly temporary or in the odd-job category).

2. Present job. On the job you now have, how would you *rate* each of these factors? Use the answers on this card. (If currently unemployed, ask question for longest job since the closing of Armour, ABC.) The factors are:

   Pay; steady work; interesting work; variety in work; people work with; use of your skills; immediate supervision; working conditions; promoting chances; company as place to work; retirement plan; other fringe benefits.

   The categories are: Very good, Good, Fair, Poor.

3. Present job. Compared to your job at Armour and Company (ABC), would you say that *on your present job* (if currently unemployed, ask for longest job since the closing of Armour)—

   The skill and training required on your job *now* is; your *present* pay is; your working conditions *now* are; you like the type of work you are doing *now;* all things considered, you like your particular job *now;* all things considered, you like working for *this* company.

For above factors, categories are Better, Worse, Same; except for first factor, where they are Higher, Lower, About same. "Don't know" is also a category for each factor.

4. (Peoria) (a) I am going to read a list of job factors (we used these in the survey we made in the plant). For each factor, I want you to tell me which answer best describes how important that factor *was* in deciding to take your first job.

(b) Present job (if different from first job and if now employed): For the job you *now* have, I want to do the same thing. How important was each of these factors in deciding to accept your present job?

For 4 (a) and (b), the factors are:

What the job paid; how steady it would be; whether it was interesting; whether it had variety; what your fellow workers would be like; whether job would use your training and education; what your supervision would be like; working conditions; your chances of promotion; the company's reputation as a place to work; what the retirement or pension plan would be like; other fringe benefits (holidays, vacations).

The categories are: Very important, Important, Fairly important, Not important, and Don't know.

E. *Economic Adjustment to Loss of Armour (ABC) Job*

1. Check marital status:

   Single, married (living together), divorced, separated, widowed.

2. Ask only of married males: Has your wife worked for pay at any time since you left Armour? Yes, No. (If "Yes") Does she usually work? Yes, No. Was she working at the time you left Armour? Yes. No. *If not,* did she start working to help out because you lost your job at Armour? Yes, No. How many hours per week does (did) she usually work? What is (was) her rate of pay? In the year since Armour shut down, about how much time (number of months) has your wife worked? In the year before Armour closed down, about how many months did she work? (If "No") Did she look for a job during any of the time since you left Armour? Yes, No. Does she usually work? Yes, No.

3. Ask only of married females: Has your husband worked for pay at any time since you left Armour? Yes, No. (If "Yes")

in the year since Armour shut down, about how much time (number of months) has your husband worked? How many hours per week does (did) he usually work? What is (was) his usual rate of pay? In the year before Armour closed down, about how many months did he work?

4. Ask of all respondents: Since you left Armour, have any other members of your household worked for pay? Yes, No. (If "Yes") Who were they (was he)? (Relationship) Does he (she) usually work? Yes, No. Was he (she) working at the time you left Armour? Yes, No. *If not,* did he (she) start working to help out because you lost your job at Armour? Yes, No. About how much per week does (did) he (she) usually contribute to your household income?

5. (Interviewer code) Respondent is (if in doubt question respondent further):

   Primary breadwinner, major source of family support, minor source of family support, housewife (out of labor force), other.

6. Other than income your household has had from wages or your unemployment compensation, has anyone in your household, including yourself, had income from any of the following during the period since you left Armour? (check those which apply)

   Social Security (OASDI), other pensions (company, military, widow), unemployment compensation (others in household than yourself), interest or dividends, rental income from property, income from a farm operation, income from other business, workmen's compensation, money from relatives or others not living with you, money from public welfare agencies (public assistance, ADC, OAA, etc.), money from private charities (church, Salvation Army, etc.), other income, none.

7. As far as family finances are concerned, which of the following would you say best describes your situation since you left Armour? Would you say that:

   You have had a great deal of difficulty, you have had some difficulty, you have had little or no difficulty?

8. (Armour studies) (If he had any difficulty) Is this due to the loss of your job at Armour? Yes, No.

9. (Peoria) In general, do you now feel better off or worse off

than when you worked at ABC? Better off, worse off, about the same.

10. As a result of leaving Armour (ABC), have you had to: Use any savings you had at the time you left Armour (ABC)? Yes, No, Had none. Cancel, cash in, or surrender, or borrow on any insurance policy? Yes, No, Had none. Sell any of your personal property to meet family expenses (such as a car, refrigerator, TV, etc.)? Yes, No. Move as a result of leaving Armour (ABC)? Yes, No. If "Yes," please explain. (Armour studies) Was there anything else that you had to cut down on? If so, what?

11. (Peoria, three cities) (a) Are you planning a vacation tirp anywhere this summer? Yes, No. If "Yes," where are you planning to go? (If "No," check whether they have already taken a vacation.)

    (b) (Peoria, three cities) How about last summer, did you take a vacation trip then? Yes, No. If "Yes," where did you go?

    (c) While you were working at Armour (ABC) or on other jobs before you worked there, did you usually take a vacation trip each year? Yes, No.

    (d–f) (Oklahoma City)

    (d) Did you plan to take a vacation trip last summer? Yes, No.

    (e) Did you actually take a vacation trip last summer? Yes, No.

    (f) (If "Yes" on [e] How long a trip was it [roughly how many miles?])

12. (Peoria) Did you receive any severance pay from ABC when you left? Yes, No. If "Yes," how much (total) did you receive?

13. (Armour studies) (a) How did you use your severance pay (separation allowance)? (After getting answer, ask:) Did you use any for:

    Job training course, household appliances, paying off debts, vacation, mortgage payments.

    (If says didn't receive severance pay, ask if he had a choice between severance pay and early retirement.)

    (b) Did the severance pay help you in any way in looking for work? Yes, No. (If "No," or "I don't think so") Why

do you say that? (If "Yes" In what ways did it help?) (Probing questions: Did it affect where you looked for work [geo-
graphic areas]? Did it affect the type of work you looked for?
Did you turn down any jobs you didn't think suitable because
you had the severance pay?)

F. *(Peoria) Earlier Work Experience*

Now I'd like to ask just a few general questions about jobs you
have had in the past.
  1. Since you first went to work, what is the longest period of time
     you ever worked for one employer? (years) Who were you
     working for? Where? Industry? (If other than job at ABC,
     ask:) What was your job there? Why did you leave this job?
  2. Since you first started working for a living, what kind of work
     (occupation) have you done for the longest period of time?
     (*If not still in it,* ask:) Why did you leave this kind of work?
  3. Of the various kinds of work you have done, which did you
     like the best? (If not still in this occupation:) Why did you
     leave this kind of work? What did you particularly like about
     this kind of work which made it better than other work you
     have done? Would you like to get back on this kind of work
     again? Yes, No. *If not,* why not? If "Yes," do you think you
     will get back on this kind of work again? Yes, No. (If "Yes")
     When? (If "No") Why not?
  4. What was your first full-time job after leaving school? Em-
     ployer, industry, location, occupation.

G. *Mobility Propensity*

  1. What do you think the chances are that: (categories are: very
     good, good, fair, poor, very poor)
        You will keep working for this company permanently (if
     self-employed, you will keep working for yourself); you will
     stay in the *same type of work* you are now doing (not neces-
     sarily the same job); you will move into a better job than
     you now have—with this company, with another company;
     you *could* get a job as good as the one you now have with
     another company?
        (Peoria) You *would* take a job as good as the one you now
     have with another company if offered to you?
  2. What *would* you do if any of the following happened?
     (a) You are offered a job at another company doing exactly

what you are now doing at 30 cents an hour more pay. Would
you take it? Yes, No. *If "No,"* why?

(b) (Peoria) You are laid off and find exactly the same type of
work with the same pay at another company. Your present
company calls you back in one month. Would you go back?
Yes, No. *If "Yes,"* why?

Your company calls you back after six months. Would you go
back? Yes, No. *If "Yes,"* why? Your company calls you back
after one year. Would you go back? Yes, No. *If "Yes,"* why?
Explanation of answer.

(c) (Peoria) Your job at (company) is eliminated for some
reason. Would you stay with the company in any other type
of work? Yes, No. *If "Yes,"* why do you think you would stay?
(Probe.) *If "No,"* why do you say "No"? (Probe.)

3. (Armour studies) (a) How long have you lived around (name
of area)? (If 10 years or less) Where did you live before you
came here? Why did you move to this area? (b) Have you any
plans for moving out of this area? Yes, No. *If so,* where and
for what reason?

4. (Peoria) Job in five years: What job do you think you'll be
in five years from now? (description or title) (Note if same.)
Do you think this job will be with your present employer or
with a different employer? Same employer, different employer.

H. *Personal Data*

1. How many persons are dependent for at least half their support
on your (your family's) income? Total number (including respondent); number of children (ages of children); number of
adults. Do they all live in this household? Yes, No. *If not,*
explain.

2. How would you describe the general condition of your health?
Would you say it is: very good, good, fair, poor? (Record
any comments.)

3. What was your father's usual occupation while you were growing up? (Be specific; for example, farmer or farmhand.)

4. Have you ever lived on a farm? Yes, No. If "Yes," between
what ages? If now lives on farm, inquire about: how many
acres worked, amount of time works on farm, annual income
from farm.

5. (Peoria) Do you own your own home or rent? Own (or buying), rent, living at home or with relations.

6. (Peoria) Interviewer fill in on basis of appearance: Race: white, nonwhite. Housing conditions: very superior, above average, average working class, below average, slum.
Interviewer's comments on interview.

SPECIAL MAIL QUESTIONNAIRE FOR MIGRANTS
(EAST ST. LOUIS, COLUMBUS, FARGO)

1. *Reason for moving* (please check the major reason):
   I couldn't find work in East St. Louis area; I was offered a job here; my family was moving; my husband came here to get a job; because where I now am is my home town area. If you had other reasons for moving, please list.
2. *Where do you prefer to work?* (answer A or B, whichever applies to you)
A. I'd rather have a job in the East St. Louis area. (If you check this, please answer the following:)
   (1) Would you go back at the same wage you were receiving when you left? Yes, No.
   (2) If not, what weekly wages would you require to return to the East St. Louis area? ($ per week)
   (3) Please list any types of work which you would particularly like and consider taking.
   (4) Please list any types of work which you would not consider taking.
B. I prefer working in the area where I now am because: (if you check this, please check all answers that apply to you)
   I like it where I am better; I have a good job here; not enough jobs in East St. Louis; too expensive to move; other (please explain).

MAIL QUESTIONNAIRE FOR RESURVEY (FIVE CITIES)

A. 1. *How many months have you worked in 1961?*
   2. Are you working now for pay? (check one)
      Yes; I am on temporary layoff. (If you check one of these, please fill out B below.)
      No, I don't have a job; check here if your have not worked at all since you left Armour (ABC). (If you check either of these, please fill out C below.)

B. *If you are working or if you are on temporary layoff, answer these:*

1. What type of work do you do? (Please give job title and describe duties. Example: Loader—I put loads on freight cars or trucks.)
2. What is your usual rate of pay? (Answer one, not all three.) Per hour, per week, per month.
3. Your usual number of hours worked each week?
4. Where do you work? City, state.
5. What company do you work for? (Check here if self-employed.)
6. Did the State Employment Service (unemployment office) refer you to this job? Yes, No.

C. *If you do not have a job now, answer these* (check the answer below that applies to you):

I have been looking for work since: (month, year). I have been doing housework at home since: (month, year). I have not been able to work since: (month, year). I have been retired since: (month, year). Other (please explain).

D. *Please answer these if you do not have a job:*

1. During the last month, how much of the total income of you and your family came from *each* of the following: From unemployment compensation? (check one) All, more than half, less than half, none. From wages of others in the family? (check one) All, more than half, less than half, none. From relief payments? (check one) All, more than half, less than half, none.
2. Please check each of the following that you used for living expenses during the last month:

   Savings, borrowed funds, old age pension, other (please explain).

If you have any comments about your problems in finding work since the Armour (ABC) plant closed, we would be glad to have them.

Index

T = Table   F = Figure

ABC Company, 23, 72, 100
Abegglen, James G., 222
Adams, Leonard P., 67, 113
Advance notice, 84, 207–209, 232
AFL–CIO, 205, 215, 225
AFL–CIO News, 251
Age
  as barrier to employment, 97–99
  and education, 56
  and family adjustment to unemployment, 79
  and industry of new jobs, 135, 136F
  and training, 249, 251
  and unemployment, 62
  see also Labor market; Labor mobility; Older workers; Unemployment, long-term
Amalgamated Meat Cutters and Butcher Workmen of North America, 25, 26, 33, 72, 232, 238, 242, 245
American Cable and Radio Corporation, 232
American Can Company, 250
American Management Association, 245
American Motors Corporation, 22
American Oil Company, 249
American Viscose Corporation, 206
Amerson, Ralph W., 184
Area redevelopment
  United States, 257–260
  Western Europe, 262–269
Area Redevelopment Act, 234, 255, 260
Armour Automation Fund Committee, 25, 26, 32, 59, 60, 76, 96, 106, 117, 118, 120, 121, 164, 211, 227, 236, 244, 252, 253
Armour and Company, 24, 26, 33, 72, 100, 203, 209, 210, 213, 232, 242
Aronson, Robert L., 67, 113
Assistance in job search, *see* Search for work

Assistance, public, *see* Public assistance
Attachment patterns
  to community, 105–109
  to company or industry, 105
Attrition, and work force reduction, 229–230
Automation, *see* Technological change
Automobile Workers of America, United (UAW), 190, 194, 201, 202, 213, 224, 225, 227, 229, 239, 245, 251, 286

Bannon, Ken, 251
Becker, Joseph M., 183, 184
Beveridge, Sir William, 181, 191
Blatnik, John A., 215
Board of Trade (Great Britain), 263
Bureau of National Affairs, 202, 223, 232, 242, 245, 246, 247, 255
Business Week, 224, 269

Cassell, Frank H., 249
Central Board of Vocational Training (Sweden), 267
Chesapeake and Ohio Railway Company, 250
Chrysler Company, 239
Civilian Conservation Corps, 214
Clague, Ewan, 284
Clark, Joseph, 215
Cohen, Wilbur J., 181, 200
Collective bargaining agreements
  advance notice, 207–209
  early retirement, 213–214
  extension of benefits to displaced workers, 206–207
  layoffs, 223–224, 230–232
  plant shutdowns, 232
  relocation allowances, 244–245
  severance pay, 204–206
  supplemental unemployment benefits, 201–203

335